# Methods of Sustainability Research in the Social Sciences

SAGE has been part of the global academic community since 1965, supporting high quality research and learning that transforms society and our understanding of individuals, groups and cultures. SAGE is the independent, innovative, natural home for authors, editors and societies who share our commitment and passion for the social sciences.

Find out more at: **www.sagepublications.com**

# Methods of Sustainability Research in the Social Sciences

Frances Fahy & Henrike Rau

Los Angeles | London | New Delhi
Singapore | Washington DC

Los Angeles | London | New Delhi
Singapore | Washington DC

SAGE Publications Ltd
1 Oliver's Yard
55 City Road
London EC1Y 1SP

SAGE Publications Inc.
2455 Teller Road
Thousand Oaks, California 91320

SAGE Publications India Pvt Ltd
B 1/I 1 Mohan Cooperative Industrial Area
Mathura Road
New Delhi 110 044

SAGE Publications Asia-Pacific Pte Ltd
3 Church Street
#10-04 Samsung Hub
Singapore 049483

Editor: Robert Rojek
Editorial assistant: Alana Clogan
Production editor: Katherine Haw
Copyeditor: Rose James
Proofreader: Dick Davis
Indexer: Bill Farrington
Marketing manager: Michael Ainsley
Cover design: Francis Kenney
Typeset by: C&M Digitals (P) Ltd, Chennai, India
Printed in India at Replika Press Pvt. Ltd

**Library of Congress Control Number: 2012941780**

**British Library Cataloguing in Publication data**

A catalogue record for this book is available from
the British Library

ISBN 978-0-85702-521-0
ISBN 978-0-85702-522-7 (pbk)

# Table of Contents

About the Editors                                                        vii
About the Authors                                                         ix
Acknowledgements                                                        xiv

**PART I: Measuring the Immeasurable? The Challenges
and Opportunities of Sustainability Research
in the Social Sciences**                                                   1

1  Sustainability Research in the Social Sciences – Concepts,
   Methodologies and the Challenge of Interdisciplinarity                   3
   *Henrike Rau and Frances Fahy*

**PART II: Researching Local Lives: Experiences of
(Un)sustainability among Individuals, Households
and Communities**                                                        25

2  Household Analysis: Researching 'green' lifestyles,
   a survey approach                                                      27
   *Stewart Barr and Jan Prillwitz*

3  Social Groups and Collective Decision-making:
   Focus group approaches                                                 53
   *Anna Davies*

4  Local Lives and Conflict: Towards a methodology
   of dialogic research                                                   72
   *Mark Garavan*

**PART III: Comparative Research on the Sustainability
Performance of Cities, Regions and Nation-states**                       89

5  Sustainable Development of What? Contesting global
   development concepts and measures                                      91
   *Su-ming Khoo*

6 Biophysical Indicators of Society–Nature Interaction:
Material and energy flow analysis, human appropriation
of net primary production and the ecological footprint 114
*Veronika Gaube, Helmut Haberl and Karl-Heinz Erb*

7 Mapping for Sustainability: Environmental noise and the city 133
*Enda Murphy and Eoin A. King*

**PART IV: Time in Focus** 153

8 Everyday Life in Transition: Biographical research
and sustainability 155
*Melanie Jaeger-Erben*

9 Time and Sustainability 173
*Henrike Rau and Ricca Edmondson*

**PART V: Current Developments and Future Trends** 191

10 Researching Complex Sustainability Issues:
Reflections on current challenges and future developments 193
*Frances Fahy and Henrike Rau*

Index 209

# About the Editors

**Dr Frances Fahy** is a lecturer in Environmental Geography at the National University of Ireland, Galway. She completed her Geography and Sociology degree (1997–2001) and PhD (2001–2005) in the Department of Geography, Trinity College Dublin. Frances formerly worked as an EPA Post-doctoral Research Fellow in the Department of Geography NUI, Galway (2005–2007) and as a lecturer in Human Geography in the School of Environmental Sciences in University of Ulster (2007–2008) before joining the department in November 2008. Frances' primary research interests are in the field of environmental planning and sustainability, specifically the social and cultural consequences of environmental change.

Frances has published widely in the field of sustainability and has led a number of research projects exploring innovative methods for public participation in planning and developing sustainable planning tools (in particular quality of life indicators and community mapping) for progressing local processes for sustainable development in local authorities. She is the current President of the Geographical Society of Ireland (2012–2014). Frances is a past Chair of the Planning and Environment Research Group (PERG) of the Royal Geographical Society (2007–2012) and is the current cluster leader of the Planning and Sustainability Research Cluster in Geography at NUIG.

**Dr Henrike Rau** is a lecturer in Political Science and Sociology at the National University of Ireland, Galway. She studied sociology and psychology at the Friedrich-Schiller-Universität Jena and the National University of Ireland, Galway. In 2008–2009 she spent her sabbatical leave as guest researcher at the Institute of Social Ecology in Vienna (Austria).

Dr Rau's research focuses on sociocultural and political aspects of consumption, especially with regard to (un)sustainable transport patterns. She currently leads research on transport, mobilities and the 'consumption of distance' as part of ConsEnSus, an EPA Ireland-funded collaborative project between Trinity College Dublin and NUI, Galway on consumption, environment and sustainability (www.consensus.ie). Her other areas of expertise include environmental sociology, social-scientific and interdisciplinary sustainability research and cross-cultural studies. She is particularly interested in the implications of human time use for sustainability, which enables her to link her previous PhD research on time cultures and temporal practices in Germany and Ireland to her current interests in sustainability.

Recent publications include the edited collection *Environmental argument and cultural difference: locations, fractures, and deliberations* (Oxford: Peter Lang, 2008, co-edited with Dr Ricca Edmondson) as well as peer-reviewed book chapters and articles in national and international journals such as *Journal of Consumer Policy, Environmental Politics* and *Nature and Culture*. Her book, *Unsustainable times? Time, culture and social change in Ireland and Germany*, is expected to be published by Peter Lang in 2013. Dr Rau is a member of the Sociological Association of Ireland (SAI) committee and the ISA-RC24 (Environment and Society) network. As a strong contributor to the sustainability research community at NUI, Galway, Dr Rau has led the development of the Environment, Development and Sustainability research group in the social sciences since 2008. In 2010 she joined the Strategy Committee of the Ryan Institute at NUI, Galway as representative of the social sciences.

# About the Authors

**Stewart Barr** graduated from the University of Exeter's Geography Department in 1998 and continued his studies at Exeter undertaking a PhD thesis entitled 'Factors influencing household attitudes and behaviours towards waste management in Exeter, Devon'. Building on this research, he worked for two years in the Department as a Research Fellow on an ESRC-funded project entitled 'Environmental Action in and Around the Home'. He became a lecturer in human geography in 2003, senior lecturer in 2008 and since 2012 has been working as an Associate Professor in Geography.

Stewart's research interests include geographies of sustainable development: environmental policy in the UK; sustainable lifestyles and citizenship; sustainable travel, tourism and mobilities, and quantitative methods in geography. He is author of *Environment and Society: sustainability, policy and the citizen* (Ashgate, 2008) and co-author of the third edition of *Statistical Techniques in Geographical Analysis* (Fulton, 2004).

**Anna Davies** is a Professor in Geography at Trinity College Dublin. Her research and teaching focuses on the realm of environmental governance. She has published extensively on areas including environmental values, governance and sustainability across a range of sectors such as land use planning, climate change, waste management and sustainable consumption. Her current research focuses on matters of environmental governance in three interrelated areas: climate justice, sustainable consumption and grassroots sustainability enterprise. In addition to focus groups her research team are also adopting and modifying collaborative visioning techniques, interactive on-line platforms and mobile diaries. Alongside her academic work Anna is an independent member of the National Economic and Social Council in Ireland and a board member of the Rediscovery Centre in Ballymun, Dublin, a grassroots sustainability enterprise.

**Dr Ricca Edmondson** was born in South Africa and brought up in England. After her D.Phil at Oxford, she taught philosophy at universities in Berlin, also working as a translator. She then carried out sociological research at the Max Planck Institute for Human Development before coming to the School of Political Science and Sociology at the National University of Ireland, Galway. As well as culture and interculturality, her interests include argumentation and (wise) reasoning, especially in relation to ageing and the environment. She is now working on the history, philosophy and ethnography of wisdom.

She is the author of *Rhetoric in Sociology* (Macmillan), *Rules and Norms in the Sociology of Organisations* (Max Planck Institute for Human Development), and *Ireland: Society and Culture* (Distance University of Hagen). She is editor of *Collective Action in Context: Power, Argumentation and Democracy* (Routledge, 1997) and co-editor of *Valuing Older People: Towards a Humanistic Gerontology* (with Hans-Joachim von Kondratowitz: Policy Press, 2009), *Environmental Argument and Cultural Difference: Locations, Fractures and Deliberations* (with Henrike Rau: Oxford, Peter Lang, 2008) and *Health Promotion: Multi-Discipline or New Discipline?* (with Cecily Kelleher: Irish Academic Press, 2000). With Anne Byrne and Tony Varley, she co-authored the hundred-page introduction to the 2001 edition of Arensberg's and Kimball's *Family and Community in Ireland*.

She has recently served as Visiting Research Fellow in the Department of Philosophy, University of Potsdam, Germany (Semester 11, 2011). She is a member of the Executive Committee of the European Sociological Association, where for 12 years she served as Co-Convenor of its Research Network on Ageing. She belongs to the international advisory boards of Ageing and Society, Poroi, Ecopolitics, and the Irish Journal of Applied Social Studies, and she is engaged in active research projects with colleagues in (among others) universities in Salford, Oxford, Helsinki and Wuhan, and is Convenor of the Galway Wisdom Project.

**Dr Karlheinz Erb** holds an MSc in ecology from the University of Vienna (1999), a doctoral degree in human ecology, University of Vienna (2003) and a habilitation ('venia docendi') in Social Ecology, University of Klagenfurt (2008). His habilitation focused on the role of land use in the Earth System and on methods for analysing drivers, patterns, processes and impacts across spatial and temporal scales.

He is member of the Scientific Steering Committee of the Global Land Project (since 2011), member of the Young Curia at the Austrian Academy of Sciences (since 2011), and member of the Commission on Ecosystem Management (CEM) at The World Conservation Union (IUCN; since 2006). In 2010, he was awarded an ERC Starting Independent Researcher Grant by the European Research Council, for the project 'Land Use Intensity from a Socio-Ecological Perspective'.

**Dr Mark Garavan** co-ordinates and lectures on the Applied Social Studies programme in the Galway-Mayo Institute of Technology, Castlebar. His PhD research was an investigation of Irish environmentalism using a variety of quantitative and qualitative research methods. It employed a number of methodologies which permitted direct comparison with an eight-nation study 'The Transformation of Environmental Activism Project' coordinated by Professor Christopher Rootes, University of Kent, Canterbury. The Irish research was carried out under the aegis of the Environmental Change Institute, NUI, Galway (Human Impact Cluster), under the supervision of Dr Ricca Edmondson, School of Political Science and Sociology, NUI, Galway.

He has written widely on the Corrib gas dispute and on sustainability issues. He is the author of *Compassionate Activism: An Exploration of Integral Social Care*. He is a Director of Feasta, the Foundation for the Economics of Sustainability. He acted as spokesperson for the Rossport Five in 2005 and 2006. These were five local men imprisoned for their opposition to the Corrib gas project.

**Dr Veronika Gaube** holds an MSc in ecology (2002) from the University of Vienna and a PhD in social ecology (2009) from the University of Klagenfurt. Her doctoral thesis examined regional sustainability initiatives with regard to land use in Austria through a combination of institutional analysis and integrated modelling. Her research interests include sustainable rural and urban development and the impacts of multi-party decision-making on land use, material, substance and energy flows at the regional level.

Methodologically, she is experienced in interlinkages of spatially explicit (GIS) models, dynamic system models and agent based models for socio-ecological systems. Other research interests include the integration of socioeconomic and ecological parameters in land-use models, material, energy and substance flow assessments and nutrients in (agro)ecosystems.

Dr Gaube recently contributed to several projects involving participative approaches ('participative modelling'). She was responsible for the development of agent-based models simulating decisions by members of farming households in several rural regions concerning their agricultural production and land use strategies. Currently, she is also involved in projects modelling residential location decisions of different household types in cities and their impact on the urban energy use. Dr Gaube has published widely in books and national and international peer-reviewed journals.

**Dr Helmut Haberl** holds an MSc in biology and mathematics, University of Vienna (1991), a doctoral degree in ecology, University of Vienna (1995) and a habilitation ('venia docendi') in human ecology, University of Vienna (2001). His doctoral thesis presented a calculation of the human appropriation of net primary production in Austria. His habilitation focused on the concept of 'energetic metabolism of societies' and its significance for analysis of society-nature interactions.

Helmut Haberl was a member of the Scientific Steering Committee of the Global Land Project and of the Scientific Committee of the European Environment Agency. He served as a lead author for two chapters of the Global Energy Assessment (published November 2011) and is currently lead author for the chapter on agriculture, forestry and other land use in working group III (mitigation) in the 5th assessment report of the IPCC (to be published in 2014). He has published more than 70 papers in international peer-review journals and co-edited several special issues of peer-review journals as well as edited volumes.

**Dr Melanie Jaeger-Erben** studied Psychology and Sociology in Germany and Sweden. During her postgraduate studies at the University of Magdeburg she acquired extensive knowledge of qualitative research methodologies. Since 2004 she has worked on topics such as social aspects of the transition to renewable energies and energy efficiency measures, gender, participation and sustainable consumption. Her PhD research deployed a practice theory approach to the study of changes in everyday consumption patterns after life events. Dr Jaeger-Erben's teaching portfolio includes courses in qualitative research methods and applied social-scientific sustainability research. She is currently working at the Center of Technology and Society at the Technische Universität Berlin.

**Dr Su-ming Khoo** is a Lecturer in the School of Political Science & Sociology, National University of Ireland, Galway. She is a member of the Sustainable Development, Governance and Changing Communities Research Cluster. Her research and teaching interests are in globalisation and development, North/South contestation, 'post-development', development theory, political economy of development, human development, human rights and sustainable development. Her recent publications have been about bridging human rights and development, citizenship, culture, consumer activism, decolonisation, ecology, democratisation and knowledge advocacy and activism, and higher education policy.

**Eoin King** is a Postdoctoral Research fellow in acoustics at Trinity College Dublin. His doctoral dissertation developed a practical framework for strategic noise mapping in Europe. In conjunction with his current position at Trinity, Eoin is also director of Infrasonic Ltd, an Irish acoustics consultancy firm. His research interests include environmental acoustics, environmental policy and strategic noise mapping techniques. He has extensive knowledge in the field of noise modelling and prediction. In 2010 he was nominated by the Irish Department of the Environment to represent Ireland on the

CNOSSOS-EU Technical Committee of experts. In 2007 he developed the largest and most complex strategic noise maps prepared in Ireland to date on behalf of the Irish National Roads Authority, in accordance with EU Directive 2002/49/EC.

**Enda Murphy** is a Lecturer in Planning at the School of Geography, Planning and Environmental Policy at University College Dublin. He obtained his PhD from Trinity College Dublin (TCD) in 2006. His research interests are broad in scope but centre on the areas of urban transportation, environmental noise, spatial planning and related issues. He has published widely in the international literature being author/co-author of more than thirty academic journal articles, book chapters, conference papers and reports. His work has been published in such journals as *Environment International*, *Journal of Environmental Management*, *Transportation Research A and D*, *Urban Studies*, *Cities*, *Growth and Change*, *Town Planning Review* and *Applied Acoustics*.

**Dr Jan Prillwitz** is a graduate of the Dresden University of Technology (TU Dresden, Germany). During his PhD research, he worked at the Helmholtz-Centre for Environmental Research, Leipzig, Germany, investigating the influence of residential relocations and other life course events on travel behaviour. In 2008, Jan received his doctorate from the Institute of Geography at the University of Leipzig. As post-doctoral researcher, Jan worked for two years on the 'Promoting sustainable travel' project at the School of Geography, University of Exeter (UK), where he explored motives and barriers for adopting more sustainable behaviour. From 2009 till 2012, Jan was Assistant Professor at the Department of Human Geography and Planning at Utrecht University in The Netherlands. At the current time, he is an independent travel behaviour researcher; his main research interests are in sustainable travel behaviour, mobility styles, concepts of new mobilities and the role of socio-psychological factors for individual travel decisions.

# Acknowledgements

The need to effectively address today's sustainability challenges has reached a previously unknown level of urgency. The threat of runaway climate change, rapid biological and cultural diversity loss, mounting pressure on the planet arising from population growth and the relentless pursuit of 'development' as well as associated potentials for social and political unrest and economic instability can no longer be ignored. At the same time, political responses to these challenges continue to be at best incremental. This makes it all the more important for those who through their theoretical and empirical work try to understand the social and political aspects of sustainability to be able to avail themselves of appropriate outlets for their thoughts and findings. This edited collection was intended to provide such an outlet. Its main aim is to show how sustainability can be understood differently (and perhaps more constructively than has hitherto been the case) if studied through the lens of the social sciences.

Of course, edited collections such as this one are only made possible because of the tireless work of many people. First and foremost, we wish to thank all contributors for their timely submissions. It was a pleasure to work with authors from Ireland, UK, Germany and Austria who are so deeply committed to theoretically informed and methodological rigorous social research on sustainability problems. The range and quality of contributions to this collection clearly demonstrates the vibrancy of the field today and gives hope for its future role and direction.

We also wish to express our gratitude to Frank Fahy for his assistance with the final manuscript. His observations and comments have greatly contributed to the success of this project. Finally, we would like to thank the editorial team at Sage Publishers for their patience and their highly professional and efficient support.

Henrike Rau and Frances Fahy
January 2013

# PART I

Measuring the Immeasurable?
The Challenges and Opportunities
of Sustainability Research in
the Social Sciences

# 1

# Sustainability Research in the Social Sciences – Concepts, Methodologies and the Challenge of Interdisciplinarity

*Henrike Rau and Frances Fahy*

## Introduction

The necessity to reconcile the needs and wants of human society with the limits of the global ecological system has resulted in proposals for alternative forms of development that prioritise human flourishing and well-being over materially intensive economic growth. Calls for development that is capable of sustaining more than seven billion people on a planet with finite resources and that ensures a good quality of life for current and future generations have shaped political agendas in the late twentieth and early twenty-first centuries. These practical and political sustainability issues are matched by equally daunting challenges with regard to its measurement. Who decides what counts as sustainable? How do we know if a new waste management policy or an initiative to encourage walking and cycling yield 'sustainable outcomes'? What time frame is needed to assess the results of a policy that claims to enhance sustainability? Perhaps some outcomes will only emerge years after the sustainability assessment of a particular initiative has been completed. Finally, who are the 'winners' and who are the 'losers' of sustainability initiatives and policies, both now and in the future? These and other pressing questions are central to the sustainability project. However, they rarely receive adequate attention from politicians, practitioners and academics.

This edited collection aims to address some of these questions through a critical examination of new and established research methodologies and tools for social research that have found application in the investigation of sustainability problems. Its contributors can draw on extensive experience and expertise with regard to both the conceptualisation of society–environment relations and the empirical study of people and places. Key methods to be covered in this collection include well-established quantitative and qualitative tools for social research such as survey questionnaires and focus groups. In addition, there is a strong emphasis on new and innovative methodologies that try to capture short- and long-term changes in human behaviour, such as problem-centred interviewing that focuses on key life events and longitudinal designs for the evaluation of sustainability programmes and initiatives. Overall, the book aims to help close a significant gap in the literature by offering an accessible and comprehensive account of current trends in the theory and practice of social-scientific sustainability research.

In this introduction we will examine past developments and current trends in sustainability research in the social sciences, concentrating in particular on contributions from sociology, geography and political science as well as recent inter- and transdisciplinary efforts. Initially, the main focus will be on the relationship between theory and empirical data. Subsequently, we will explore the (political) relevance and practicability of key approaches to measuring sustainability and sustainable human development. Following on from this, we will turn our attention to recently emerging inter- and transdisciplinary approaches to social research methodology and practice that represent interesting departures from more conventional ways of viewing and doing science. Throughout this introduction we will touch on some epistemological and methodological challenges inherent to social-scientific sustainability research in general, and recent trends towards greater disciplinary integration in particular. This discussion will encompass the potential benefits and drawbacks involved in combining social and natural science research methods. The concluding section of this introductory chapter will outline the overall structure of this edited collection and make visible the connections between individual chapters.

## Linking theory and data: sustainability concepts and their measurement

There is still great uncertainty about the use of the term 'sustainable development' (SD) and its precise meaning: people who use the term in conversation or public debate may not necessarily talk about the same thing at all. The concept of SD has also had many critics who have taken issue with both its normative and prescriptive nature and its definitional breadth. Some have even described it as a paradox or an oxymoron whose deployment in the context of public and political debates is likely to perpetuate the existing discursive and practical hegemony of progress and economic growth (Sachs, 1997; Latouche, 2007). This raises the question whether conceptual agreement can ever be reached, given the diversity of ideas and initiatives that are subsumed under the umbrella concept of sustainable development (see also Mebratu, 1998; Parris and Kates, 2003).

This said, many actors involved in SD politics, research and practice have more or less explicitly adopted the definition by the World Commission on Environment and Development (WCED), or variants thereof. The 1987 WCED report *Our Common Future*, also commonly referred to as the Brundtland report, is seen as a watershed moment in the history of sustainable development theory and practice. It defines sustainable development as development that 'meets the needs of the present without compromising the ability of future generations to meet their own needs' (WCED, 1987: 24). The Brundtland report recognises the various threats to society and environment that emanate from the over-consumption of resources and proposes measures to address this problem. While there is a strong focus on the role of the economy throughout the document, the role of politics in bringing about sustainable development is also explored in detail.

There are also proposals to substitute 'sustainability' for sustainable development to address (or perhaps avoid) some of the deep-seated conceptual uncertainties and ideological and moral tensions associated with the latter, many of which appear to resist any immediate resolution. We would argue here that concerns over sustainability can be traced back to pre-modern subsistence economies and traditional cultures but that by linking the issue of sustainability to modern growth and development logics, these older roots are frequently ignored. It is worth noting here that all of the contributors to this collection have adopted a nuanced and cautious approach to SD terminology which rejects the uncritical use of the word 'sustainable' but recognises the high importance of sustainability as a concept.

Regardless of the outcome of these conceptual debates, it is clear that sustainability research has gained huge momentum both in the social and the natural sciences, partly in response to the seriousness of social and environmental problems today. This raises important questions about the implications for social research of this 'sustainability turn'. Surprisingly, this is hardly ever explicitly recognised. This lack of attention to fundamental methodological questions that arise from the growing influence of SD thinking more generally, and specific choices of sustainability concepts and terminology in particular, has been a key motivation for this edited collection and all chapters will cover these and related issues.

So what are the possible methodological implications of adopting either the Brundlandt definition itself or one of its variants? Firstly, to do so means to also think about the issue of intergenerational justice and how to operationalise and measure it. How can we capture trends in human development and resource consumption that stretch across multiple generations? Are commonly used cross-sectional research designs adequate for the measurement of long-term change? And how effective are conventional social science approaches to longitudinal data analysis for the study of society–environment relations? Ultimately, cross-sectional country data collected at regular intervals remain the dominant method for capturing and reporting social, economic and ecological change. At the same time, longitudinal data collection, that is, the recording of information over an extended period of time using the same sample (of people, households, organisations, etc.) continues to be the exception. This has significant implications for the analysis of social and ecological changes and how they occur.

Secondly, while the Brundlandt report and its various successors are explicitly global in focus, they nevertheless ascribe a significant role to the nation-state as a key administrative unit. While this clearly reflects the historical context of the WCED meeting in 1987, it has implications for the kinds of sustainability research that can be meaningfully conducted using this definition. National-level data continues to dominate mainstream sustainability research. While this focus on countries and their sustainability performance is useful on many levels, it cannot adequately capture many cross-national challenges to sustainability. As will be shown throughout this book, the growing complexity of global flows of people, goods, waste products and ideas and their capacity to transcend national boundaries cannot be ignored (cf. Rau, 2010). Importantly, this shift towards flows and mobilities brings to the fore wider issues about the adequate scale of social research as well as its generalisability, which will be central motives of this collection.

Comparative efforts are central to the investigation of sustainability, though there is great diversity with regard to the unit of analysis used. While classical comparative studies have often been cross-national in focus, there is now a much greater emphasis on 'peer-group' and regional approaches that group together individual nation-states. For example, Flynn's (2007) recent comparative study of Ireland's environmental performance adopted a peer-group approach that included three other countries: two that were seen as similar to Ireland (Portugal, Greece) and one that was judged to be different (Denmark). The many benefits of this innovative approach to sampling are evident throughout Flynn's study and highlight the need to move beyond conventional frameworks for cross-national comparison.

Similarly, definitions of sustainability that deviate from or challenge mainstream SD concepts require alternative ways of thinking about and measuring sustainability. Many of the contributions to this collection will discuss alternative approaches to comparative research that differ from more traditional work in terms of scale, focus and choice of unit of analysis. For example, recent calls by academics and sustainability advocates for the (re)localisation of economic activity as a way of addressing social and ecological problems raise interesting questions about how to adequately measure the success (or otherwise) of small-scale initiatives such as Transition

Towns. Similarly, prominent sustainability studies have focused on cities rather than nation-states, which is also reflective of a renewed interest among social scientists in urban life.[1]

It is likely that current and future challenges to the theory and practice of sustainable development will also change the measurement of sustainable outcomes. For example, it could be argued that a commitment to bid 'farewell to growth' (Latouche, 2010) would also imply a clear departure from established indicators and measurements of economic activity. In addition, certain topics that were previously confined to the margins of sustainability politics and research are now pushing through to the centre of debate, requiring the development of new indicators. For example, the impending threat of large-scale displacement of people both within and between countries due to climate change and associated environmental disasters can no longer be ignored. The implications of mass migration for global social and political stability, including the threat of social disintegration and the disappearance of indigenous cultures, have only recently received adequate attention from decision makers. In June 2011, UN High Commissioner for Refugees António Guterres urged countries to develop new approaches to climate-induced displacement of people. In his speech at the *Nansen Conference on Climate Change and Displacement in the 21st Century* in Oslo he referred to climate-induced movement of people as the 'defining challenge of our time' and criticised the lack of political will to tackle climate change.[2] This clearly has significant implications for the kinds of sustainability research projects that are needed to inform policy and shape public discourse. For example, it now seems vitally important to connect information about local and regional environmental degradation with migration data. Similarly, there is a need for more reliable and detailed information about the relationship between violent conflicts and environmental destruction, as well as more nuanced analyses of such data (cf. Salehyan, 2008).

To conclude, while more conventional approaches to data collection and analysis such as large-scale surveys are likely to remain dominant, partly because existing research capacity and infrastructure depend on their continued use, novel approaches can be expected to emerge to compete for recognition and funding. These include the increased deployment of visualisation methods aided by developments in information and communication technology, more widespread use of participatory and collaborative methods for data collection and analysis and modifications to conventional methodological approaches and tools to capture hitherto neglected social and environmental phenomena. However, the task of translating sustainability concepts into meaningful empirical observations will remain the ultimate challenge in the field. All contributions to this edited collection capture current practices in relation to the operationalisation of theoretical concepts and explore potential future developments.

## Sustainability and social research: Methodological challenges

The social-scientific measurement of sustainability throws up a range of questions to do with *what* to measure, *why* and *how*. Some of these questions relate to the nature of social research more generally, and have been central to methodological debates since the inception of many social science disciplines in the nineteenth century. These include methodological issues to do with objectivity and subjectivity or ways of assessing the quality of social inquiry. Broader questions to do with the nature of human knowledge, how people make sense of their social and physical environment and how they know what they know also continue to emerge in the context of social-scientific sustainability research, albeit often only as a subtext.

How we measure social and material conditions shapes and reflects how we think and talk about them. The rhetoric of measurability – the widely established idea that things do not matter (or perhaps do not even exist) if they cannot be measured – has influenced the sustainability debate in diverse ways. It seems important to remember here that the emergence of sustainability research in the late 1960s and early 1970s coincided with the rise of environmentalism and the re-emergence of Malthusian arguments with regard to population and resource consumption in many developed countries. Key research reports and academic publications such as Ehrlich and Ehrlich's (1968/2009) *The population bomb*, the *Limits to growth* report (Meadows et al., 1972) and its 30-year update (Meadows et al., 2004), the *Stern review on the economics of climate change* (Stern, 2006) and the various Intergovernmental Panel on Climate Change (IPCC) climate change assessment reports published since 1990 have fuelled and shaped the global sustainability debate.

What these publications have in common is a focus on quantifying and modelling the consequences of (un)sustainability. This methodological emphasis on quantification is also reflected in public debates that frequently revolve around directly measurable and numerically expressible aspects of environmental degradation. Predicted increases in global temperature as a result of climate change, or the anticipated rise in sea levels as a result of thawing pole caps and glaciers, have received significant media attention and have captured the public's imagination. Al Gore's popular documentary *An inconvenient truth* (2006) captures this type of sustainability discourse, which draws mostly on conventional large-scale quantitative data.

While there are countless benefits to using large-scale data and numeric indicators to investigate, represent and compare the sustainability performance of countries and regions, for example to draw attention to global inequalities, there is still considerable uncertainty about what indicators are most appropriate (see Khoo, Chapter 5 and Gaube et al. Chapter 6 in this

volume). The measurement of human development has long been dominated by economistic ways of thinking which prioritised economic growth
and its measurement using gross domestic product (GDP) and gross
national product (GNP). However, the dominance of economics has been
challenged in recent years, in particular, following the onset of the financial
crisis in 2008. Composite indicators of sustainability such as the Human
Development Index (HDI) and the Happy Planet Index (HPI) have emerged
and gained in popularity. This new generation of indicators combine a focus
on economic activity with measurements of ecological improvement or
decline, and human well-being. These alternative indicators thus reflect new
ways of thinking about development which recognise that a continued
focus on economic growth will destroy vitally important ecosystems and
threaten humanity.

How can this shift in sustainability research towards more integrated
indicators be explained? Even as recently as 1995 Kaufmann and Cleveland
argued that lack of agreement between natural and social scientists about
indicators represents a major barrier to sound sustainability research and
that much greater integration is needed. Much has happened with regard to
integration since Kaufmann and Cleveland published their work. Importantly, we record a rapid increase in the number of sustainability studies
that purport to have adopted an interdisciplinary approach, that is, that
bring together people from a variety of academic disciplines to study complex problems.[3] While many of these studies claim to be theoretically, con-
ceptually and methodologically integrated, few of them describe explicitly
how this integration has been achieved. Some key issues of interdisciplinarity will be discussed in more detail in the next section.

However, many current approaches to measuring sustainability continue
to overlook important social and cultural aspects, partly because capturing
the latter requires alternative modes of social inquiry whose epistemological
and practical features are distinctly different from mainstream methods
based on quantification. Recent publications such as Juliet Schor's (2010)
*Plenitude* and Helena Norberg-Hodge's (1991/2009) *Ancient futures: learning from Ladakh* as well as popular documentaries such as *The economics
of happiness* (2010) have sparked interesting debates about cultures of happiness and human well-being, quality of life and localisation as a form of
resistance to globalisation. Many of these contributions have adopted innovative methodological approaches that either complement or altogether
replace more conventional methods with novel tools for researching the
social world. For example, Helena Norberg-Hodge's (1991/2009) work on
traditional Ladakhi culture and its exposure to modern global capitalism
combines cultural anthropological fieldwork and ethnographic inquiry with
action research elements, including 'reality tours' for members of Ladakhi
society. These tours are intended to provide Ladakhi community leaders

with opportunities to experience first hand the merits and demerits of 'Western culture' and to potentially dispel common misconceptions among the Ladakhi about life in a highly developed country when the leaders return to their home region. These 'reality tours' included visits to a shopping mall, nursing home and municipal waste dump. The growing popularity of visioning techniques and backcasting workshops to tap into local knowledge and lay expertise in innovative ways represents another main strand of qualitative inquiry that is (re-)shaping sustainability research in the social sciences (cf. Quist and Vergragt, 2004; Davies et al., 2012).

Different methodological approaches in sustainability research do not only represent diverse methodological and practical options. They also reflect divergent ontological and epistemological views. For example, it is possible to distinguish between constructivist and (critical) realist strands that differ not only with regard to their methodology but also in *how society is viewed* and *how members of society are expected to interact with each other and with their biophysical environment*. Here, views of environmental problems as 'socially constructed' contrast with perspectives that emphasise the material realities of environmental (and societal) problems as well as their social causes and consequences. A researcher's commitment to a particular methodological approach, therefore, reflects their underlying ontological and epistemological assumptions, at least to some degree, though this is rarely explicitly recognised. Instead, many sustainability researchers appear to adopt a 'technical view' (Bryman, 1988) that assumes methodological choices to reflect pragmatic-instrumental decisions rather than broader concerns about the nature of human social life and its investigation.

Such a technical view has many advantages, including its strong emphasis on the practicalities of research as well as a potentially greater propensity towards mixing methods and unconventional and innovative study designs. However, its tendency to treat researchers' methodological choices as separate from their views of the social world and human behaviour, including people's interactions with the biophysical environment, can eclipse important tensions and divergences within sustainability research whose theoretical treatment could potentially advance the field. It is argued here that this lack of debate among sustainability researchers about the relationship between researchers' 'world views', which may be more or less compatible, and their methodological choices represents a serious obstacle to greater methodological clarity and enhanced harmonisation, especially within the context of inter- and transdisciplinary projects. It remains to be seen whether a fully-fledged, robust methodological debate will characterise the field of social-scientific sustainability research in the future, given its current focus on developing pragmatic solutions to sustainability problems and its leaning towards 'weak' interdisciplinarity.

# Beyond disciplinarity? Efforts towards integrated sustainability research

The inherent complexity and multidimensionality of most sustainability challenges has called into question many existing disciplinary boundaries within the social sciences and beyond. But is it possible, or indeed desirable, to abandon disciplinary traditions to solve pressing social and environmental problems, as some social scientists suggest? If so, what are the consequences for existing disciplines, especially those whose prominence has somewhat waned over the last few decades? What innovations with regard to social scientific research are necessary to be able to study different forms of social and economic organisation *and* their material consequences? Efforts to answer these and related questions are manifold and reflect the diversity of the field. Some have defined sustainability research as a subdiscipline in its own right that connects different disciplines. 'Sustainability is multiple things at once and navigates interesting territory – it is a goal, an ideal, an umbrella, *and a sub-discipline of multiple disciplines*' (Stock and Burton, 2011: 1091, emphasis added). Social scientists who are actively engaged in national and international sustainability debates and research, including many of the contributors to this edited collection, thus adopt and advocate inter- and transdisciplinary work as a way of addressing the pressing problem of reconciling economic development with social equity and environmental integrity (e.g. Schor, 2010: 11). In other words, a commitment to interdisciplinarity is often seen as a necessary precondition for successful sustainability research: it is much less clear what this type of research is expected to look like and what ontological, epistemological and methodological foundations it is supposed to rest upon.

Undoubtedly, there are significant 'hidden' barriers to interdisciplinary collaboration, many of which only become visible during the actual research process. As mentioned in the previous section, these barriers may be rooted in fundamental differences in how researchers with different disciplinary backgrounds and training define the object, nature and goals of scientific inquiry. In other words, disagreements over methodological choices are rarely *just* about technical or practical matters. Instead, members of different disciplines may hold diametrically opposed views of human behaviour, the nature and composition of society and its dependence on natural resources. For example, fundamental differences exist both within and between major social science disciplines with regard to explanations of people's actions and, by extension, their interactions with the environment. Sociologists, economists and human geographers may hold very different and at times incompatible views of the motives of human behaviour.

Similarly, different theoretical traditions in the social sciences are often underpinned by different and perhaps incompatible views of the human condition, including fundamental divergences with regard to the degree of rationality ascribed to human social (inter)action, the importance of societal structures vis-à-vis agency or the role of the individual within social organisations and institutions. By default, these different views exert considerable influence over a researcher's choice of research methodology, for example whether to focus on individuals' self-reported views and practices or to collect information about directly observable group behaviour. For example, consider the issue of (un)sustainable consumption which has major consequences for society and the environment. Here, rationalistic perspectives of consumers as 'utility maximisers' who make rational decisions based on complete information contrast with views that stress the culturally diverse and socially negotiated nature of everyday consumption practices, such as what people eat or how they move around. These views are in turn underpinned by disparate notions of the structures and functions of human society and its significance for individuals' attitudes and actions.

Fundamental differences in how human behaviour is viewed and conceptualised are not merely semantic; they also influence the choice of research methodology. As stated previously, questions remain with regard to the connection between a researcher's epistemological commitments and convictions, that is, what he or she considers to be an appropriate way of generating knowledge about the social world, and their methodological choices. Here, we could ask whether it is actually possible to decouple certain research methods such as choice experiments used by economists to measure consumer decisions from their theoretical–conceptual base, in this case a rational choice approach to human behaviour. Is it not the case that theoretical claims which focus on *meaning*, that is, the ways in which people make sense of their social and biophysical environment, require tools for empirical testing that tap into the nuances of these meanings (rather than establish their frequency or spread within the population)? Clearly, these and related questions represent a continuation and expansion of, rather than a break from, methodological debates in the social sciences around the issues of multi-method research and methodological integration (Bryman, 1984, 1988). In fact, some of the current debates about the merits and demerits of interdisciplinary sustainability research closely resemble past debates among social scientists on combining qualitative and quantitative methods.

As interdisciplinary research has grown in popularity over the past few years, attempts have been made to divide or categorise interdisciplinary studies in line with their key features (e.g. Lyall et al., 2011). Recent categorisations include various distinctions between 'strong' and 'weak' forms of interdisciplinarity, with the former describing work that links widely dissimilar social and natural science disciplines while the latter captures collaborations between members of cognate disciplines. Distinctions between interdisciplinarity and transdisciplinarity also continue to be debated. Although interdisciplinarity and transdisciplinarity have been used interchangeably by many authors, there are a number of important arguments in favour of distinguishing between them to achieve greater conceptual clarity. Recent contributions by Gertrude Hirsch Hadorn and colleagues on the nature and role of transdisciplinary sustainability research deserve particular attention in this context, because they show the enormous potential of projects that involve academic and non-academic research and knowledge communities and that focus on providing solutions to complex sustainability problems (Hirsch Hadorn et al., 2006, 2008; see also Costanza, 1997).

Yet others have gone further by asking whether academic disciplines should remain in place but work together, or whether they should be dissolved altogether. Some prominent social scientists have recently argued that disciplinary parochialism hampers the advancement of social scientific knowledge, and that the notion of disciplines itself needs to be challenged (e.g. Sayer, 1999; Jessop and Sum, 2001). This concern clearly resonates in Andrew Sayer's (1999) critique of disciplinary bastions in social research which informs his plea for postdisciplinarity:

> I believe we should celebrate rather than mourn the decline of disciplines. We should encourage the development of not merely interdisciplinary studies but postdisciplinary studies. I believe this identification which so many academics have with their disciplines is actually counterproductive from the point of view of making progress in understanding society (1999:2).

Interestingly, these calls for greater disciplinary integration and overlap have been connected to broader debates around what constitutes 'normal' scientific practice (cf. Funtowicz and Ravetz, 1991; Hirsch Hadorn et al., 2006, 2008). While an in-depth discussion of post-normal approaches to science is beyond the scope of this introduction, it is important to note that arguments in the literature for a scientific paradigm shift towards post-normality have often resulted from scientists' engagement with 'wicked' sustainability challenges. Efforts to understand and potentially solve seemingly intractable social–environmental problems with very high levels of uncertainty and risk quickly revealed the limitations of conventional scientific approaches (e.g. Funtowicz and Ravetz, 1991).

The realities of sustainability research, policy and practice are often far removed from the twin goals of disciplinary integration and joined-up thinking and problem-solving discussed above. As regards disciplinary input into policy, conventional economic contributions continue to dominate the policy landscape. In many policy contexts, including many of those found in Ireland, it seems almost impossible to influence policy decisions without providing estimates of potential costs and benefits as well as time frames for implementation. This clearly contradicts much sustainability research which shows that the benefits of sustainable solutions (whether financial or otherwise) may be indirect and difficult to measure or quantify and that they may emerge only after a prolonged period of time. Similarly, social-scientific efforts to study sustainability questions remain wedded to disciplinary conventions in terms of what kinds of questions to ask and how to answer them. This also coincides with a strong focus on large-scale quantitative work. Much work conducted in more conventional public and private research settings, including universities, state agencies and private research consultancy firms, remains firmly disciplinary in focus.

While inter- and transdisciplinary work carried out by research teams from the social and natural sciences undoubtedly remains the exception, some research institutes and centres have specialised in more integrated approaches to sustainability research. For example, major research institutes in Europe involved in sustainability research such as the Stockholm Environment Institute (SEI) in Sweden, the Potsdam Institute for Climate Impact Research (PIK), the Wuppertal Institute for Climate, Environment and Energy in Germany and the Institute of Social Ecology in Vienna (Austria) have adopted explicitly inter- and transdisciplinary approaches. This points towards a set of distinct problems that arise whenever a distinctly interdisciplinary field such as sustainability research is confronted with existing disciplinary-centred systems of knowledge production and dissemination, many of which have very real material consequences in terms of organisational structures, research funding and impact assessment.

Ultimately, the success or otherwise of efforts towards greater inter- or transdisciplinarity in sustainability research will depend on whether and to what extent funding structures, institutional conditions, quality indicators and output metrics used to measure the impact of scientific work can be modified to accommodate greater linkages between social science disciplines as well as between social and natural scientists. While the pressing nature of many social and environmental problems may raise doubts in some people's minds about the appropriateness of drawn-out debates on the merits and demerits of disciplines and discipline-specific methodologies, this edited collection sets out to show that the issue of disciplinary boundaries simply cannot be ignored because they go right to the core of sustainability research.

# Structure of the book

This collection introduces scholars and students to a range of approaches to social research that are considered highly suitable for the social-scientific investigation of sustainability questions. Each chapter complements theoretical considerations with case study material and practical advice to enable readers to plan and conduct their own research and to engage in interdisciplinary conceptual and empirical work. The book assembles international contributions from social scientists whose expertise in the field of sustainability research is widely recognised.

There are three core themes that connect the different chapters in this collection. First and foremost, all chapters draw attention to the fact that the views and actions of individuals are both shaped by and reflected in their social, political and infrastructural context. This perspective challenges many conventional approaches to the study of human behaviour that assume people to be rational actors whose individual decisions and attitudes translate more or less directly into measurable behaviour. Many of the contributions to this book caution against approaches to sustainability research that uncritically embrace methodological and epistemological individualism and that conceptualise human social life as the mere aggregate of individual actions. Instead, there is ample evidence presented throughout the collection that synergies and interactions between individuals, groups and organisations across different temporal and spatial scales can produce outcomes for society and the environment that amount to much more than the sum of their parts and that require novel and innovative ways of doing research.

A second key theme revolves around two questions: how to conceptualise the relationship between societal development and resource consumption and how to effectively translate these concepts into suitable and effective measurements. Many contributions to the book stress the need to connect the study of human social life to assessments of its material foundations and impacts. This is perhaps one of the most significant challenges that social scientists working on sustainability issues face, both in terms of conceptual orientation and operationalisation. Most authors included in this book acknowledge that the ways in which societies use resources, including time, space and material objects, cannot be separated from the wider social processes that underpin them. For example, Gaube et al. (Chapter 6) provide ample evidence for the major link between societal organisation and resource consumption.

Thirdly, the collection draws attention to features of human behaviour that have significant implications for the environment and that have hitherto received limited attention. For example, Rau and Edmondson's chapter shows that human behaviour is inextricably linked to time and that future sustainability research in the social sciences must take seriously the material effects of human time use. At the same time, they emphasise the need to examine the social and cultural meanings of time and their relevance to social organisation as a possible strategy for enhancing sustainability research and policy. Other contributors to the collection argue that a central task for social-scientific sustainability research is to connect more traditional social-scientific concerns with current work on the environment. Classic sociological themes such as democracy and public participation, the material conditions of social inequality or the contested nature of development cannot be treated in isolation from their material conditions; instead, their investigation needs to give adequate attention to both their socio-economic and their environmental causes and effects. While this 're-materialisation' of social theory and research presents considerable challenges, the contributions to this collection show that many traditional demarcation lines between the social and the natural sciences have become untenable and obstructive to sustainability thinking.

The book presents an extensive catalogue of methodological approaches and tools for social-scientific sustainability research and maps their deployment in concrete empirical projects. To group the different approaches effectively and to facilitate selective reading, chapters are allocated to three thematic areas: (1) work that focuses on the local level; (2) comparative studies that draw on different social and geographical units of analysis; and (3) investigations that give priority to time-related aspects of sustainability. We believe that each one of them captures a central area of current social-scientific sustainability research with regard to both conceptual orientation and methodological choice. Adopting this threefold structure represents an alternative approach to classifying social research that moves beyond more traditional qualitative/quantitative/multi-methods distinctions and dichotomies such as small- versus large-scale or positivist versus interpretivist. At the same time, this division into sociopolitical *and* time–space categories was deliberately chosen to acknowledge and make visible the critical departure from conventional ways of doing research that characterise much social scientific sustainability research today.

Part II covers methodologies and tools aimed at the investigation of attitudes and behaviour at the *local level*, that is among individuals, in families, households and individual organisations and within communities. All three chapters in this section demonstrate that a strong thematic and methodological focus on local- or micro-level phenomena can offer important insights into the development of social norms, conventions and processes and culture-specific views and practices that are much less visible at higher levels of social organisation. Importantly, a focus on the local explicitly recognises the significance of primary social relations, that is, those within the family or community but also in work, for people's everyday social and material practices, and thus for sustainability.

Part III focuses on *comparative approaches* that measure the sustainability performance of cities, regions and nation-states. The contributors to this part of the book also attend to some pressing conceptual and practical issues that have affected the comparative investigation of sustainable development to date. An in-depth discussion of the contested nature of sustainable development as a concept as well as discernible convergences and divergences with regards to its measurement are central themes in this part of the book.

Part IV explores the issue of time and its significance to sustainability. Here, arguments are put forward for a critical, in-depth engagement with temporal dimensions of social and ecological change. This in turn challenges social scientists to move beyond more conventional research methodologies that are largely atemporal and indifferent to the complexities of time and to embrace new and innovative approaches that take time seriously. A critical examination of biographic and longitudinal research designs and their epistemological foundations forms a central aspect of this section of the book. The concluding section, Part V, presents a critical assessment of current and future trends in social-scientific sustainability research.

All three chapters in Part II share a concern for the local as the main focus of sustainability inquiry and explore the merits and drawbacks for both researcher and researched of social-scientific inquiries into local lives. In Chapter 2, Stewart Barr and Jan Prillwitz explore the ways in which sustainability researchers approach the challenge of understanding pro-environmental behaviours. They review how most research to date has focused on citizens and consumers, drawing attention to the challenges that arise when trying to understand the motives and actions of individuals. They argue that many debates within sustainability policy stress the importance of behavioural change as a way of tackling global issues like climate change. However, there is still relatively little known about the processes that lead to shifts in everyday consumption patterns, especially with regard to social influences on individuals' habits and practices.

Barr and Prillwitz also note the recent acknowledgement by researchers in the sustainability field that environmental behaviours occur in everyday contexts that involve others, and warn of researching individual pro-environmental behaviour outside of this context. Proffering households as the most exigent and 'important unit for analysis of sustainability', Barr and Prillwitz present a brief overview of the theoretical approaches that have traditionally informed research on household sustainability before turning to examine the various methodological approaches. Here, they focus primarily on the use of survey questionnaires as a means of recording individual and household commitments towards the environment. They critically examine key theoretical and methodological concepts that inform the quantitative measurement of human behaviour, before detailing each stage of the survey approach. From framing appropriate aims and objectives, through survey design, construction and sampling, to implementation, Barr and Prillwitz's chapter provides valuable insights into each essential element of this quantitative research approach. Importantly, their contribution offers some practical advice for researchers in the field, such as what to do if a randomly sampled respondent is not home. While such detailed material is rarely found in traditional research methods books, it can be invaluable for researchers attempting to grapple with the practicalities of fieldwork.

Following on from their comprehensive and practical overview of the research process, Barr and Prillwitz draw on a recent case study of travel behaviour in the UK to illustrate the specific application of the survey technique. Indeed, such detailed descriptions of 'real-world' research projects are used throughout this entire collection, whereby authors introduce and critically examine individual case studies and projects to illustrate the benefits and drawbacks of a specific research technique or methodological approach. Barr and Prillwitz's chapter concludes with a brief exploration of the potential for survey research 'beyond the household as a unit for analysis defined by residential location' and a call for researchers to explore 'alternative sites of practice' if the survey-based sustainability assessment of households is to be advanced beyond its current remit.

The need for sustainability research to place individual's views and actions firmly within their wider social and political contexts forms an integral and recurring theme of the book. Anna Davies' theoretically framed examination of the merits and demerits of focus groups (FG) for the study of collective decision making (Chapter 3) demonstrates this very vividly. The contemporary prominence of public participation within sustainability strategies provides the context for her analysis. While the need for broad participation of society in sustainability decision making has long been acknowledged, it is only in recent years that researchers and practitioners have developed a suite of tools which specifically aim to address this 'deliberative turn' in sustainability engagement.

In her chapter, Davies first explores the wide range of tools and techniques to facilitate such participation. She examines critically how these tools and techniques vary with regard to type of engagement and the extent to which that engagement is connected to decision-making processes, before turning to focus groups as one such tool. Following a brief discussion of the nature of focus groups more generally as well as their methodological specificities, Davies purposely centres the chapter on the applications of the FG approach for sustainability and collective decision making. She provides a critical appraisal of how the focus group approach has been adopted and adapted to the purpose of progressing sustainability in a range of geographical and administrative contexts. Specifically, this chapter reviews some recent sustainability-related studies that adopt a focus group approach before detailing a specific case study of the use of FG research in exploring public environmental values and planning for sustainability in the UK. Davies concludes that FGs certainly can provide a means through which social groups can be involved in decision making, but warns that that if the outcomes or products that are formed during these processes cannot be accommodated within wider systems of governance, their impact will be limited at best.

Mark Garavan's chapter revolves around his experiences in the early- to mid-2000s researching and representing a community in North County Mayo in Ireland whose members have resisted the construction of a large-scale gas pipeline project. He argues for a dialogic approach to social research that takes seriously the concerns and voices of the participants and adopts a long-term view of human life and the research process. In addition, he cautions against efforts to exclude emotions from the research process because, while doing so may appear to reduce undue subjectivity, it also eclipses a major aspect of the human condition that is central to social inquiry. Garavan shows that local responses to the pipeline development involve culture-specific cognitive and linguistic efforts as well as visceral reactions by people who feel that the future of their place, community and livelihoods is under threat. This shows how local people's concepts of sustainability are often very different from rational-scientific discourses that dominate most sustainability debates. Instead they may involve feelings that cannot easily be articulated and that may only come to the fore whenever people are confronted with dominant discourses of 'development'. This poses some significant challenges to researchers who wish to capture and convey these culture-specific sustainability concepts.

Garavan refers to some existing ethnographic studies in sociology and anthropology to remind the reader of the culture-specific nature of concepts of rationality, which are often central to people's actions and protests. This allows him to connect his own work to major methodological debates that have influenced the investigation of cultures in the past and that remain highly relevant in the context of contemporary culture-sensitive sustainability research. Drawing on J.B. Peires' work, he is able to show that outside interpretations of unfamiliar social rituals such as the Great Xhosa Cattle Killing Movement (1856–7) are frequently inadequate and do not capture their culture-specific meanings. Culturally sensitive modes of inquiry, on the other hand, may produce accounts of protest events that capture both the why and the how. Garavan subsequently refers to Paolo Freire's work to make the case for a dialogic approach to social research that helps to address and potentially overcome some of the conceptual and methodological challenges that affect inquiries into local concepts of sustainability and their contestation.

Recent efforts to compare and contrast the sustainability performance of different cities, regions and nation-states are the focus of Part III of the collection. All three contributions offer a critical assessment of major conceptual and practical issues that have both helped and hindered the comparative study of sustainability. Naturally, a major focus of this part of the book is on the contested nature of sustainability concepts and indicators and their political relevance. In Chapter 5, Su-ming Khoo compares key indicators of human development and critically examines their connections with wider sustainability debates. Her detailed analysis of existing work in the field reveals some of the problems that have limited the applicability and usefulness of more traditional ways of measuring development. Many of these relate to the dominance of economistic thinking and its overemphasis on GDP, which has marginalised discussions about other significant areas of human social life.

Subsequently, Khoo argues that alternative ways of thinking and talking about sustainability such as the 'limits to growth' debates in the 1960s and 1970s have only partially captured the complexity of the problem, partly because these debates have remained firmly wedded to economic arguments. She also critiques how the dominance of narrow economistic approaches in sustainability policy has marginalised many qualitative aspects of sustainability, including people's quality of life and their capacity to reach their full potential and use their capabilities. Her discussion of alternative concepts and indicators of human development such as the three-dimensional Happy Planet Index (HPI) developed by the New Economics Foundation (NEF) and the notion of Ecological Space (ES) demonstrates both their advantages as well as limitations.

In Chapter 6, Veronika Gaube, Helmut Haberl and Karlheinz Erb examine key quantitative measurements of society–environment interaction to explore their suitability or otherwise for the interdisciplinary investigation of sustainability issues. Their chapter offers a detailed comparison of three internationally recognised environmental sustainability indicators: Material and Energy Flows Analysis (MEFA), Human Appropriation of Net Primary Production (HANPP) and Ecological Footprint (EF). All three indicators make visible the human consumption of natural resources both in numeric terms as well as through visual representation; however, they do so in very different ways. Through their systematic comparison, Gaube and colleagues are able to cast light on the usefulness, limitations and comparability of these three socio-ecological indicators. Importantly, they show how these indicators have become modified over time in response to changes in the nature and trajectory of society–environment interactions and subsequent shifts in their scientific measurement. This clearly demonstrates the highly fluid and dynamic nature of many sustainability indicators, a fact that deserves much greater attention than has hitherto been the case.

Drawing on examples from Austria's transition from an agrarian to an industrial society, Gaube and colleagues argue that complex interactions between society and the biophysical world can be only partially captured by methods that focus solely on the quantification of ecological sustainability. Moreover, it is evident from the discussion that the choice of indicator has significant implications for sustainable policy and practice, thereby contradicting proposals by some sustainability scientists for a decoupling of the politics and measurement of sustainability. They conclude their chapter with a plea for more inclusive indicators that incorporate environmental, social, economic and political factors and that could find application in different policy arenas.

Mapping as a tool for sustainability research enjoys growing popularity, partly because of the increasing significant of socio-spatial indicators of human development and its environmental consequences such as the Ecological Footprint (EF) or the Human Appropriation of Net Primary Production (HANPP) discussed by Gaube and colleagues in Chapter 6. Geographical Information Systems (GIS) enable the analysis and visual representation of diverse phenomena across a region – for example, topology, census data, or soils. Such information is vital for supporting sustainability planning. Indeed, there is now a substantial body of literature on the technological dimensions and the development of GIS-based sustainability indicators (see for example Carmichael et al., 2005; Ghose and Huxhold, 2005). In Chapter 7, Enda Murphy and Eoin King draw on their respective geographical and engineering backgrounds and expertise to demonstrate the importance of mapping as a method for assessing environmental sustainability. Situating their discussion at the city level, their chapter draws upon the issue of urban noise pollution as an illustrative example of the potential of mapping in sustainability research. Murphy and King discuss the link between noise pollution and environmental sustainability and review a number of key studies which have demonstrated that preservation of a good sound environment is important for the maintenance of public health, human well-being and a high quality of life.

Using the case study of Ireland's capital city Dublin, Murphy and King outline their approach to noise mapping and present some of their key findings. The authors conclude that graphical representations of environmental problems such as noise maps can serve to raise public awareness of major sustainability issues. They also highlight the transferable nature of these mapping techniques and their potential to identify and visualise trends in different types of social and environmental data, which can aid current and future understandings of sustainability issues and contribute to possible solutions.

In Part IV, Chapters 8 and 9 explore the many connections between time and sustainability, with a view to identifying areas of sustainability research, policy and practice that require 'temporalisation'. It is argued that while many conventional approaches to social-scientific research have remained largely atemporal, sustainability research clearly requires time-sensitive epistemological and methodological approaches. Melanie Jaeger-Erben's contribution (Chapter 8) focuses on the impact of life events on consumption patterns. She argues that a longitudinal approach to the investigation of (un)sustainable consumption patterns can shed light on why and how people change their everyday practices in ways that cross-sectional designs cannot. These findings may open up opportunities for policy makers and sustainability advocates to tailor their efforts towards the promotion of more sustainable consumption patterns to people's specific needs at various stages of their lives. However, Jaeger-Erben also shows that in some cases disruptions in people's everyday routines caused by life events such as relocation or the arrival of the first child may in fact further entrench existing practices that may or may not have significant resource implications.

While time plays a central role in society–environment interactions more generally, it is particularly relevant in the context of current sustainability debates and initiatives. In Chapter 9, Henrike Rau and Ricca Edmondson put forward arguments for the further 'temporalisation' of social-scientific sustainability research, that is, for the development and deployment of time-sensitive methodologies and tools for data collection and analysis. Their contribution examines recent proposals in the sustainability literature for a much greater engagement with the issue of time use and its implications for society and the material world. Importantly, they show how time-sensitive qualitative approaches can reveal important information about the meanings people attach to temporal aspects of sustainability, such as the issue of intergenerational justice.

The diversity of insights and approaches to sustainability research provided in Parts II, III and IV of this book clearly indicate the immense contribution of social-scientific research to the investigation of sustainability problems. In the concluding section of this volume, Part V, we, the editors, summarise the key themes emerging from the preceding chapters and identify some of the future challenges regarding social scientific research in the sustainability arena. Increasingly, many projects in this field are expected to be policy relevant in their questions and outputs. In our view, the opportunities and challenges of undertaking policy-relevant research are integral to the future shaping of social-scientific contributions to the sustainability debate. Through our own experiences of working in this field, we conclude the edited volume with a critical reflection on the methodological challenges involved in undertaking policy-relevant research and consider how newly emerging methodological approaches in the field of sustainability can challenge expectations among many policy makers about how sustainability research should be done.

## Notes

1 The FP7-funded project Sustainable Urban Metabolism for Europe (SUME) 2008–2011 exemplifies this new interest in urban societies, the built environment and broader issues of development (www.sume.at).
2 UNHCR, The UN Refugee Agency Press Release, 6 June 2011, http://www.unhcr.org/4decc5276.html (accessed 23 August 2011).
3 Note that definitions of the terms 'interdisciplinarity' and 'transdisciplinarity' differ significantly in the social sciences literature. In some cases, the two terms are used interchangeably. However, in this chapter we clearly distinguish between inter-, trans- and postdisciplinary work. Interdisciplinary research encompasses efforts to bring together researchers from different academic disciplines. The resulting exchange of ideas can be more or less detached from individuals' disciplinary background. The term 'transdisciplinarity' is useful to label projects that involve academic and non-academic experts and knowledge communities and that focus explicitly on solving 'real world' problems (cf. Hirsch Hadorn et al., 2008). Finally, postdisciplinary approaches explicitly set out to challenge common forms of disciplinary parochialism and imperialism (cf. Sayer, 1999).

# References

Bryman, A. (1984) 'The debate about quantitative and qualitative research: a question of method or epistemology', *The British Journal of Sociology*, 35 (1): 76–92.

Bryman, A. (1988) *Quantity and Quality in Social Research*. London: Routledge.

Carmichael, J., Talwar, S., Tansey, J. and Robinson, J. (2005) 'Where do we want to be? Making sustainability indicators integrated, dynamic and participatory', in R. Phillips (ed.), *Community Indicators Measuring Systems*. Aldershot: Ashgate. pp. 178–204.

Costanza, R. (1997) *Frontiers in Ecological Economics: Transdisciplinary Essays*. London: Edward Elgar.

Davies, A. R., Doyle, R. and Pape, J. (2012). Future visioning for sustainable household practices: spaces for sustainability learning? *Area*, 44 (1): 54–60. doi: 10.1111/j.1475-4762.2011.01054.x

Ehrlich, P.R. and Ehrlich, A.H. (1968) *The Population Bomb*. New York: Ballantine Books.

Ehrlich, P.E. and Ehrlich, A.H. (2009) 'The population bomb revisited', *Electronic Journal of Sustainable Development*, 1 (3): 63–71.

Flynn, B. (2007) *The Blame Game: Rethinking Ireland's Sustainable Development and Environmental Performance*. Dublin: Irish Academic Press.

Funtowicz, S. and Ravetz, J.R. (1991) 'A new scientific methodology for global environmental issues', in R. Costanza (ed.), *Ecological Economics: The Science and Management of Sustainability*. New York: Columbia University Press. pp. 137–52.

Ghose, R. and Huxhold, W. (2005) 'Role of multi-scalar GIS-based indicators studies in formulating neighbourhood planning policy', in R. Phillips (ed.), *Community Indicators Measuring Systems*. Aldershot: Ashgate. pp. 157–77.

Hirsch Hadorn, G., Bradley, D., Pohl, C., Rist, S. and Wiesmann, U. (2006) 'Implications of transdisciplinarity for sustainability research', *Ecological Economics*, 60 (1): 119–28.

Hirsch Hadorn, G., Hoffmann-Riem, H., Biber-Klemm, S., Grossenbacher-Mansuy, W., Joye, D., Pohl, C., Wiesmann, U. and Zemp, E. (eds) (2008) *Handbook of Transdisciplinary Research*. Dordrecht: Springer.

Jessop, B. and Sum, N. (2001) 'Pre-disciplinary and post-disciplinary perspectives', *New Political Economy*, 6 (1): 89–101.

Kaufmann, R.K. and Cleveland, C.J. (1995) 'Measuring sustainability: needed – an interdisciplinary approach to an interdisciplinary concept', *Ecological Economics*, 15 (2): 109–12.

Latouche, S. (2007) 'Sustainable consumption in a de-growth perspective', in E. Zaccai (ed.), *Sustainable Consumption, Ecology and Fair Trade*. London: Routledge. pp. 178–85.

Latouche, S. (2010) *Farewell to Growth*. London: Wiley.

Lyall, C., Bruce, A., Tait, J. and Meagher, L. (2011) *Interdisciplinary Research Journeys: Practical Strategies for Capturing Creativity*. London: Bloomsbury.

Meadows, D.H., Meadows, D.L., Randers, J. and Behrens III, W.W. (1972) *The Limits to Growth*. New York: Universe Books.

Meadows, D.H., Meadows, D.L. and Randers, J. (2004) *Limits to Growth: The 30-Year Update*. White River Junction, VT: Chelsea Green Publishing.

Mebratu, D. (1998) 'Sustainability and sustainable development: historical and conceptual review', *Environmental Impact Assessment Review*, 18 (6): 493–520.

Norberg-Hodge, H. (1991/2009) *Ancient Futures: Learning from Ladakh*. San Francisco, CA: Sierra Club.

Parris, T.M. and Kates, R.W. (2003) 'Characterizing and measuring sustainable development', *Annual Review of Environment and Resources*, 28: 559–86.

Quist, J. and Vergragt, P.J. (2004) 'Backcasting for industrial transformations and system innovations towards sustainability: relevance for governance?', in K. Jacob, M. Binder and A. Wiezorek (eds), *Governance for Industrial Transformation. Proceedings of the 2003 Berlin Conference on the Human Dimensions of Global Environmental Change*. Berlin: Environmental Policy Research Centre. pp. 409–37.

Rau, H. (2010) '(Im)mobility and environment–society relations: arguments for and against the "mobilisation" of environmental sociology', in M. Gross and H. Heinrichs (eds), *Environmental Sociology: European Perspectives and Interdisciplinary Challenges*. Dordrecht: Springer. pp. 237–53.

Sachs, W. (1997) '"Sustainable Development"', in M. Redclift and G. Woodgate (eds), *The International Handbook of Environmental Sociology*. Cheltenham: Edward Elgar. pp. 71–82.

Salehyan, I. (2008) 'From climate change to conflict: no consensus yet', *Journal of Peace Research*, 45 (3): 315–26.

Sayer, A. (1999) 'Long live postdisciplinary studies! Sociology and the curse of disciplinary parochialism/ imperialism'. Lancaster: Department of Sociology Online Papers, http://www.lancs.ac.uk/fass/sociology/papers/sayer-long-live-postdisciplinary-studies.pdf (accessed 2 October 2011).

Schor, J.B. (2010) *Plenitude*. New York: The Penguin Press.

Stern, N. (2006) *Stern Review on the Economics of Climate Change*. London: HM Treasury.

Stock, P. and Burton, R.J.F. (2011) 'Defining terms for integrated (multi-inter-trans-disciplinary) sustainability research', *Sustainability*, 3 (8): 1090–113.

WCED (World Commission on Environment and Development) (1987) *Our Common Future: A Global Agenda for Change*. Oxford: Oxford University Press.

# PART II

Researching Local Lives: Experiences of (Un)sustainability among Individuals, Households and Communities

# 2

## Household Analysis: Researching 'green' lifestyles, a survey approach

*Stewart Barr and Jan Prillwitz*

## Introduction: disciplinary methods for an interdisciplinary challenge?

This first chapter on 'doing' sustainability research will focus on what many policy makers have argued is the most challenging and important unit for analysis of sustainability. As will be seen later in this chapter, however one defines 'households' (as individuals, consumers or units based on living circumstances) the relationship between this 'micro' or 'meso' scale and global environmental challenges is becoming increasingly important for policy makers keen to generate a widespread change in the way societies live and consume resources (DEFRA, 2005, 2008). Yet despite the enthusiasm with which national and local authorities have embraced the 'behaviour change' agenda at this scale, the magnitude of the task is such that there continues to be an increase in the volume of literature dedicated to understanding and promoting behaviour change (Jackson, 2005). This chapter will explore the ways in which this agenda has been pursued methodologically by focusing on a number of considerations that researchers need to address when exploring household sustainability. In this introductory section, the definition and disciplinary boundaries of 'household sustainability' research will be examined, before exploring the scales of household research (households – consumers – individuals). Then, the chapter will explore the theoretical and methodological approaches that have been adopted to study household sustainability, before providing a worked case example from an Economic and Social Research Council (ESRC) project in the south-west of England. It should be noted that the chapter will focus specifically on quantitative methods of survey design and analysis: the reader is encouraged to look at other chapters in this volume for details of qualitative methodologies. Finally, the chapter will conclude by exploring the scale of households, as individuals, consumers and units of 'everyday' life, through the lens of alternative contexts for behaviour beyond 'the home', such as leisure and work-based environments.

The first major task in an exploration of sustainability at the household scale is to examine what is meant by 'sustainability' in this context. As indicated by this chapter's subtitle, the term 'sustainability' has become synonymous with 'environment', yet it should be noted that defining household practices related to sustainability is fraught with problems and researchers have often adopted flexible approaches for exploring 'green' household behaviour. These have often been on what could be argued as the periphery of environmental concerns, for example, the focus on ethical consumption (Seyfang, 2005) and local food networks (Little et al., 2009). In both of these cases, 'environmental' concerns were framed in a broader sustainability context, encompassing economic, social and ethical concerns, whereas in other studies (e.g. Anable's study of 'green' travel behaviour, 2005) the environmental focus has been more pointed. Indeed, it should be noted that despite surface evidence to the contrary, nearly all of the research that has described and explored sustainable behaviours is based on an environmental framing of sustainability.

A second issue relates to the terms used in the literature relating to 'green lifestyles'. The terms 'green' and 'lifestyles' are both somewhat problematic because a wide range of definitions has been used to frame both constructs. This relates partly to the environmental focus on sustainability practices discussed previously. However, when used together, the notion of 'green lifestyles' implies clearly demarcated practices that can be identified, codified and measured that constitute an environmentally sustainable set of behaviours. Indeed, the use of the term 'lifestyles' implies particular formations of practices that can be used to identify groups of individuals sharing broadly similar behavioural traits. As will be seen in this chapter, such an approach has come to dominate UK public policy for behavioural change, but it is important to note that in strictly academic terms, the notion of lifestyles represents a broad range of concepts well beyond these approaches and encompasses disciplines such as sociology, psychology, anthropology, marking and geography. Indeed, the term is often used interchangeably with notions of pro-environmental behaviour, environmental practice and environmentally responsible behaviour. In most cases, researchers using these terms are referring to sets of behaviours that have a direct impact on environmental sustainability, such as recycling waste, reducing thermostats or using less water, although those using the term 'practice' would argue that what is important to understand is not the relationship of the behaviour to the outcome, but rather the behaviour itself. In most cases, differences between these terms are largely semantic, but underlying these are important epistemological variations.

The third and final issue to consider when approaching the study of household sustainability is therefore the disciplinary perspective adopted, or indeed whether to adopt such a perspective. While visiting the University of British Columbia's Institute for Resources, Environment and Sustainability in 2009, we asked one colleague for his disciplinary background. He replied, 'I have no home discipline. I focus on problems and the solutions we can find to resolving them. A disciplinary focus cannot do that.' This remark struck us not only for its boldness but also the universal truth that it portrays. Yet reading the numerous research papers that have been published on sustainable living, it seems obligatory for writers to argue the case for their preferred disciplinary approach. This has much to do with the internal workings of the academic system, which often rewards evidence of 'contribution to the discipline' over inter- or cross-disciplinary research that is both innovative and problem-centred, and funding and monitoring schemes such as the Research Assessment Exercise (RAE) in the UK have done very little to incentivise researchers to cross the divide between disciplines.

A useful illustration of the divisions that can develop and often hamper progress on understanding a research challenge is the issue of travel behaviour research. As Banister (2008) has noted, transportation studies have come to be broadly defined by two epistemological and methodological approaches, which in turn have knock-on effects on the ways in which researchers define, explore and explain travel behaviour. On the one hand, proponents of the 'transport planning and engineering' concept argue that travel is based on a derived demand and research should focus on enhancing mobility, reducing travel times and be based on modelling approaches. In contrast to this focus on physical dimensions, the 'sustainable mobility paradigm' has sought to focus on social dimensions, where travel is a valued activity and the focus should be on enhancing accessibility, stressing reasonable travel times and reliabilities, and placing focus on people as the primary users of transport networks. These two approaches necessarily drive different methodological agendas, with the first being mainly centred on large-scale modelling of travel behaviour based on the interaction of physical factors. In contrast, the second places emphasis on smaller-scale studies of values, attitudes, practices and wider social concerns that place mobility in the context of social and cultural norms for travel and consumption. Such differences in approach are important to appreciate when considering the study and promotion of green lifestyles; in many instances, the researcher is forced to make a choice between different epistemological and methodological strategies, both to serve the coherence of their research, but also to satisfy the peer review community of the validity of their work.

Accordingly, despite numerous calls for more interdisciplinary working, there is still a tendency to focus on conventional approaches to research and, in the wider context of green lifestyles, the remainder of this chapter will seek to signpost these issues as they arise.

## The 'Household' Scale: citizens – consumers – households

When the term 'household' is used, it commonly evokes notions of family units living within a given residential unit. Yet this catch-all term masks a range of micro scales and networks within which green lifestyles have been measured and explored. Although it may be a crude distinction, research at the household scale can broadly be categorised into three groups. First, there has been a focus on the 'citizen' as an individual who has ascribed responsibility for acting in an environmentally responsible manner. Second, the notion of citizenship has been extended to incorporate the various acts of consumption that pervade modern, everyday life and places citizen responsibilities alongside the choice-ethic typified by contemporary market economies. Third, these individual elements can be placed in the wider context of household units, groups of individuals who through the mundane practices of everyday life co-organise their acts of consumption and daily routines.

The majority of pro-environmental behaviour research has focused on the first two of these categories, placing the individual at the centre of understanding environmental practices. Spaargaren and Mol (2008) describe the ways in which the 'citizen-consumer' construct has become prevalent in framing the various theoretical approaches towards pro-environmental behaviour in Western capitalist societies. Indeed, this focus on the individual is one that marks a wider political shift in understandings of the rights and responsibilities of citizens and consumers in neo-liberal economies (Giddens, 1991). As Clarke et al. (2007) have noted, an analysis of public services in the UK since the 1980s reveals how the responsibilities of good citizenship have been framed within notions of consumer rights and choice. Thus in the environmental realm, it is no longer acceptable or adequate to simply frame 'individuals' as key actors; they are both citizens and consumers:

> The act of consumption is becoming increasingly suffused with citizenship characteristics and considerations. It is no longer possible to cut the deck neatly between citizenship and civic duty, on one side, and consumption and self interest, on the other. (Scammell, 2000: 351–52)

Such an assertion is significant from a methodological perspective, because research that only views individuals participating in 'environmentally responsible' behaviour as an act of good citizenship fails to recognise the ways in which policy and the state have come to promote consumption as an equally valid approach to environmental sustainability (Slocum, 2004; Berglund and Matti, 2006). This is a departure from earlier writings of social theorists on environmentally responsible behaviour (e.g. Leonard-Barton, 1981), who argued for reduced consumption and frugality as a way to promote sustainability. In contrast, the mainstream logic of the consumer-citizen approach does not question the need to consume, but rather places emphasis on the power of consumer choice in making the 'right' decisions.

Nonetheless, such an approach is not without its critics, and recent research by social scientists has called for an appraisal of the comfortable alignment of consumption and citizenship. Johnson (2008: 62) has argued that:

> the citizen-consumer hybrid provides relatively superficial attention to citizenship goals in order better to serve three key elements of consumerist ideology: consumer choice, status distinction, and ecological cornucopianism.

In this way, researchers need to recognise the boundaries of what constitutes the green lifestyle and to question the logic of the ways in which policy frames such lifestyles in normative settings. To make the point, a recent World Wildlife Fund (WWF) paper on behavioural change warned that:

> The comfortable perception that global environmental challenges can be met through marginal lifestyle changes no longer bears scrutiny. The cumulative impact of large numbers of individuals making marginal improvements in their environmental impact will be a marginal collective improvement in environmental impact. Yet we live at a time when we need urgent and ambitious changes. (Crompton and Thogersen, 2009: 6)

Accordingly, individuals as consumers and citizens pose a series of challenges for researchers interested in exploring green lifestyles, from questioning the normative understandings of what environmentally 'responsible' behaviour constitutes to understanding the ways in which individuals balance consumer rights and citizen responsibilities. Yet there is also a further complication that arises when considering the green lifestyle, and this is related to the scaling of environmental behaviours; for while the individual has become the standard frame of reference for exploring pro-environmental behaviour, researchers have come to recognise that such behaviours occur in everyday contexts that involve others, most often in the household.

Accordingly, researchers of pro-environmental behaviour need to be mindful of the pitfalls of studying individuals outside of this context. Recent research by scholars such as Nicky Gregson and Elizabeth Shove (Gregson, 2006; Gregson and Crewe, 2003; Gregson et al., 2007; Shove, 2003; Shove et al., 2007) has stressed the importance of household practices through explorations of the materialities of everyday life and has placed emphasis on the household as a key frame of reference, exploring the ways in which materials and technologies are purchased, consumed, used and disposed by household members. This research, based on in-depth qualitative methods, has demonstrated the importance of viewing the household as a site where practices are negotiated between and influenced by other household members, thus stressing the importance of context when exploring individual behaviours.

In reality, many social researchers do not have the logistical capability or funding to undertake such detailed research at the household level, but it is nonetheless critical for researchers to recognise the importance of households, their metabolism and collective practices as part of any investigation of green lifestyles.

## Exploring household sustainability: theoretical approaches

Having outlined a range of definitional, disciplinary and contextual factors that researchers of green lifestyles need to consider, the final piece of background information necessary for studying households and sustainability is to appreciate the various theoretical approaches that have been adopted to explore pro-environmental behaviour. Such an appreciation is critical to understand the epistemological basis for the methodological approaches deployed to empirically investigate pro-environmental behaviour, and an overview of research in this field is no simple task – any attempt to generalise types of research into categories inevitably leads to crude simplifications. However, for the sake of brevity and understanding, three broad traditions can be identified: social–psychological, sociological and policy-driven.

The first of these approaches, related broadly to the field of social and environmental psychology, has dominated pro-environmental behaviour studies at the individual and household level for a number of decades (Barr, 2008), and has contributed a wealth of empirical understanding to the psychological prossesses involved in environmental decision making. Using both established theoretical models from social psychology, such as Ajzen's (1991) theory of planned behaviour, and wider research from the quantitative social sciences, researchers have attempted to identify the factors influencing environmental behaviours using measures of values (e.g. Dunlap et al., 2000), attitudes (e.g. Oskamp et al., 1991) and contextual factors (Guagnano et al., 1995). These are often explored through the use of statistical techniques to identify the most important influences.

A second tradition in environmental social science relates to research on the role of the environment in framing everyday social practices (Shove, 2003). Informed by an understanding of 'practice' as the representation of consumption norms in contemporary society, research by authors such as Shove et al. (2007), Gregson et al. (2007) and Bulkeley and Gregson (2009) has largely utilised qualitative methods to explore the ways in which 'the environment' is framed within everyday settings and is inextricably linked with overarching consumption practices that come to form the mundane and yet richly diverse practices of daily life.

Finally, and often unrelated to these two preceding traditions, both academics and policy makers have recently begun to engage in wider debates concerning the viability of generating behavioural change. Accordingly, such research is by definition applied and action-centred, with the emphasis on using appropriate concepts and methods to understand and effect change (Barr, 2008). Indeed, in recent publications by the UK's Department for the Environment, Food and Rural Affairs (DEFRA, 2005, 2008) considerable research effort has been focused on the use of market-oriented techniques to understand and promote behavioural change through tools like social marketing, which relies heavily on the segmentation of populations using statistical techniques such as cluster analysis (Wheeler et al., 2004).

In reality, presenting three discrete 'traditions' in this way is somewhat misleading, given the tendency for much new research to adopt a postdisciplinary perspective. Nonetheless, in both interpreting the ways in which others have designed their surveys and in considering the function of a survey in one's own research, the theoretical diversity in environmental social science is often a key consideration.

## Methodological approaches to household sustainability

A consideration of the many contextual factors (notably disciplinary and theoretical concerns) involved in pro-environmental behaviour research at the household and individual levels can be daunting and, therefore, has to be guided by the epistemological considerations of the research involved alongside the practicalities of the research project concerned. This section will explore these considerations in two ways. First, it will provide an overview of the ways in which researchers can utilise surveys (a necessarily broad term) to examine behavioural, attitudinal and situational characteristics of household sustainability. Second, it will use a case study from recently completed research in the UK that has focused on the complex issue of travel behaviour. This example will demonstrate the practicalities of survey design, implementation and analysis, as well as the limitations of using this type of method.

## The survey approach

As Bryman (2008) has noted, the term 'survey' describes any empirical tool that is researcher-led within the social sciences, but its common use is often applied only to questionnaire surveys that contain both quantitative and qualitative items. In this section, therefore, the term 'survey' refers to this popular definition that ostensibly relates to questionnaire design, and the section will aim to explore the stages that researchers need to go through in designing, testing, implementing and analysing household survey data.

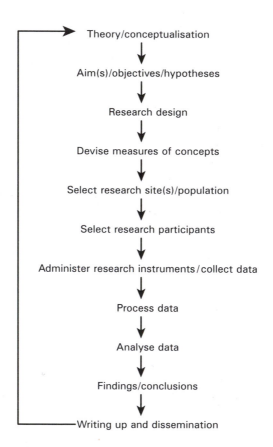

**Figure 2.1** The survey process.

As a guide to appreciating the importance of a logical research process, Bryman (2008) provides an excellent flow diagram demonstrating the ways in which much quantitative social research proceeds from a series of questions and hypotheses right through to the generation of results and further research (Figure 2.1 is a shortened and adapted version). The crucial point to take from this diagram is the importance of linking the aims, objectives and theoretical considerations of the research with the study instrument's (i.e. survey) questions and the analysis of these items to yield data to address the initial aims and objectives. This is of particular importance with research that uses large amounts of quantitative data, where it is too easy to get lost in the mass of information collected and thus avoid addressing the critical questions. Accordingly, the following subsections aim to provide brief pointers to good practice in the design, implementation and analysis of a household survey.

## Aims and objectives for household surveys

Framing appropriate aims and objectives is critical for the outcomes one wants to achieve at the end of the research process, so these need to be both distinct and focused, which ultimately enables one to design a better survey instrument.

A research *aim* should seek to provide an overview of the purpose of the research, without being definitive in terms of the particular methods or the specific data unit to be collected. In household survey research on sustainability, it is quite common for an aim to frame the theoretical or conceptual approach being adopted and to identify the geographical or demographic population being considered. Good examples would include those which sought to:

- Identify the barriers and motivations involved in promoting greater use of sustainable transport modes in London;
- Examine the efficacy of the Theory of Planned Behaviour (TPB) in determining the uptake of recycling behaviour in student households;
- Explore the role of gender and ethnicity in determining levels of water conservation in low-income households.

These three examples provide a range of combinations for the composite elements of a good research aim; each one is theory- or concept-led (with either a reference to a particular theoretical idea or a hypothesis) and states the population to be examined (geographic, demographic, social). However, the aims listed above do not stipulate the ways in which they will be addressed methodologically. This is the role of *objectives*, which provide the direct link to the survey instrument and provide the guide for designing sections and questions in the survey. To take the first aim as an example, this might have the following three objectives:

1  To measure reported daily travel behaviour amongst a random selection of individuals in three London boroughs;
2  To assess the motivations and barriers for engaging in more sustainable travel modes amongst this sample of individuals;
3  To use segmentation analysis to define specific 'travel lifestyles' and to examine the behavioural, attitudinal and demographic characteristics of these groups.

These objectives have a number of important properties. First, they are analytically incremental, moving from descriptive measurement to analytical complexity. Second, they clearly define what is to be measured (i.e. behaviour, attitudes and so on). Third, they give an indication of the outcome of the analysis (in this case, a segmentation model). Indeed, a further policy-oriented objective could be added to make the links between research and practice more evident.

## Survey design considerations

Perhaps the most problematic element of household survey design is the relationship between the survey instrument and deciding how it will be implemented (e.g. by mail, face-to-face). In one sense, a decision about implementation has to be borne in mind before a final decision on the type of survey instrument can be made, because of issues such as practicality, length and likely response rates. While mail surveys and questionnaires hand-delivered for respondents to complete can be of some considerable length, those undertaken on the doorstep or 'on the street' require brevity that is often hard to achieve when the research has numerous objectives. Thus the relationship between survey type and implementation method is something of a conundrum, and it is likely that the definitive choice in one area will direct a commensurate approach in the other.

Alongside the challenge of deciding on a survey type, a further problem specific to environmental behaviour research is the ways in which the research seeks to measure and report pro-environmental behaviour. This is a particular concern within the sustainability field, because researchers are often concerned with 'measuring' behaviour and attitudes towards issues that are both emotive and governed by complex normative assumptions. One of the most contentious issues has been the measurement of pro-environmental behaviour using reported behavioural indices (for example, asking people how frequently they engage in a range of practices like recycling or energy conservation). These measures are evidently proxies of behaviour, and because pro-environmental behaviour can often be governed by a perceived norm to 'conform' to specific sets of practices, there have been concerns that individuals tend to overestimate the extent to which they are environmentally active (Corral-Verdugo, 1997). Despite these concerns, the research of Corral-Verdugo and his colleagues (Corral-Verdugo et al.,

1994–1995) has demonstrated that while reported behaviour is not a strictly accurate measure of actual commitment, the differences between individuals are proportionate and so assumptions can be made with a degree of certainty concerning the relative commitments of different respondents.

Accordingly, despite the legitimate concerns researchers have about measuring behaviour, in many ways the proxies derived from surveys are the most cost-effective and practically realistic. Attempts at observed environmental behaviours are fraught with problems, not least because so much environmental practice is habitual in nature and thus is not simply observed by measuring quantities of one sort or another. Indeed, even in cases where detailed analysis of issues such as waste arisings occur (e.g. Tucker, 1999) the final amounts are not particularly helpful in explaining why these have occurred. It is therefore the case that most survey approaches are based on the measurement of reported behaviour through a range of common indices, which will be explored later in this chapter.

The final issue to consider in survey design is the ways in which the instrument will align the stated objectives with the survey instrument itself, to ensure that the objectives can be successfully met. If we take a look at the objectives outlined in the previous section, we should now be able to expand on how these could be measured in our survey (in italics below each objective):

- To measure reported daily travel behaviour amongst a random selection of individuals in three London boroughs:

  *Use a range of travel behaviour indices to explore type of travel, travel mode and frequency of use, and whether this is for single or multiple journeys.*

- To assess the motivations and barriers for engaging in more sustainable travel modes amongst this sample of individuals:

  *Use a range of theoretically defined measures to explore motivations and barriers, perhaps adopting measures used in previous research or those which enable comparisons to other frameworks or models.*

- To use segmentation analysis to define specific 'travel lifestyles' and to examine the behavioural, attitudinal and demographic characteristics of these groups.

  *This requires that the data are collected and measured in such a way that the segmentation analysis can be undertaken, i.e. the measures are usable with the type of analysis to be undertaken.*

Accordingly, survey design for pro-environmental behaviour studies at the household level requires consideration of the implementation approach to be adopted, the ways in which behaviour will be measured and the conditions necessary for the survey to address the various objectives of the research.

## Survey construction

With the various survey considerations in mind, the practical construction of a survey instrument (or questionnaire) is often viewed as being a simple process, requiring relatively little thought and sophistication. However, survey questions are open to potential different interpretations, which requires the researcher to pay particular attention to their formulation and presentation. Dillman (1978) provides an excellent guide to the construction of mail and telephone surveys, and highlights the numerous pitfalls of sloppy survey design and question wording. What follows is a simple but specific guide to ensuring that a survey exploring pro-environmental issues is both effective and comprehensive.

First, the presentation of the survey is a key issue. Although questionnaires that are researcher completed do not require a professional design, the way the research is presented orally to the respondent is equally important. As Dillman (1978) notes, all surveys should look as professional as possible, within the limits of time and financial constraints that may not permit glossy or colour designs. If the survey is on paper and to be completed by the respondent, the underlying messages conveyed by the title and images on the cover are critically important; for example, is the title value-laden or leading? Consider the difference between a survey entitled 'Encouraging environmental behaviour' and 'Investigating environmental behaviour'. Clearly the first example indicates a particular position that aims to promote behavioural change, while the second takes a more neutral position. Indeed, images can also send particular messages; consider the value (or not) of including official logos on the front of a questionnaire. While public opinion surveys still demonstrate widespread trust of academic research, the presence of logos from other organisations can be a mixed blessing. Take the example of placing a local authority logo on the front cover of a survey about waste management. Ostensibly, this may appear to add credibility and authority to the survey, but it may also be viewed as an endorsement of the local authority's policies and thus reframe a respondent's views on the research and their responses to it.

The same basic principles apply to surveys undertaken on the street or door-to-door, where the researcher completes a series of answers provided by the respondent. In this case, verbal indicators are crucially important in the ways respondents perceive the research and it is also worth considering the presentation of the researcher; does a business suit denote a corporate or 'official' stance, whereas a very casual appearance gives a sense of amateurism?

A second issue is the introduction to the survey. Whether administered verbally or in writing, the instructions and introduction to a survey are major determinants of whether a respondent will decide to complete the questionnaire or not. This section of a survey is often complex and requires considerable fine editing to reduce the size to a manageable level, yet there are certain key elements that are required. First, the respondent needs to become familiar with the aims of the research and its potential use; again, as with the survey title, care must be taken to ensure that the aims are neutral and do not act as a deterrent to those who may not be pro-environmental. Second, the introduction needs to ensure that the respondents are familiar with the uses the survey data will be put to and the ways in which their information will be kept both confidential and anonymous. This can cause some problems if the survey is being used as a recruitment tool for further (usually qualitative) research, and a simple way of ensuring respondents' anonymity is to state that their personal details will be separated from the survey on its return. Finally, clear instructions need to be provided about the survey's completion. In household surveys, there may be a requirement that a particular member of the household completes the questionnaire, or that each adult member completes a section. In most cases, this will be beyond the researcher's control, but it is prudent to ensure that every effort to get the right person to complete the survey.

Aside from issues of presentation and the introduction, there are several other points that need to be considered as general principles of good survey design:

- For self-completion questionnaires, the format should be logical, well-spaced and of an appropriate design that most individuals could read the survey (although large print copies should be made available on request);
- Dividing the survey into sections helps the respondents to manage their completion of the questionnaire and enables them to fill it out in stages. It also makes it look less menacing!
- Each section should be introduced to provide a short rationale for its inclusion, especially where personal data are requested (such as age, gender, income and other demographic data);
- Question wording is evidently critical, yet often overlooked by researchers. Simplicity and the use of familiar language are vital and there is a need to avoid jargon. For example, the term 'sustainability' is often used in surveys without much thought, and yet this term is both unfamiliar and often contested by respondents;
- In cases where specific value or attitude inventories need to be used, these should be explained and, in some cases, respondents should be encouraged to give their immediate reactions rather than dwelling at length over what could appear as complex questions. This is often a problem with psychological value scales where individuals are asked to rate abstract notions of 'simplicity', 'nature' and 'environment';

- Finally, with surveys that are related to environmental issues, there are often ethical issues that need to be considered in terms of respondent learning and knowledge transfer. In many cases, surveys can act as spurs to new ways of thinking for respondents and, therefore, it is important to provide a way for individuals to obtain more information and feedback from the survey.

## Sampling and implementation

The final consideration in survey design is evidently the means of sampling and collecting the data from the questionnaire according to the study's objectives. In the first instance, the sampling frame will be determined mostly by the population of interest and the desired outcomes from the research (i.e. a representative sample based on a known population or a sample based on factors such as convenience or prior knowledge). Standard methodological textbooks (see Bryman, 2008; Wheeler et al., 2004) provide clear explanations of the main ways of sampling for questionnaire surveys, but in essence the choice between probabilistic sampling (for representative samples of a given population) and non-probabilistic sampling (for convenience, purposive or quota samples) is driven by the outcomes one wishes the survey to attain; representative samples can go some way to enabling the researcher to make broad statements about the population based on the sample, while non-probability samples are necessarily more limited in their scope to generalise. However, there may also be other considerations in the choice of a sampling frame, such as the time, resources and data availability for selecting samples based on random or systematic random techniques. In many cases lack of funding, time and labour necessitate approaches based on convenience and purposive techniques.

The second consideration, that of implementation, is necessarily determined in part by the sampling framework adopted, but is also often influenced by the practicalities of collecting sufficient data on a limited budget and within a short time frame. As standard textbooks indicate, the number of potential implementation strategies ranges from on-street, door-to-door, contact and collect (where the survey is left with the respondent to complete), to telephone, mail and Internet. In an environmental social science context there are no preferable approaches, but rather an appreciation is needed that the more contact the researcher can have with respondents, the higher the response rate will be. Inevitably, this is a consideration that has to be based on the specific project parameters.

There are clearly many more considerations for environmental social scientists in the design and implementation of surveys that cannot be included in this short chapter, but these constitute the major points. The final substantive sections of this chapter considers these using a specific case study of travel behaviour that provides a practical example of survey design.

# A UK case study of travel behaviour

To illustrate some of the points made in the previous section, this part of the chapter will discuss a typical example of environmental behaviour research that adopted a survey approach. The example is drawn from an Economic and Social Research Council (ESRC) project on Promoting Sustainable Travel undertaken from January 2008 to July 2010 (www.exeter.ac.uk/prost). The project as a whole aimed to explore the motivations and barriers for individuals to engage in more environmentally sustainable forms of travel behaviour, such as walking, cycling, public transport use, as well as a consideration of travel behaviour in a tourism context and the motivations and barriers towards adopting low-carbon forms of travel for tourism and leisure. The research consisted of five stages, involving survey instrument design through both stakeholder engagement and a preliminary set of focus group discussions. These initial stages were used to design and implement a questionnaire survey to 2000 households in and around the city of Exeter in south-west England. Subsequently, respondents to the survey participated in both further focus group and in-depth interview research. The following sections describe the three stages of survey design, sampling and implementation, and demonstrate the process of undertaking a survey from the setting of objectives to the implementation of the questionnaire.

# Conceptual and theoretical underpinnings

In line with the comments at the start of this chapter, it is worth exploring the intellectual basis for the research, given that this has a major bearing on the survey design adopted. Like many areas of environmental social science, travel behaviour research is characterised by a number of different theoretical and conceptual perspectives, drawn from social psychology, economics and sociology. Indeed, as Banister (2008) has noted, the disciplinary differences in travel research have fundamental implications for how individuals are perceived within the transport system. The research reported in this chapter adopted a pragmatic approach and framed the research around the developments in UK environmental policy that have placed individual consumers at the centre of efforts to promote sustainable development (DEFRA, 2005, 2008). This approach has begun to explore the ways in which segmenting the population into groups defined by their environmental attitudes can be used to target tailored policies at these different segments. Within this context, the research aimed to evaluate this strategy through exploring travel behaviour in a range of residential and spatial contexts, and drew on a range of theoretical ideas from previous work by social psychologists (e.g. Anable, 2005), sociologists (e.g. Shove, 2003) and policy analysts (e.g. Darnton and Sharp, 2006). Indeed, the research also sought to examine the role of climate change as an emergent discourse in debates on travel behaviour (Becken and Hay, 2007). Accordingly, rather than being defined by one particular discipline or theoretical model, the research used both qualitative and quantitative methods to evaluate the effectiveness of segmentation as a technique for promoting sustainable travel behaviour, and thus drew on a range of perspectives.

## Objectives and survey design

The objectives of the research were as follows:

- First, to identify and measure a series of 'sustainable travel behaviours' using a sample of individuals from the general public;
- Second, to explore the empirical and conceptual links between different types of sustainable travel practices amongst the sample;
- Third, to use segmentation analysis to identify a series of lifestyle groups based on these behavioural data;
- Fourth, to use an established framework of environmental behaviour to identify the motivators and barriers for adopting different forms of behaviour according to lifestyle group;
- Fifth, to use the results from objectives 1–4 to assist local and national policy makers in promoting sustainable lifestyle practices through social marketing techniques.

Objectives 1 to 4 clearly relate to the types of data and analysis that were required from the quantitative survey (amongst other methods), while objective 5 is an impact-oriented task relating to the wider dissemination and longer-term influence of the research.

As noted previously, the quantitative survey design was developed both with theoretical ideas and issues raised by local and regional stakeholders (such as local authorities, interest groups and government agencies) and the results from ten preliminary focus groups. Two of these groups were held in each of the study's five sample locations. These were defined on the basis that travel behaviour is partly linked to residential location and thus household access to services. Accordingly, the five study locations represented a series of different urban environments: high-density inner city, medium-density suburbs, low-density outskirt suburb, rural commuter estate and rural town centre.

Given that information for items to be used in the survey was derived from three different sources, the number of potential themes to explore was considerable, and this was compounded by the recognition that respondents would only have limited tolerance in answering large numbers of questions. Accordingly, the process of designing the survey commenced in May 2008, directly after the first stakeholder meeting, and continued until August 2008 when the results of the ten focus groups held in early July 2008 were considered.

The process of questionnaire construction often seems both simple and linear in nature, but this research demonstrated that numerous iterations were needed before the questionnaire was ready for publication. First, the principal investigator of the project drafted the initial survey, which was then altered by the project researcher, a process that continued for several months. Second, a draft of the survey was sent to key stakeholders for comments. Third, the market research company also commented on the survey to provide advice on the practicalities of its implementation.

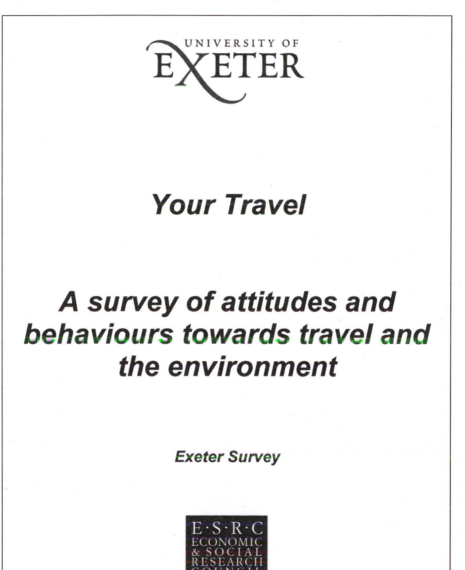

**Figure 2.2** Cover page of travel questionnaire.

## Introduction

Thank you for agreeing to complete this survey. It is designed to gauge your attitudes and opinions over a wide range of travel and transport issues that concern Exeter, Devon and the UK. It is funded by the Government's Economic and Social Research Council (ESRC) and is part of a large research project into travel and transport in Devon by University of Exeter.

It is important to the research team that you answer ALL sections relevant to you and your household. This will help us achieve a more accurate account of everyone's views. We would ask that one adult individual in your household completes the survey, in the main about themselves only. Once completed a representative of our team will collect it at an agreed time.

The research seeks to examine the links between people's attitudes and their behaviour for a range of travel and lifestyles activities. You can be sure that the responses you give will not be written in vain. The final results of the research will be sent to the City and County Councils for inspection before being used by both central and local government to shape provision of better services for local residents.

**Prize Draw:** We are offering the opportunity to win one of five prizes for participants who complete this survey. Winners will be selected at random in a prize draw once all responses have been received in March 2009. The first two prizes will be a First Class Open return rail ticket from Exeter to London and the remaining three prizes will be day return standard rail ticket from Exeter. If you would like to be entered into the prize draw, please fill in your details below*.

**Participation:** If you would like to take part in a follow-up focus group as part of this research, please fill in your details below*. If selected, we will contact you during the spring of 2009.

**Feedback:** If you would like to receive a brief written report on the results of your work, please fill in your details below*. We will send you the report during summer 2009.

| I would like to: | Enter the prize draw (please tick) ☐ | Take part in a follow-up focus group (please tick) ☐ | Receive written feedback on the research (please tick) ☐ |
|---|---|---|---|
| **Name** | | | |
| **Address** | | | |
| **Telephone** | | | |
| **E-mail** | | | |

**\*Confidentiality:** If you have completed your details above, <u>please remove this sheet from the rest of the survey and hand it back separately to the person who collects your questionnaire.</u> This will ensure that your responses in the rest of the survey are kept separate from this information. The following questions in the survey cannot be used to identify you or your household.

*If you require* further information about this questionnaire, please do not hesitate to get in touch:

| | |
|---|---|
| **Research Team Co-ordinator:** | **Dr. Jan Prillwitz** |
| Postal address: | University of Exeter, Department of Geography |
| | Amory Building, Rennes Drive |
| | Exeter, EX4 4RJ |
| Telephone: | 01392 263347 |
| E-mail: | J.Prillwitz@exeter.ac.uk |
| Project website: | http://www.ex.ac.uk/prost |

**A <u>large print</u> version of this questionnaire is available on request.**

**Figure 2.3** Introduction page from travel questionnaire.

---

**SECTION 1: Travel behaviours**

In this first section, we need to collect some information about the types of travel you use, both for everyday activities and also for any holidays or breaks.

1. Thinking about travel **YOU** undertake on a **daily or weekly basis,** please tell us **the main** mode of travel **YOU** <u>use most frequently</u> for the following activities. **Please only tick <u>one box per activity</u>.** If an activity does not apply to you. Please tick 'Not applicable'.

| *Most frequent travel mode for:* | Car | Motor-bike | Bus/Coach | Train | Taxi | Bicycle | Walk | other | Not applicable |
|---|---|---|---|---|---|---|---|---|---|
| Shopping | ☐ | ☐ | ☐ | ☐ | ☐ | ☐ | ☐ | ☐ | ☐ |
| Travel to work | ☐ | ☐ | ☐ | ☐ | ☐ | ☐ | ☐ | ☐ | ☐ |
| Travel whilst at work | ☐ | ☐ | ☐ | ☐ | ☐ | ☐ | ☐ | ☐ | ☐ |
| Local leisure travel | ☐ | ☐ | ☐ | ☐ | ☐ | ☐ | ☐ | ☐ | ☐ |
| Visiting friends and relatives locally | ☐ | ☐ | ☐ | ☐ | ☐ | ☐ | ☐ | ☐ | ☐ |
| Taking children to school or nursery | ☐ | ☐ | ☐ | ☐ | ☐ | ☐ | ☐ | ☐ | ☐ |
| Other local travel | ☐ | ☐ | ☐ | ☐ | ☐ | ☐ | ☐ | ☐ | ☐ |

2. Continuing to think about **YOUR daily and weekly travel,** please indicate below if **YOU** use any of these travel modes <u>**less frequently or as an alternative to your main mode**</u> for each activity. You can tick more than one box per line if you use more than one travel mode for an activity less frequently/as an alternative. **If you only use travel mode stated in question 1 for certain or all activities, please tick 'Not applicable'.**

| *Less frequent travel mode for:* | Car | Motor-bike | Bus/Coach | Train | Taxi | Bicycle | Walk | other | Not applicable |
|---|---|---|---|---|---|---|---|---|---|
| Shopping | ☐ | ☐ | ☐ | ☐ | ☐ | ☐ | ☐ | ☐ | ☐ |
| Travel to work | ☐ | ☐ | ☐ | ☐ | ☐ | ☐ | ☐ | ☐ | ☐ |
| Travel whilst at work | ☐ | ☐ | ☐ | ☐ | ☐ | ☐ | ☐ | ☐ | ☐ |
| Local leisure travel | ☐ | ☐ | ☐ | ☐ | ☐ | ☐ | ☐ | ☐ | ☐ |
| Visiting friends and relatives locally | ☐ | ☐ | ☐ | ☐ | ☐ | ☐ | ☐ | ☐ | ☐ |
| Taking children to school or nursery | ☐ | ☐ | ☐ | ☐ | ☐ | ☐ | ☐ | ☐ | ☐ |
| Other local travel | ☐ | ☐ | ☐ | ☐ | ☐ | ☐ | ☐ | ☐ | ☐ |

**Figure 2.4** Example of reported behaviour measurement from travel questionnaire.

**28.** How would you describe **Your home** (please tick one)?

| | |
|---|---|
| Detached ☐ | Linked detached ☐ | Semi-detached ☐ |
| Terrace (with passage) ☐ | Terrace (no passage) ☐ | Purpose-built flat ☐ |
| Flat in older property ☐ | Mobile/park home ☐ | Other ☐ |

**29.** Please let us know the gender and age of each person living in your household by completing the table below. Please remember, if you live in a shared house or flat, please consider only yourself and – if applicable – persons you are living with (spouse/ partner, family). You should tick two boxes per line, one for each person's gender and then one for their age group.

| | Male | Female | Under 16 | 16–19 | 20–29 | 30–44 | 45–59 | 60–74 | 75 and over |
|---|---|---|---|---|---|---|---|---|---|
| **You** | | | | | | | | | |
| **Spouse/ partner** | | | | | | | | | |
| **Dependent Child 1** | | | | | | | | | |
| **2** | | | | | | | | | |
| **2** | | | | | | | | | |
| **4** | | | | | | | | | |
| **5** | | | | | | | | | |
| **Other adult 1** | | | | | | | | | |
| **2** | | | | | | | | | |
| **3** | | | | | | | | | |
| **Lodger 1** | | | | | | | | | |
| **2** | | | | | | | | | |
| **Other** | | | | | | | | | |

**30.** How many cars (including motor homes) does **your household own or have access to?** _____

**(This can include access through a car club)**

**31.** How many bicycles **does your household have?** _____

**32.** How many motorbikes **does your household have?** _____

**33.** Do **you or does anyone in your household** have a concessionary travel pass, such as a National Bus Pass (e.g. for concessionary travel, or a 'Coach Card') or Railcard?

Yes ☐ Continued to **Question 34**    No ☐ ➔ Please go to **Question 35**

**34.** Who **in your household** has such a travel pass (tick all that apply)?

You ☐ Other members of the household ☐

**35. Do you or does anyone in your household** have a disability (a disability is any physical, sensory or mental impairment which has, or had, a substantial and long-term adverse effect on a person's ability to carry out normal day to day activities)?

Yes ☐ Continue to **Question 36**    No ☐ ➔ Please go to **Question 37**

**36.** Who **in your household** has a disability (tick all that apply)?

You ☐ Other members of the household ☐

**Figure 2.5** Example of measuring socio-demographic variables from travel questionnaire.

Eventually, the finished product emerged. The following key points can be derived from the completed survey:

- The front page is simple and could therefore be printed in black and white, offering an economic option for producing the survey (Figure 2.2). The title attempts to relate the survey directly to the individual concerned and also uses neutral language to describe the questionnaire. Both the University's and funder's logos are used to lend credibility to the survey;
- The introductory page is necessarily long, but attempts to set out both the aims of the research and also the ways in which the research will be used (including the protection of personal data, Figure 2.3). It also encourages participation in the research by offering entry into a prize draw for the chance to win rail tickets, as well as the invitation to participate in further, qualitative research;
- The two sample pages provided in Figures 2.4 and 2.5 provide an illustration of the layout of the survey and the ways in which the research team sought to make the questionnaire as user-friendly as possible within the constraints of the need to gather a large amount of data. In particular, note the introductions to questions, the use of Likert-style items and the section formatting.

## Sampling and implementation

The sampling approach adopted for the research was probabilistic and sought to achieve as representative a sample as possible in the five study locations. This was only possible because of the financial support from the funding council (ESRC) which allowed for the adoption of a systematic random sampling technique. The desired sample for each location (400 households) was used to calculate a 'sampling interval' from which to draw from the population (i.e. every tenth household for a population of 4000). This was undertaken using the Royal Mail's address list.

The survey was implemented using the contact and collect method, where a researcher calls at the specified address and introduces the survey. If the residents agree to complete the survey, it is left for them to complete over three or four days; if the residents decline to participate, the researcher moves to the household immediately next door and continues to visit houses until the residents agree to complete the survey. The benefit of such an approach is that return rates are generally high given the form of 'social contract' between the researcher and respondent; the problem can be that there is a disproportionate number of individuals who respond to the survey who have an interest in the topic, thus compromising the survey's representativeness.

This sampling problem is challenging, although in comparison with the very low return rates of mail surveys it can be regarded as a sound investment. More broadly, the approach adopted in this case study was largely successful, but there were also drawbacks. First, the survey was aimed at 'an individual' and it should be recognised that travel behaviour is something governed both by individual and household motivations and barriers and that travel practices represent these tensions. Second, the complexity of measuring travel behaviour in both a daily and tourism context was challenging, and the survey may not have captured the level of detail that these practices entail. Third, it is questionable whether issues such as human-induced climate change can be explored with appropriate levels of accuracy in social surveys, especially given the conflicting media discourses on both the role of individuals and the potential solutions.

## Survey analysis

The possible drawbacks of using a survey approach to explore travel behaviour are not limited to the potential 'representativeness' of the survey's findings, but also the ways in which the data collected can be used. Indeed, survey analysis is perhaps the most neglected area of questionnaire design, yet the implications of not collecting the right sort of data are fundamental and can mean that the original study objectives cannot be met. To this extent, it is worthwhile attempting to include a notion of what types of analysis will be required in one's objectives as a way of confining the types of data one seeks to include in the questionnaire. For example, the case study outlined previously used terms such as 'measure', 'segmentation analysis' and 'framework of environmental behaviour' as a way of indicating how the data would be treated.

Although there is not space here to outline the range of quantitative analyses possible with survey data (see Bryman and Cramer, 2009 and Wheeler et al., 2004 for detailed technical guides), there are some important general principles that can be outlined. First, it is important for survey design that the researcher is familiar with both the types of analysis and the computer package in which these will be performed before the questionnaire is completed; this ensures both that the questions being posed are appropriate and that analysis can proceed rapidly once the data are collected. Second, it is important to define the types of analysis necessary to meet the study's objectives as a way of inferring the tests needed for the data. In general terms, researchers are interested in exploring the following with environmental social science data:

- Descriptions of behaviours, attitudes, values and social characteristics;
- Inferring differences between samples and groups, such as differences between those who appear to be pro-environmental and those less committed to environmental issues;

- The relationship between one variable and another, for example between attitude and behaviour;
- The relationships between three or more variables, such as the correlation between a series of attitude statements;
- The identification of different segments or types (for example, 'green traveller', 'committed car user' and 'cycle enthusiast');
- The explanation of behaviours, attitudes and values.

Looking once again at the case study on travel behaviour, the following analyses may seem appropriate in relation to the research objectives:

- First, to identify and measure a series of 'sustainable travel behaviours' using a sample of individuals from the general public: *simple descriptive statistics using frequency tables, frequency graphs and clustered bar charts to compare between variables.*
- Second, to explore the empirical and conceptual links between different types of sustainable travel practices amongst the sample: *this could be undertaken using bivariate statistics to explore relationships between variables or a multivariate factor analysis to examine the links between a number of travel practices.*
- Third, to use segmentation analysis to identify a series of lifestyle groups based on these behavioural data; *cluster analysis could be used to segment the data into groups.*
- Fourth, to use an established framework of environmental behaviour to identify the motivators and barriers for adopting different forms of behaviour according to lifestyle group; *multiple regression could be used to establish the relative influence of different variables on travel behaviour.*

These forms of analysis are the most common in environmental social science, although the list above is not comprehensive and it is worth consulting a text such as Bryman and Cramer (2009) for both details of further tests and the technical information on their implementation with a computer package. Indeed, scientific reporting of the results from studies adopting a survey approach is most effectively obtained from scholarly articles published using such data in journals like *Environment and Behavior* and the *Journal of Environmental Psychology*.

## Beyond households: analysing social context

As a conclusion to this chapter and a way of looking forward, this final section explores the potential for survey research beyond the household as a unit of analysis defined by residential location. As seen in this chapter, households present some major challenges for researchers, not only because of their diversity but also because they are dynamic units of consumption, becoming (re)-constituted in different consumption contexts and spaces. These alternative 'sites of practice' for the household are critical to appreciate if the challenges of surveying households and their sustainability are to be met. As recent research on tourism has demonstrated (Barr et al., 2010), household consumption while on holiday and attendant attitudes towards the environment while on holiday can often be very different to those expressed in the home or daily context. To this extent questions of how waste is managed, energy is consumed and water is used become ones framed by consumption context and the extent to which individuals carry across attitudes and practices from one site to another.

Such a conclusion raises important and difficult questions for researchers seeking to grapple with designing surveys that accurately represent the complexity of environmental practices in different consumption contexts for something as diverse as 'the household'. As noted in this chapter, designers of such surveys need to consider not only the theoretical needs of their research but also the very practical (and often defining) characteristics of their research – its funding, time constraints, respondents and implementation method. Designing a survey may appear simple at first glance, but there is much to consider if high-quality and useful data are to be generated.

# References

Ajzen, I. (1991) 'The theory of planned behavior', *Organizational Behavior and Human Decision Processes*, 50: 179–211.

Anable, J. (2005) '"Complacent car addicts" or "aspiring environmentalists?" Identifying travel behaviour segments using attitude theory', *Transport Policy*, 12: 65–78.

Banister, D. (2008) 'The sustainable mobility paradigm', *Transport Policy*, 15: 73–80.

Barr, S. (2008) *Environment and Society: Sustainability, Policy and the Citizen.* Aldershot: Ashgate.

Barr, S., Shaw, G., Coles, T.E. and Prillwitz, J. (2010) '"A holiday is a holiday": practicing sustainability home and away', *Journal of Transport Geography*, 18: 474–81.

Becken, S. and Hay, J.E. (2007) *Tourism and Climate Change.* Clevedon: Channel View.

Berglund, C. and Matti, S. (2006) 'Citizen and consumer: the dual role of individuals in environmental policy', *Environmental Politics*, 15: 550–71.

Bryman, A. (2008) *Social Research Methods.* Oxford: Oxford University Press.

Bryman, A. and Cramer, D. (2009) *Quantitative Data Analysis with SPSS 14, 15 and 16: A Guide for Social Scientists.* London: Routledge.

Bulkeley, H. and Gregson, N. (2009) 'Crossing the threshold: municipal waste policy and household waste generation', *Environment and Planning A*, 41: 929–45.

Clarke, J., Newman, J., Smith, N., Vidler, E. and Westmarland, L. (2007) *Creating Citizen-Consumers; Changing Publics and Changing Public Services*. London: Sage.

Corral-Verdugo, V. (1997) 'Dual "realities" of conservation behaviour: self reports vs observations of re-use and recycling behaviour', *Journal of Environmental Psychology*, 17: 135–46.

Corral-Verdugo, V., Bernache, G., Encinas, L. and Garibaldi, L. (1994–1995) 'A comparison of two measures of reuse and recycling behaviour: self-report and material culture', *Journal of Environmental Systems*, 23: 313–27.

Crompton, T. and Thogersen, J. (2009) *Simple and Painless? The Limitations of Spillover in Environmental Campaigning*. London: WWF UK.

Darnton, A. and Sharp, V. (2006) *Segmenting for Sustainability*. Didcot: Social Marketing Practice.

DEFRA (Department of the Environment Food and Rural Affairs) (2008) *Framework for Environmental Behaviours*. London: DEFRA.

DEFRA (Department of the Environment Food and Rural Affairs) (2005) *Securing the Future*. London.

Dillman, R.A. (1978) *Mail and Telephone Surveys*. New York: Wiley.

Dunlap, R.E., Van Liere, K.D., Mertig, A.G. and Jones, R.E. (2000) 'Measuring endorsement of the new ecological paradigm: a revised NEP scale', *Journal of Social Issues*, 56: 425–42.

Giddens, A. (1991) *Modernity and Self-Identity*. Cambridge: Policy Press.

Gregson, N. (2006) *Living With Things: Ridding, Accommodation, Dwelling*. Oxford: Sean Kingston Publishing.

Gregson, N. and Crewe, L. (2003) *Second-hand Cultures*. Oxford: Berg.

Gregson, N., Metcalfe, A. and Crewe, L. (2007) 'Identity mobility and the throwaway society', *Environment and Planning D: Society and Space*, 25: 682–700.

Guagnano, G.A., Stern, P.C. and Dietz, T. (1995) 'Influences on attitude–behavior relationships: a natural experiment with curbside recycling', *Environment and Behavior*, 27: 699–718.

Jackson, T. (2005) *Motivating Sustainable Consumption: a Review of Evidence on Consumer Behaviour and Behavioural Change*. London: Sustainable Development Research Network/RESOLVE.

Johnson, J. (2008) 'The citizen-consumer hybrid: ideological tensions and the case of Whole Foods Market', *Theory and Society*, 37: 229–70.

Leonard-Barton, D. (1981) 'Voluntary simplicity lifestyles and energy conservation', *Journal of Consumer Research*, 8: 243–52.

Little, J., Ilbery, B. and Watts, D. (2009) 'Gender, consumption and the relocalisation of food: a research agenda', *Sociologia Ruralis*, 49: 201–17.

Oskamp, S., Harrington, M.J., Edwards, T.C., Sherwood, D.L., Okuda, S.M. and Swanson, D.C. (1991) 'Factors influencing household recycling behaviour', *Environment and Behavior*, 23: 494–519.

Scammell, M. (2000) 'The Internet and civic engagement: the age of the citizen-consumer', *Political Communication*, 17: 351–55.

Seyfang, G. (2005) 'Shopping for sustainability: can sustainable consumption promote ecological citizenship?', *Environmental Politics*, 14: 290–306.

Shove, E. (2003) *Comfort Cleanliness and Convenience: the Social Organization of Normality*. Oxford: Berg.

Shove, E., Watson, M., Hand, M. and Ingram, J. (2007) *The Design of Everyday Life*. Oxford: Berg.

Slocum, R. (2004) 'Consumer citizens and the cities for climate protection campaign', *Environment and Planning A*, 36: 763–82.

Spaargaren, G. and Mol, A.P.J. (2008) 'Greening global consumption: redefining politics and authority', *Global Environmental Change*, 18: 350–59.

Tucker, P. (1999) 'Normative influences in household recycling', *Journal of Environmental Planning and Management*, 42: 63–82.

Wheeler, D., Shaw, G. and Barr, S. (2004) *Statistical Techniques in Geographical Analysis*, 3rd edn. London: Fulton.

# 3

# Social Groups and Collective Decision-making: Focus group approaches

## *Anna Davies*

## Introduction

Those seeking to influence policy for sustainability, as outlined in the land-mark document *Agenda 21*, published as part of the suite of statements emanating from the Rio Earth Summit in 1992, have long argued that greater participation of a wide spectrum of social groups in decision making is essential to promote more sustainable development (Macnaghten and Jacobs, 1997):

> The broadest public participation and the active involvement of the non-governmental organizations and other groups should also be encouraged. (*Agenda 21*, Chapter 1, Preamble, Paragraph 3)

> It is imperative that youth from all parts of the world participate actively in all relevant levels of decision-making processes because it affects their lives today and has implications for their futures. In addition to their intellectual contribution and their ability to mobilize support, they bring unique perspectives that need to be taken into account. (*Agenda 21*, Chapter 25 Children and Youth In Sustainable Development, Paragraph 2)

> Delegating planning and management responsibilities to the lowest level of public authority consistent with effective action; in particular the advantages of effective and equitable opportunities for participation by women, should be discussed. (*Agenda 21*, Chapter 8, Integrating Environment And Development In Decision-Making, Paragraph 5, (g))

In particular, calls to engage marginalised groups who have not traditionally had either access or influence in decision-making fora, including women and young people as identified above, but also people with disabilities, ethnic minorities and the elderly, have become familiar elements of strategic statements by governments and non-government bodies alike. These calls have led to the development and use, by academics and other governance stakeholders, of a suite of tools for engaging the public in matters of sustainability so that their input may be considered in decision-making processes. These tools vary both in the type of the engagement that is required by participating groups[1] and the extent to which that engagement is tied into decision-making practices. Typically types of engagement enshrined in sustainability activities resonate with a range of public participation approaches in planning systems as detailed in the now classic work of Arnstein (1969) and her conceptualisation of 'ladders of participation', and many other typologies subsequently (see Creighton, 2005; Davies and Gaythorne-Hardy, 1997; Kavanagh and Davies, 2007). These typologies categorise participation from non-participation (manipulation and therapy according to Arnstein), through tokenism (information, consultation and placation), to citizen control (partnership, delegated power, citizen control).

Much of the current sustainability engagement work focusing on social groups may be considered to be located at the lower end of Arnstein's spectrum of participation, focusing on information provision through awareness campaigns, exhibitions or limited consultation through opinion poll surveys and/or public meetings. In particular, studies of environmental and sustainability opinions, attitudes and behaviour were dominated by quantitative surveys and opinion polls through organisations such as MORI (1995) and the annual findings of surveys such as British Social Attitudes (Witherspoon, 1994) well into the 1990s. These surveys were, and continue to be, useful indicators of concern detailing reported views, values and behaviour of representative samples of populations, but they are of little value for exploring deeper reasoning behind concerns about unsustainable development. Such research is then valuable as an 'extensive' framework (Massey and Meegan, 1985; Sayer, 1984), but the constrained format generally fails to address the ambivalence and ambiguities inherent in the complex concepts and disputed practices that characterise the arena of sustainable development.

However, there has been a parallel burgeoning of more deeply interactive and deliberative practices that provide publics with alternative and potentially more empowering mechanisms for engaging in matters of sustainability (see Stirling, 2001). This deliberative turn in sustainability engagement incorporates a range of activities including future searches, visioning, citizens' juries, summits or panels, world cafés, consensus conferencing, appreciative inquiries, forum theatres, planning for real, Regener8 and the focal point of this chapter, focus groups (People and Participation Portal, 2010).[1] At this juncture it is important to note that focus groups do not take a singular form, they are not necessarily inherently deliberative, for example, just as the products of focus groups are not always integrated into decision-making frameworks (Davies, 1999). Equally focus groups have been used to different objectives, both as a forum to discuss aspects of participation in and for sustainability and as a space for the co-generation of ideas about how current patterns of development can be made more sustainable (Davies, 2001). Despite the complexity of the focus group form and function, it has been used in a variety of settings for the purpose of engaging publics in issues of sustainability, and as such it continues to be a significant tool in the armoury of sustainability researchers and practitioners alike. Before examining the applications of the focus group technique in the realm of sustainability, however, it is useful to outline some of the main features of the approach and its methodological specificities.

## The nature of focus groups

Fundamentally, and unsurprisingly, all focus groups allow a number of people (the group) to discuss a topic (the focus) about which they might not be experts, but on which their views are important nonetheless. Most significantly the focus group environment, while being supportive, must generate opportunities for interaction, dialogue and discussion amongst the group's members. It is this interactive and discursive component that differentiates the research outputs (the group discussion) from standard one-to-one interviews when the questioning normally moves from interviewer to interviewee and the responses from the interviewee are then recorded. This process is used to gain insight into participants' natural vocabulary on a topic. It is possible through the focus group to see if people will challenge others, and how they will respond to such challenges. The focus group can be a self-contained means of collecting data or a supplement to quantitative or other qualitative methods. Typically it has been seen as a preliminary, exploratory tool, but Morgan (1988), argues that focus groups should not be confined to this role. He suggests that focus groups are useful for, 'orienting oneself to a new field; generating hypotheses based on informants' insights; and evaluating different research sites or study populations' (Morgan, 1988: 11). A simple test of whether focus groups are appropriate for a research project is to ask how actively, and easily, participants would discuss the topic of interest or when there appears to be a gap between professional and public thinking on a particular matter (Kreuger, 1994). In the case of sustainability and environment-related matters, past research suggests that people can articulate their socio-economic and environmental concerns (Burgess, 1988a, b; Hedges, 1985; Mostyn, 1979).

The roots of the group approach can be found in two very different contexts: market research and psychology. The difference between these two areas is reflected in the nature and content of the groups which are conducted. Market research tends to use one-off groups, while psychology groups work with an in-depth approach. In-depth groups have been conducted most comprehensively within the environmental arena by Burgess et al. (1988a, b), who draw on psychotherapy and the pioneering work of Foulkes (1948). In-depth groups allow a special group dynamic to develop over a number of meetings so that views and values can be revisited and qualified, which avoids superficial results. By the same token they demand considerable commitment on the part of participants and the dynamic created is not always favourable. Participants may become dependent on the group or feel exploited.

The once-only group, favoured by market research, is cheaper and more time efficient than one-to-one interviews, as a greater number of people can be involved in the research process in a shorter period of time. This approach has been used in the past to examine people's views of planning developments (Hedges, 1985): to explore cultural values of landscapes (Little, 1975); and to address the physical, intellectual, social and emotional benefits from participating in wildlife projects (Mostyn, 1979). One problem with this type of research is the possible superficiality of the remarks and values that are expressed, which can lead to predictable results and stereotyping. However, once-only groups are still significant because they can provide a forum for people to share and test out their views with others rather than responding in an isolated interview.

Focus group textbooks, of which there are many (see Barbour, 2008; Kreuger and Casey 2000), suggest that groups of between 6–10 people should be brought together on a preset number of occasions to discuss selected topics. The discussion is directed by the moderator who ensures that a free debate ensues, including all members of the group, avoiding confrontation and keeping the process focused on the topic at hand. The moderator is usually a key figure as facilitator, recording the discussion and taking supplementary notes, prompting questions and initially screening participants. The moderator is also pivotal in shaping the form and content of focus group discussions and influencing moderator–group dynamics, a matter that will be returned to in the concluding section of this chapter. The selection of participants for focus groups does not usually seek to achieve a statistically representative sample of the public, although they can capture a range of views from across society unless the aim is to access views of a particular target group.

A major concern with focus groups is addressed by Burgess et al. (1988a, b) who ask, 'how does one find a number of "ordinary" citizens who are not necessarily members of organisations with direct interests in environmental matters, but who are willing to give up the time to discuss environmental values?' (1988a: 316). Incentives can be offered for attendance, but unless the sums are considerable they are unlikely to persuade reluctant individuals to participate and also bring attendant concerns about 'buying', or commodifying, the activity of research. Previous research concludes that the most productive methods of persuasion, particularly for vulnerable groups, include researchers being familiar to, and trusted by, the people whose involvement is sought and where group sessions occur in accessible places at appropriate times for the participants. Ultimately the usefulness and validity of data collected through focus groups is affected by the extent to which participants feel comfortable about openly communicating their ideas.

A key strategy for encouraging participation within a group once it has been established is to develop a positive group dynamic where people feel able to speak freely. The process of conducting focus groups, therefore, raises important issues regarding the power relationships inherent in, and between, groups drawn from potentially different socio-economic, gender, ethnic and age ranges. The group dynamic can be moulded by those who have the social or institutional power to impose their own interpretations and representations on the group.[2] The role of the moderator is also key here in terms of preventing the destructive development of negative group dynamics, but it has been suggested also that group interaction is easier, and positive group dynamics developed, when individuals have some common ground or communities of interest (Hedges, 1994). Ultimately, unavoidably and central to the very purpose of focus group research it is the case that '[a]ttitudes and perceptions relating to concepts, products, services, or programs are developed in part by interaction with other people. We are the product of our environment and are influenced by people around us' (Kreuger, 1994: 11).

The basic introduction to focus groups in sustainability research detailed above is not intended to be a 'cookbook' for conducting focus groups; there are many resources available online and in journals and books that provide such guidance.[3] Essentially, as will be seen from the following section, the focus group technique is often tailored to meet the specific demands of a particular issue (or focus) being considered.

## Applications of focus groups for sustainability and collective decision making

Within the broad but contested area of sustainability, focus groups have been employed in a wide variety of contexts. For example, focus groups were explored as a means to combat social exclusion and encourage empowerment alongside local development in Preston in the north of England (Clarke and Cox, 2003). More recently Seymour et al. (2010) have used focus groups to elucidate resident perceptions of urban alleys and the potential for alley greening as a means to rejuvenate local environments. Within the realm of agricultural sustainability research focus groups have been used as a means to see the potential of farmer participation in the development of sustainability indicators (King et al., 2000), while Tiwari et al. (2008) used a mixed-method approach, which included focus groups, to analyse the sustainability of upland farming systems in the Middle Mountains region of Nepal. Within the USA, Selfa and colleagues adopted a focus group approach in a number of agricultural studies: to examine the challenges in governing biofuels production in Kansas and Iowa, engaging in complex ideas regarding the scalar split of burdens and benefits that such production might entail (Selfa, 2010); and to compare producer and consumer attitudes and practices toward environmentally friendly food and farming in Washington State (Selfa et al., 2008). Remaining within the agricultural sustainability arena, Fan (2009) examined how stakeholders perceive genetically modified crops and foods through focus groups and interviews. This work illustrated how such qualitative methods permitted non-traditional interpretations of sustainability, in this case through different religious perspectives, to enter the decision-making fora.

Issues related to nature conservation and biodiversity protection have also been approached using the focus group technique, often in conjunction with other methodological tools. For example, in Ireland, the Biochange project (http://www.biochange.ie) included research examining the politics that shaped the management of biodiversity within the state. Nine focus groups were conducted with community groups within the case study region of County Clare and the Burren to try to elucidate greater insights into public understandings of biodiversity and gauge people's perceived role in its protection. These focus groups supplemented stakeholder interviews with representatives from public, private and civil society sectors that had an interest in, or impact on, biodiversity. In a similar vein but entirely different geographical location, Tessema et al. (2010) used focus groups and household surveys to examine community attitudes toward wildlife and protected areas in Ethiopia. The work found that despite potential tensions between wildlife protection and local use of resources there was a relatively positive attitude toward the need for biodiversity protection. In the work of Christie et al. (2006) a range of different methods including focus groups and contingent valuation was used to identify publicly relevant ecological concepts of biodiversity and their relative importance (or value). They concluded that the discursive spaces provided the optimum spaces in which to deliberate issues of biological worth amongst publics.

Adopting focus groups as part of a multi-method approach is also present in research examining sustainable waste management practices. Refsgaard and Magnussen (2009), for example, generated data from interviews with municipal employees, questionnaires and multi-criteria mapping alongside focus groups with regard to recycling food waste. Meanwhile Davies et al. (2005) developed a nested questionnaire, focus group and action research framework for engaging similarly with barriers and motivations to sustainable waste management practices in Ireland. In this research project focus groups were appropriated to engage with young people about their waste behaviours because adults' responses to earlier questionnaires had identified young people as both the cause of, and potential actors to resolve, waste problems (see Fahy, 2005). The focus group format provided an open and non-judgemental forum to explore this apparently contradictory conceptualisation of young people.

In the energy arena Oltra et al. (2010) analysed, through focus groups, public perceptions of carbon capture and storage technology in Spain. Kasemir et al. (2000) used focus groups to explore citizens' engagement with climate change. Specifically Kasemir et al. (2000) developed Integrated Assessment (IA)-Focus Groups which, they argue, are designed primarily for involving citizens in integrated assessments of complex issues like climate change.

In the forestry sector Carvalho-Ribeiro et al. (2010) examined multifunctional forest management in northern Portugal through participatory mechanisms, including two focus group meetings, conducted within two parishes in order to establish whether adaptive governance systems could be developed to deliver more sustainable forest management futures. More broadly McGregor (2005) followed on from work of Burgess et al. (1988a, b) and Davies (1999, 2001) in terms of exploring how small group discussions can reveal the ways in which people articulate their engagements with nature.

The multifunctional characteristics of focus groups are illustrated by a number of research studies which have used them as a tool to examine the very notion of participation within decision making. For example Klinsky et al. (2010) used focus groups to evaluate the impact of two geographical information systems (GIS)-based tools that were aimed at promoting discussions about sustainability and, particularly, connecting local and global issues in a suburban context in Montreal, Canada. Through the medium of group discussions Macnaghten and Jacobs (1997) explored cultural barriers to greater public participation in sustainability initiatives.

From the brief outline of focus group adoption in sustainability-related research areas detailed above, it is clear that while focus groups themselves may be considered a deliberative tool they are frequently used as a means to evaluate particular groups' (this can be publics but can equally include stakeholders) views of policy interventions or to gain understanding of responses to particular sustainability challenges. In the remainder of this section one particular case of focus group research for sustainability is outlined in detail.

# Public environmental values and planning for sustainability in the UK

During the 1990s it became clear that there was growing public concern with, and political attention directed towards, environmental degradation around the globe. At the same time increasing attention was paid to the role of environmental values, both in academic studies and in public policy fora, and how such values should be incorporated (or not) into planning policies and decisions for sustainability (English Nature, 1995; Countryside Commission, 1995; Cowell, 1992). This issue was, and remains, particularly acute in conditions of conflict over land-use developments such as nuclear energy facilities, road building and even wind farms. In order to look at these interconnected issues of value–policy–decision making for sustainability, two contrasting locations within the county of Bedfordshire in the UK were selected; Luton and south Bedfordshire, and focus groups with publics undertaken in the mid-1990s (see Davies, 1999, 2001).

Luton's physical image had suffered from pressure for development in an already built-up area, and the surrounding Green Belt and AONB (Area of Outstanding Natural Beauty) landscape designation provided a strong physical boundary to future developments. In contrast with Luton, south Bedfordshire's environment was predominantly rural with Green Belt and the Chilterns (designated in 1964 and renewed in 1989) covering large sections of the area. Yet there was little known about how people actually living in the two locations felt about their local environments, how those environments and experiences had changed over time and, importantly for sustainable development, how they should change in the future. It was this issue of place and change that was used as a way to focus on what people valued about their local areas and why they did so.

The research adopted a two-session group discussion format with members of the public in both locations to allow the researcher and participants time for reflection between sessions with the aim of reducing the superficiality of responses, but without excluding people on the grounds of limited time to participate in the research. Twelve focus groups were conducted in total, six in Luton and six in south Bedfordshire. Participants were drawn from pre-existing community groups (see Box 3.1), which have been called 'natural groups' (Holbrook, 1996). The benefit of this approach was that the groups were self-supporting prior to, during and after the research process, and there was no need to spend the initial session developing a group dynamic. There were still unavoidable power relationships within these natural groups, but the voluntary and independent nature of their construction suggested that individuals would feel relatively free to participate in discussions. Inevitably, a new dynamic was created to some extent by the presence of the moderator and how she was perceived by the various groups, but the location of the group sessions in the place that the group normally met aimed to ensure the groups were comfortable in their surroundings as far as possible.

There were difficulties in recruiting people from exactly targeted groups using the natural focus-group approach because group members of organisations, such as parents' associations, are members of many communities simultaneously. However, the focus groups were not intended to form a representative sample of the population. Rather the aim was to elucidate a detailed range of views from different sections of society. An explicit effort was made to incorporate groups who were commonly under-represented in decision-making systems. Access to these community groups was achieved by approaching community development officers, visiting community centres (including leisure centres and public houses), village halls and contacting societies directly with details gathered at local libraries. Non-environmental groups were specifically selected in order to gain views and values from people who were not regularly involved in planning and environmental practices. Indeed, it was revealed during the sessions that not one of the participants had engaged in any formal participation channels for local planning. Environmental values and concerns operate in a variety of organisational contexts, public, private and voluntary, and informal agendas of environmentalism are present outside the official organisations (Myerson and Rydin, 1994).

---

**Box 3.1   Focus group composition**

**Luton:**

(1) (Sixth formers – urban) Luton Sixth Form College April 1996

   No. in group: 7 Age: 16–19

   Gender: mixed Ethnicity: mixed

(2) (Playgroup – urban) Farley Hill Playgroup April 1996

   No. in group: 6 Age: 30–50

   Gender: female Ethnicity: white

(3) (Ethnic – urban) Luton Ethnic Minorities Support Group May 1996

   No. in Group: 6 Age: 30–60

   Gender: female Ethnicity: mixed

(4) (Unemployed–urban) Luton Day Centre, NVQ Group May 1996

   No. in group: 6 Age: 30–50

   Gender: male Ethnicity: mixed

*(Continued)*

(Continued)

(5) (Rotary – urban) Luton Rotary Club June 1996

No. in group: 9 Age: 40–70

Gender: male Ethnicity: white

(6) (Table tennis–urban) Luton 50+ Table Tennis Club May 1996

No. in group: 6 Age: 55 +

Gender: mixed Ethnicity: white

**Totternhoe area:**

(1) (Playgroup – rural) Totternhoe Playgroup May 1996

No. in group: 6 Age: 20–40

Gender: female Ethnicity: white

(2) (Women's Institute–rural) Totternhoe WI June 1996

No. in group: 7 Age: 40 +

Gender: female Ethnicity: white

(3) (Luncheon – rural) Totternhoe OAP Luncheon Group May–June 1996

No. in group: 7 Age: 60 +

Gender: mixed Ethnicity: white

(4) (Roteract – rural) Roteract Club October 1996

No. in group: 9 Age: 18–30

Gender: mixed Ethnicity: white

(5) (Parents Association–rural) Totternhoe PA August 1996

No. in group: 6 Age: 35 +

Gender: mixed Ethnicity: white

(6) (Fellowship – rural) Totternhoe Fellowship September 1996

No. in group: 11 Age: 45 +

Gender: female Ethnicity: white

The sessions followed a flexible topic guide, the first beginning with a discussion of the local area in order to put members at ease and encourage open conversation. The second session focused more specifically on 'environmental values', the changing value of the local environment and how the groups perceived the links between local, national and global environmental values. It also discussed issues related to community participation in policy making, encouraging participants to talk about their views and experiences of planning and local government. Focus group sessions were recorded and the discussions were transcribed verbatim as soon as possible after the event. The first two discussions were videotaped, which permitted a more detailed analysis of the physical interactions of the group and the influence of the facilitator, which was deemed useful for training purposes but ultimately unnecessary for all group discussions.

In the transcription process, participants were allocated a pseudonym in the coding to allow for anonymity. Any significant pauses were noted along-side the text in the transcripts as were phrases said in jest or with irony, in order to reduce possible misinterpretation at later analysis stages. Any words that were added to the extracts to improve readability were clearly marked by placing square brackets around the inserted text. During analysis tran-scripts were manually coded, themes were identified, noted and then sorted on a word processor which enabled a basic content analysis to be under-taken.[4] A simple overview grid was used to allow a comparison of focus groups and topics and establish commonalities between responses. These were compared with other interview themes and points of interest recorded. Relationships and patterns were then identified and clusters of ideas formed.

Although there is limited space here to exemplify the range and depth of environmental values found during the research, it is useful to provide an example of the type of environmental values that were expressed through the focus groups (for more in-depth analysis see Davies, 1999, 2001, 2006). The following extracts from the rural section of the case study provide one illustration of the detailed information that was gathered regarding the participants' statements of value about their local areas. In general people did not make a distinction between tangible and intangible environmental values, but firmly linked concrete experiences and activities with feelings and emotions. The first extract from a rural Roteract group discusses the value of their surrounding rural environment because of its impact on their sense of well-being and how that is eroded by the loss of countryside to built development:

*Jane:* I know I rely on the countryside for my own well-being. Whether I'm walking, or on a bike, or whatever, we can just go down the road and it's really special. Without it I would feel hemmed in, a bit claustrophobic, like it's all on top of you and there's no escape.

*Marian:* What I don't think they realise is that when they allow the countryside to be lost. People feel a great sense of loss. You feel cheated like you've lost something you owned, even though you didn't.

*Jane:* But it was sort of owned by us though. I mean it is owned by all of us, it's part of us, it's our history and identity and stuff.

*John:* It's part of our heritage, isn't it?

*Sally:* Yeah, but it's not like it's conscious or deliberate. It's more instinctive. You know you need to recharge your batteries with a countryside hit.

*Tim:* I don't think they appreciate these things when they make a decision. They can't know what it means to us in this way, like for well-being and that, if they don't ask and they never do. (Roteract – rural)

This discussion is important because within it the participants recognise that the values they are talking about are often subconscious and difficult to articulate in ways which would be expected in formal policy arenas, 'it's not like it's conscious or deliberate. It's more instinctive.' It is the intuitive, felt nature of the participants' environmental values that is difficult for a structured policy system like planning, with its aspiration to instrumental rationality, to deal with. One participant recognises the limitations of current policy processes when he says, 'I don't think *they* appreciate these things when *they* make a decision. *They* can't know what it means to us in this way, like for well-being and that, if they don't ask and *they* never do.' In this passage there is another interesting feature which plays an important role in the difficult relationship between the public and public policy. The participants refer to an unspecified 'they' when talking about policy makers. The public appear uncertain who is responsible for actually making decisions, whether it is planners, politicians or some other body, but what they are sure about is that 'they' are powerful and 'we', the public, are not. Other public groups, such as the Womens' Institute below, also recognise tensions between powerful professional judgements and their own values which they feel are often ignored or discarded:

*Elsie:* I mean just recently we have been petitioning to save some open ground by the school. They want to develop it.

*Carol:* For us it's like the village green we don't have. People play there, meet and have a chat, walk the dog, mess around, you name it. I used to go berrying there as a kid, all that sort of stuff you know.

*Linda:* It has history and memories for us all in different ways.

*Elsie:* It would be a real loss because where would we go to get those things then?

*Janet:* The council won't budge; they say it's been designated for development. It all seems one way, like what we want has to be negotiated, but what they want goes without any negotiation or explanation, or really justified at all on our terms against what we value it for. (WI – rural)

This discussion is framed by the public's feeling of their council's inattention to their values, views and opinions. There is a sense of exclusion and inefficacy which reinforces what appears to be an existing lack of public trust in the council's decisions and motivations. The final comment in this extract is particularly salient: the mismatch between the justification requirements of professional and public value judgements. There is tangible frustration in the group that the council fails to appreciate what the public valued the land for; that the council is by the very nature of its established political and professional analysis unable to access and process their deeply felt values. It is this point which suggests that the value mismatch between public and policy, highlighted through the environmental focus-group process, cannot simply be attributed to public exclusion from environmental decision making.

The situation is made doubly difficult by the prevalence of intangible, non-material environmental values when responses are freed from the confines of structured questionnaires and traditional policy concerns. In this particular case the problem for the planners was that the land that the Womens' Institute was trying to keep as open space had been designated for development for a number of years (and in a number of past development plans). Therefore, the planners had little choice but to accept development proposals because of historical decisions. Because of the public's lack of knowledge of the planning system, and the development plan process in particular, they were not aware of the land's status or even what it meant, nor had they been involved in any public local inquiries to express the level of environmental value that the land had for them. It appeared that the public did not see the planning process as the place to express their positive environmental values. Only when the land was threatened by development did they feel compelled to voice their concerns.

The planning system and those who work with it seemed unable to challenge past decisions on the basis of the socio-environmental values that the public were now expressing through the focus group. The values that the publics expressed were not of the type that was generally admitted to planning decisions. The land was not designated as being particularly rare scientifically, or of particular historical value, for example. The local quality of life value expressed by publics was acknowledged by planners (who were also interviewed in the research)[5] but often just not seen as legitimately defensible in the adversarial planning process. Authors such as Patsy Healey (1993; 1997) had already described a shift, particularly following the adoption of sustainable development as the dominant environmental narrative in planning, towards greater emphasis on scientific quantification and less concern with the subjective, aesthetic and moral considerations. But as Susan Owens (1994) has suggested, with scientific advancement and tighter controls on pollution and health standards, the hardest environmental decisions to make in the future will be about quality of life, sense of place and local distinctiveness, which cannot be dealt with through greater quantification. Such decisions will require mechanisms that permit a shift in emphasis away from elitist judgement and quantification to a more democratic system where subjectivity is legitimised through majority judgements. Such mechanisms would need to embrace expanded democratic pragmatism where deliberative forums, for example, could enable debates about such intersubjective judgements (Dryzek, 1996, 1997). Of course planning is by no means an entirely scientific activity. Planning is a political process through which decisions are made by a complex cocktail of administrative rationality (expert judgement), democratic pragmatism (popular participation) and economic rationalism (the market imperative) mediated through a morass of power structures (Flyvberg, 1998).

## Conclusion: merits and limitations

Much of the general literature on focus groups examines their construction, conduct and ethics (see Barbour, 2008; Kreuger and Casey, 2000). While these are important areas of concern for those considering taking up the technique in the arena of sustainability (the process and practice of focus groups is complex and contested), it is equally important to consider how the products of focus groups will be analysed and used (or potentially not used) to shape decision making. Although more deliberative techniques, such as focus groups, certainly provide a means through which social groups can be involved in matters of sustainability decision making, if the products that they create cannot be accommodated within wider systems of governance, then their direct influence will be limited at best. Following Davies (1999), three issues need consideration: the relationship between research and policy, the level of reflexivity in policy structures, and the mechanisms through which the research products of focus groups can be admitted into planning for sustainability. For, as detailed in the work of Stirling (2007; 2008), Burgess et al. (2007), while deliberative decisions can provide space for alternative views to be aired, all participatory spaces are subject to power dynamics and to the vagaries of overarching systems of governance, which themselves vary across regions and through time. Ultimately, focus groups are not a catch-all approach to be used in all sustainability research focused on social groups or collective decision making.

Focus groups, like other techniques, are flexible tools which can be shaped to a particular research context even though focus group textbooks may sometimes present what appear to be rigid guidelines. Group discussions have to be sensitive to the particular needs and situation of the participants as well as to the aims of the research.

The benefits of the technique can be summarised as allowing meaningful participation by social groups, in particular by marginalised minorities, in research and policy issues. The interactive and discursive nature of the discussions means that people become active subjects rather than objects of research. The method acknowledges and embraces the complexity of social values and actively encourages discussion. Responses can be clarified through follow-up questions and non-verbal responses can be taken into consideration. The large amounts of rich data that are captured reflect the subtle nuances in discussion and therefore avoid repetition of received wisdom. In this way focus groups allow synergism, security, spontaneity and serendipity.

However, there are attendant limitations related to the focus group method in terms of representativeness, potential researcher bias and the possibility of replicability. They require a considerable commitment on the part of participants to the research process and it may be difficult to persuade certain groups to participate in research without some external incentive. Within any group the influence of dominant personalities can be detrimental to the wider group dynamic, impairing equitable participation and requiring considerable moderator skill to manage. Finally, summarising and interpreting results, as with all qualitative research, can be a difficult and lengthy process. Further to this, even if methodological problems can be reduced or even removed, the information that focus groups produce (such as in the case study presented in the previous section) may not fit easily into the structures and remit of planning policies. Yet to view the root cause of the tensions between focus-group data and planning policy as being located solely in the focus-group method, is flawed.

The recognised role of the researcher in qualitative research often leads to criticism that the resulting data is idiosyncratic, impressionistic and non-verifiable.[6] It is true that qualitative research can be viewed as a 'messy' process (Allen, 1991), however, this need not imply a lack of rigour. Indeed, an important advantage of qualitative work is its flexibility, allowing the interviewer to develop themes with respondents as they emerge. The researcher, inevitably, influences research findings, but qualitative methods allow for greater reflexivity about the effect that has on data so that 'qualitative methods can be replicable in purpose, if not in detailed procedures' (Allen, 1991: 182). It is also the case that quantified data can be interpreted in as many ways as qualitative information. The process of analysis in both approaches is not theoretically or practically 'objective'. The interpretation of empirical research results is a subjective process where researchers make sense of data, drawing out themes and conclusions which they feel relate most significantly to the research questions and aims. Even with technical and computerised methods of analysis the process of information-gathering and interpretation is as much an art as a science. Whatever methodological framework is chosen, the researcher needs to be open about the interpretation process and aim for a transparent system of analysis of the data collected.

The structure, process and products of focus groups themselves may provide a forum for reasoning and argumentation which could improve public policy formation (Jacobs, 1997). Yet the focus groups should not be used uncritically, for like any research method they are open to misuse and misinterpretation. There remains a lack of experience amongst researchers and policy makers in translating focus group information into policy. A mutual learning experience between the public, researchers and policy makers needs to take place so that false expectations are not raised amongst the public about possibilities for policy change, and also that unrealistic demands are not placed on policy makers to implement blindly the results of focus groups.

## Notes

1   The People and Participation Portal is an online resource which details a whole range of methods for public participation: http://www.peopleandparticipation.net led by Involve, a not-for-profit organisation and Headshift, an innovative media organisation. The portal was developed following a book of the same name published in 2005 to ensure up-to-date information on public participation issues.
2   The behaviour of the individual in group settings has been widely addressed in psychology research (Pines, 1983; Blumberg et al., 1983; Oakley, 1980; Brown, 1988; Smith, 1987) and while it is not possible to address the issues here, it is important to recognise the relevance of group dynamics in group settings.
3   Relevant academic material is widely referenced in this chapter. For free and accessible web-based guidance see *The Handbook for Excellence in Focus Group Research* http://www.globalhealthcommunication.org/tools/60 and the People and Participation Portal: http://www.peopleandparticipation.net
4   Qualitative software packages were relatively under-developed at the time of the research although they have become much more user-friendly in recent years – see http://www.qsrinternational.com
5   The research also incorporated in-depth interviews with 35 stakeholders in the planning process including planners, politicians, private sector companies, environmental non-governmental organisations, regulators and advisory bodies.
6   Qualitative researchers would argue that verification is not the aim of their research, but this leads to problems of generalising conclusions of qualitative research beyond the research context and eradicating overt researcher bias.

## References

Allen, G. (1991) 'Qualitative research', in G. Allen and C. Skinner (eds), *Handbook for Research Students in the Social Sciences*. London: Falmer Press, UK. pp. 177–89.

Arnstein, S.R. (1969) 'A ladder of citizen participation', *JAIP*, 35 (4): 216–24.

Barbour, R. (2008) *Doing Focus Groups*. New York: Sage.

Burgess, J., Limb, M. and Harrison, C. (1988a) 'Exploring environmental values through the medium of focus groups 1. Theory and practice', *Environment and Planning A*, 20 (3): 309–326.

Burgess, J., Limb, M. and Harrison, C. (1988b) 'Exploring environmental values through the medium of focus groups 2. Illustrations of a group at work', *Environment and Planning A*, 20 (4): 457–476.

Burgess, J., Stirling, A., Clark, J., Davies, G., Eames, M., Staley, K. and Williamson, S. (2007) 'Deliberative mapping: a novel analytic–deliberative methodology to support contested science-policy decisions', *Public Understanding of Science*, 16 (3): 299–322.

Carvalho-Ribeiro, S., Lovett, A. and O'Riordan, T. (2010) 'Multifunctional forest management in northern Portugal: moving from scenarios to governance for sustainable development', *Land Use Policy*, 27 (4): 1111–22.

Christie, M., Hanley, N., and Warren J., Murphy, K., Wright, R.and Hyde, T. (2006) Valuing the diversity of biodiversity, *Ecological Economics*, 58 (2): 304–317.

Clarke, M. and Cox, S. (2003) 'Combating social exclusion: focus groups, local empowerment and development: a Preston case study' in S. Buckingham and K. Theobald (eds), *Local Environmental Sustainability*. Abington: Woodhead Publishing. pp. 93–112.

Countryside Commission (1995) *Environmental Capital for the Countryside: a Final Report*. Cheltenham: Countryside Commission.

Cowell, R. (1992) 'Environmental compensation: a legitimate niche for the quid pro quo?', *ECOS*, 13 (4): 27–33.

Creighton, J.L. (2005) *The Public Participation Handbook: Making Decisions through Citizen Involvement*. London: John Wiley and Sons.

Davies, A. (2001) 'What silence knows – planning, public participation and environmental values', *Environmental Values*, 10 (1): 77–102.

Davies, A., Fahy, F. and Taylor, D. (2005) 'Mind the gap! Householder attitudes and actions towards waste management', *Irish Geography*, 10: 151–68.

Davies A.R. (1999) 'Where do we go from here? Environmental focus groups and planning policy formation', *Local Environment*, 4 (3): 295–316.

Davies, A.R. (2006) 'Nature in place: public visions of nature–society relationships in the UK', in J.G. Riyan, W.T. van den Born, W. de Groot and H.J. Lenders (eds,) *Visions of Nature: a Scientific Exploration of People's Implicit Philosophies Regarding Nature in Germany, The Netherlands and the United Kingdom*. Münster: LIT Verlag. pp. 85–106.

Davies, A.R. and Gaythorne-Hardy, F. (1997) *Making Connections: Community Involvement in Environmental Initiatives – a Good Practice Guide*. Cambridge: Committee for Interdisciplinary Environmental Studies.

Dryzek, J. (1996) 'Foundations for environmental political economy: the search for Homo Ecologicus?', *New Political Economy*, 1 (1): 27–40.

Dryzek, J. (1997) *The Politics of the Earth: Environmental Discourses*. Oxford: Oxford University Press.

English Nature (1995) *Criteria for Identifying Critical Environmental Capital of the Terrestrial Environment. Discussion paper 141, English Nature Research Reports*. Peterborough: English Nature.

Fahy, F. (2005) 'The right to refuse', *Local Environment: The International Journal of Justice and Sustainability*, 10 (6): 551–69.

Fan, M. (2009) 'Stakeholder perceptions and responses to GM crops and foods: the case of Taiwan', *Sustainable Development*, 17 (6): 391–99.

Flyvberg, B. (1998) *Rationality and Power*. Chicago, IL: University of Chicago Press.

Foulkes, S.H. (1948) *Introduction to Group-Analytic Psychotherapy*. London: Maresfield Reprints.

Healey, P. (1993) 'The communicative work of development plans', *Environment and Planning B: Planning and Design*, 20 (1): 83–104.

Healey, P. (1997) *Collaborative Planning: Shaping Places in Fragmented Societies*. Basingstoke: Macmillan.

Hedges, A. (1985) 'Group interviewing', in R. Walker (ed.), *Applied Qualitative Research*. Aldershot: Gower. pp. 71–91.

Hedges, A. (1994) *Community Involvement in the Chilterns Natural Area Trial. Final Consultancy Report for English Nature*. Bedford: Billington Manor.

Holbrook, B. (1996) 'Shopping around: focus group research in North London', *Area*, 28 (2): 136–42.

Jacobs, M. (1997) 'Environmental valuation, deliberative democracy and public decision-making institutions', in J. Foster (ed.), *Valuing Nature? Ethics, Economics and the Environment*. London: Routledge. pp. 211–31.

Kasemir, B., Dahinden, U., Swartling, A.G., Schule, R., Tabara, D. and Jaeger, C.C. (2000) 'Citizens' perspectives on climate change and energy use', *Global Environmental Change – Human and Policy Dimensions*, 10 (3): 169–84.

Kavanagh, R. and Davies, A. (2007) *Increasing Public Knowledge and Awareness of Biodiversity: A Reference Manual*. Dublin: Biochange, Trinity College Dublin, available from: http://www.biochange.ie/Reference%20manual.pdf

King, C., Gunton, J. and Freebairn, D. (2000) 'The sustainability indicator industry: where to from here? A focus group study to explore the potential of farmer participation in the development of indicators', *Australian Journal of Experimental Agriculture*, 40 (4): 631–42.

Klinsky, S., Sieber, R. and Meredith, T. (2010) 'Connecting local to global: geographic information systems and ecological footprints as tools for sustainability', *Professional Geographer*, 62 (1): 84–102.

Krueger, D. (1994) *Focus Groups*. London: Sage.

Kreuger, R. and Casey, M. (2000) *Focus Groups: A Practical Guide for Applied Research*. New York: Sage.

Little, C.E. (1975) 'Preservation policy and personal perception: a 200 million acre misunderstanding', in R. Bruch, J.G. Fabos and E.H. Zube (eds), *Landscape Assessment: Values, Perceptions and Resources*. Stroudsburg, NJ: Dowden, Hutchinson and Ross. pp. 46–58.

Macnaghten, P. and Jacobs, M. (1997) 'Public identification with sustainable development – investigating cultural barriers to participation', *Global Environmental Change – Human and Policy Dimensions*, 7 (1): 5–24.

Massey, D. and Meegan, R. (1985) *Politics and Method: Contrasting Studies in Industrial Geography*. London: Methuen.

McGregor, A. (2005) 'Negotiating nature: exploring discourse through small group research', *Area*, 37 (4): 423–32.

Morgan, D. (1988) *Focus Groups as Qualitative Research*. London: Sage.

MORI (1995) *MORI Business and the Environment Survey*. London: MORI.

Mostyn, B. (1979) *Personal Benefits and Satisfactions Derived from Participation in Urban Wildlife Projects*. Shrewsbury: Nature Conservancy Council.

Myerson, G. and Rydin, Y. (1994) 'Environment and planning: a tale of the mundane and the sublime', *Environment and Planning D*, 12 (4): 19–34.

Oltra, C., Sala, R., Sola, R., Di Masso, M. and Rowe, G. (2010) 'Lay perceptions of carbon capture and storage technology', *International Journal of Greenhouse Gas Control*, 4 (4): 698–706.

Owens, S. (1994) 'Land, limits and sustainability: a conceptual framework and some dilemmas for the planning system', *Transactions of the Institute of British Geographers, N. S.*, 19 (4): 439–56.

Refsgaard, K. and Magnussen, K. (2009) 'Householder behaviour and attitudes with respect to recycling food waste – experience from focus groups', *Journal of Environmental Management*, 90 (2): 760–71.

Sayer, A. (1984) *Method in Social Science: A Realist Approach*. London: Hutchinson.

Selfa, T. (2010) 'Global benefits, local burdens? The paradox of governing biofuels production in Kansas and Iowa', *Renewable Agriculture and Food Systems*, 25 (2): 129–42.

Selfa, T., Jussaume, R. and Winter, M. (2008) 'Envisioning agricultural sustainability from field to plate: comparing producer and consumer attitudes and practices toward environmentally friendly food and farming in Washington State, USA', *Journal of Rural Studies*, 24 (3): 262–76.

Seymour, M., Wolch, J. and Reynolds, K. (2010) 'Resident perceptions of urban alleys and alley greening', *Applied Geography*, 30 (3): 380–93.

Stirling, A. (2001) 'Inclusive deliberation and scientific expertise: precaution, diversity and transparency in the governance of risk'. In *PLA Notes No.40*. London: IIED. pp. 66–71. Available from http://www.iied.org/NR/agbioliv/pla_notes/pla_backissues/40.html

Stirling, A. (2007) 'Deliberate futures: precaution and progress in social choice of sustainable technology', *Sustainable Development*, 15 (5): 286–95.

Stirling, A. (2008) 'Opening up' and 'closing down': 'power, participation, and pluralism in the social appraisal of technology science', *Technology and Human Values*, 33 (1): 262–94.

Tessema, M., Lilieholm, R., Ashenafi, Z. and Leader-Williams, N. (2010) 'Community attitudes toward wildlife and protected areas in Ethiopia', *Society and Natural Resources*, 23 (6): 489–506.

Tiwari, K., Nyborg, I., Sitaula, B. and Paudel, G. (2008) 'Analysis of the sustainability of upland farming systems in the middle mountains region of Nepal', *International Journal of Agricultural Sustainability*, 6 (4): 289–306.

Witherspoon, S. (1994) 'The greening of Britain: romance and rationality', In R. Jowell, L. Brock, G. Prior and B. Taylor (eds), *British Social Attitudes 11th report*. Dartmouth: SCPR. pp. 107–40.

# 4

## Local Lives and Conflict: Towards a methodology of dialogic research

### Mark Garavan

On the coast of North Mayo, if you undertake the short walk from the quay at Portacloy to the headland overlooking the Stacks of Broadhaven, you will walk across some of the following placenames: *Tóin a'Choire* (the bottom of the cauldron), *Poillín a Mhúin* (the small urine hole), *Teacháin a'tSalainn* (the little salt house, where sea water was boiled to extract the salt). Nearby, on the cliffs, are other intriguing placenames such as *Strapa Tabac* (the ledge of the tobacco), *Fothair na luchóige* (precipice of the mice), *Fothair a'Bhoic* (precipice of the playboy). The earthy and spiritual imaginations of the communities who gave these names are revealed in place names of other close-by features such as *Na Magairli* (the testicles), *An Chailleach Chrom* (the crooked hag or witch) and *Strapa na gCailleach Dhubh* (the ledge of the black hag).[1]

These place names, with their mix of the old and new, the physical and religious, the humorous and serious, show the vibrant character of a community's interaction with place. Ancient names and events are joined with contemporary happenings to record, in geographical space, the continuity of the living community. In this way, a connection is made to previous generations through a landscape that is not just physical but imaginative too.

Into this cultural landscape of North Mayo came, in 1999, the proposal to construct an enormous gas refinery and pipeline complex. How was such a proposal understood by the local community? How did local lives respond? In a sense the question became what is the meaning of this development, to this specific community, in this specific time? What language could be used to make sense of it? Could the refinery project be absorbed into this cultural framework or did it undermine and threaten it? Does its existence pose a threat to the continuity and integrity of the whole? Was it merely an object to be inserted into the accumulative sequence of geographically located place names, or was it something far deeper, operating at a psychological and cultural depth dimension which upset the local people's conception of the integrity and safety of place itself and by extension their sense of selves?

In our effort to understand this contemporary instance of a dispute involving a local community, social science researchers are confronted with the challenge as to how to methodically investigate the micro-dynamics of the conflict and whether investigating local lives in these settings requires specific research methodologies. In this chapter I wish to tentatively suggest that one appropriate methodology for understanding local lives in conflicts over sustainability is what I will call dialogic research. By dialogic research I mean a process of empathic listening with local actors over a prolonged time period in a wide variety of settings, formal and informal, which involves a slow unravelling of local meanings and language, recognising that these meanings emerge from social interaction. In this sense, local views are never of course 'uncovered' or 'discovered'. They are produced in a dialogic exchange with numerous interlocutors, including the academic researcher. This methodology encompasses the conventional tools of ethnographic research, such as participant observation and interviews. But I wish to lay emphasis on the centrality of dialogue in order to highlight the importance of questioning as a mode of discovery for both researcher and local actor, and also to recognise the centrality of rhetorical considerations in shaping how actors articulate their concerns. The suggestion being proposed here is that views are uncovered through the multiple processes of dialogue with others in the course of a dispute. In short then, when we try to understand the specific concept of sustainability as deployed by local actors, we need to recognise how the term is employed, refined and transformed through the course of collective action itself.

In focusing on dialogue in this way I want to particularly acknowledge the ideas of the Brazilian educator Paulo Freire (1921–1997). Freirean methodology, while developed in a specific sociocultural pedagogical context, nonetheless offers us the crucial exhortation to understand social reality from 'within', from the arena of local conflict itself, and in so doing to utilise the language of the participants themselves. This involves the researcher in investigating the social reality of the community in a genuine and committed process of engagement over time. The researcher's first move therefore is to avoid a naïve and uncritical imposition of an imposed theoretical framework, but rather to engage in a humble (and even loving) human process of listening through dialogue. The second step in such an approach is to try and reflect on the language which emerges between researcher and participants to determine whether it truly conveys the views of the local actors, but in such a way that it can also make sense to outside audiences. I shall attempt to further elaborate on such a proposed methodology in the specific case of local lives and sustainability using the Corrib gas conflict as an illustration, before concluding by recognising some obvious limits and risks in such an approach. Indeed, it is important to emphasise that methodological proposals such as this are selected to investigate specific disputes in specific circumstances and are not being proposed as necessarily having general application or to be the only appropriate methodology. Two factors appear of particular importance in suggesting such a method of close dialogue: where cultural identity is explicitly raised by local actors and where the dispute occurs over a significant time period involving a diverse set of actors, thus obliging local views and articulations to become subject to refinement and development.

## Towards dialogic research

Given these features, what methodologies can be used to make sense of local lives battling to protect themselves from perceived harm or, more ambitiously perhaps, to affirm a mode of sustainable living in the world?

I wish to draw on my dual role in the Corrib gas conflict both as academic and participant in offering some cautious suggestions towards answering this. Drawn first to this issue as an academic researcher I became in time, for some 18 months between 2005 and early 2007, the official spokesperson for the local campaign. In this latter role, I had to balance the requirement of making sense of the issues to a national audience and yet remaining true to the spirit of local opposition. This made me acutely aware of the frequent dissonance between these two concerns. My awareness of local views and modes of expression made me realise how hopelessly inadequate were the available discourses of public debate and contestation in addressing the core issues mobilising local opposition. Land-use criteria, Special Area of Conservation protection, environmental pollution limits served to frame a debate that, for many locals,[2] was about far deeper issues such as cultural integrity and psychological well-being. These inadequacies in terms of public debate could in turn be reflected in the academic temptation to mis-categorise the dynamics of the evolving campaign. The closer we get to social reality, the more complex it turns out to be.

## Corrib Gas dispute – a methodological challenge

The engagement with the refinery and pipeline complex required that many local inhabitants attempt to articulate into rhetorically meaningful language their views and responses to the gas project. Thus, they were obliged to engage with the language of engineering and gas-processing technicalities, with the language of land-use and sustainable planning, with the language of safety risk assessment and with the necessity to produce media-friendly precise statements of their often complex and nuanced points of view. Indeed, in the course of the community's response to the gas project proposal even the language of opposition itself became increasingly drawn from outside sources, and thus became part of the matrix of cultural and linguistic translation and negotiation. This occurred in response to the influx of allies and politically mobilised actors from outside the community. Thus, 'oppositional' discourses, whether of the environment, sustainability, globalisation, anti-capitalism or resource nationalism, were invoked on different occasions. All of these engagements with interlocutors, particularly with decision-making bodies to which the community was subject, served not only to shape their expressions of views, but also to confine and limit their voice. These imposed languages set necessary horizons to the sayable, the thinkable, the imaginable. The result appeared to be that during the course of over a decade of campaigning, it became increasingly difficult for local actors to speak straightforwardly in their own terms to outside audiences about what was animating their opposition to the gas project.

This observation serves as a crucial factor in considering an appropriate methodology for investigating local lives in conflicts over place and community. Part of the consequence of the rhetorical and discursive structure facing local actors in the case of the Corrib gas conflict is that many of the deep-rooted concerns at the heart of their opposition were effectively silenced in the public sphere. If, as is probable, this feature of the dispute applies in other local-based prolonged conflicts in Ireland (the Hill of Tara road conflict might be one further example), then the result is likely to be that the local voice is not heard, either because it does not get articulated or because, even if expressed, it makes little sense to interlocutors. A form of 'cultural invasion' takes place whereby one version of 'reality' becomes imposed and, potentially, internalised by putative dissenters. Cultural invasion amounts to a process by which

> dominant ideas, which mystify the social and economic arrangements, concealing their exploitative nature, become part of a person's 'common sense'. They become the taken for granted aspects of 'reality' which enable a human being to consent to the existing arrangements, no matter how exploitative they might be in her or his regard. (Mayo, 2004: 41)

If all of this is true, what then might really be going on in local protest? Are the issues potentially at stake being missed or glossed over? Might the pejorative designation of 'NIMBY'[3] often applied to such activism be obscuring what might in fact be conflicts concerning far deeper and systemic matters? The crucial challenge which this in turn poses for the researcher or the observer of local lives in conflict is whether we can be sure that we fully understand the issues and claims in contestation. Do we need a process of deeper investigation than we may think in order to properly excavate the meanings and implication of micro-level collective action? This is of particular importance when we are trying to make sense of conflicts over a claim as potentially universal as 'sustainability', which may take on quite specific forms when examined at the local level of local lives. It is in this specific context that a method of dialogic research suggests itself as a possibility.

---

### Box 4.1   Cultural Sensitivity and Deep Comprehension: Great Xhosa Cattle Killing

The requirement for a process of deep and culturally-appropriate comprehension is illustrated in J.B. Peires' (1989) book on the Great Xhosa Cattle Killing Movement of 1856–7. During this brief period of months large numbers of Xhosa in parts of South Africa slaughtered their cattle. Hundreds of thousands of cows were killed, resulting in famine and impoverishment which led to the deaths of thousands of Xhosa. The consequence was to strengthen British imperial rule. Why did they carry out this apparently irrational action? Peires' immensely detailed investigation attempts to answer that and reveals a number of different interpretations. The British thought it was a 'Chiefs' Plot' designed to trigger a Xhosa uprising and therefore was simply part of their ongoing war with native groups. It appeared to many others to be a form of cultural suicide – a final act of desperation by a disintegrating people.

But in fact the event is entirely explicable in terms of factors within Xhosa culture. It was specifically triggered by dramatic prophesies foretelling a rejuvenation of the country if cattle were killed. The prophecies suggested these cattle would be replaced by healthier animals and a great renewal would occur. 'the main concern of the believers was not the expulsion of the settlers but the advent of a "happy state of things for all"' (Peires 1989: 133). In other words, killing cattle constituted a deeply rational and culturally appropriate response to precarious outside conditions that made sense to the local people.

'The central beliefs of the Xhosa Cattle Killing were neither irrational nor atavistic. Ironically, it was probably because they were so rational and so appropriate that they ultimately proved to be so fatal' (1989: 138).

---

## The local character of Irish environmental conflict

The question of how we are to understand local mobilisations, collective action and campaigns becomes even more compelling when we consider the extent to which much Irish 'environmental' protest, or protest over sustainability, appears to be local in its scope. Despite the claim that Irish environmentalism is broadly similar in structure and concerns to 'mainstream' European activism (Baker, 1990), it appears to be the case that activism in Ireland is largely local in character. Protest event data from 1988 to 2002 (Garavan, 2007)[4] show that protest in the Irish setting is far more likely to be employed by local actors in prosecuting local disputes rather than by national actors in national campaigns. During this period, reported environmental protest mobilisation occurred exclusively at a local level in two-thirds of cases. Three-quarters of all reported grievances were subnational in scope. Perhaps this extraordinary localism by comparison with many other developed European states (see Rootes, 2003 for an overview of European environmental protests) suggests that Irish environmentalism is somehow flawed or aberrant (Yearley, 1995; Tovey and Share, 2001; Tovey, 2007)? As suggested above, localism seems to imply a narrow, 'NIMBY'-style focus on immediate issues and grievances with a concomitant failure to address wider social and political matters.

In any event, it is clear from the data that protests by local actors occurred largely in response to the incidence of development. The increase in development projects during the 'Celtic Tiger' period of national economic growth in the late 1990s and early 2000s seems to have given rise to a reactive series of conflicts with local actors who were determined either to mitigate, or prevent entirely, perceived negative consequences for local areas arising from those projects. Thus, reported environmental claims seemed to be issue-dependent and therefore largely confined to the redress of particular matters, rather than addressing wider environmental problematics. For example, local actors may protest against a specific proposal to site an incinerator in their area, but are less likely to protest against the national policy on incineration if they are not being directly affected. Given that social movements are 'meant' to be about structural transformation, this raises the possibility that actors with a local horizon are not the real thing and are not in fact components of an environmental social movement.

Social movements are identified by a number of apparent characteristics such as the cultural and political character of the claims they raise, the perception of their activists in regards to the meaning and purpose of the mobilisation, and the extent and density of their networks (see, for example, Della Porta and Diani, 1999; Eyerman and Jamison, 1991; Melucci, 1988). The sociological assumption in regards to social movements thus may lead researchers investigating local conflicts over the siting of unwanted projects to seek out the social movement apparently latent or manifest in it (Leonard, 2006).

But if, in fact, we find local actors apparently not trying to change a social or political system, then what might they be trying to achieve? What does the protest and campaign look like from 'within'? There seems little doubt that if the dispute is prolonged over time the possibility arises that far deeper issues emerge that render what may appear mere 'local' protest far more challenging to the contemporary social and political order than may otherwise seem to be the case, especially given that local actors may not invariably utilise conventional social movement discourses and frames. This may occur because 'local' issues may, over the course of an extended dispute, be conceptualised as instances or manifestations of wider, more macro, problems. In such cases the requirements to engage with 'outside' or national-level actors, whether they be adversaries or allies, seem to be critical factors in stimulating this deepening problematic. This in turn suggests the appropriateness of longitudinal research methodologies in attempting to understand such disputes, and reminds us of the essential requirement to refine our research methodologies in light of the character and circumstances of the object of that research.

## The culture of silence – listening and giving voice

When we examine a local protest mobilisation, what do we expect to hear? As I have suggested above, the first step is one of listening with compassion and uncovering the local language. Local lives are not public lives. One implication of this is that local actors, as suggested above, may not necessarily express their views in terms of conventional or formal political or philosophical categories. In the specific case of articulations regarding 'sustainability' there are two immediate constraints to their mode of expression: rhetorical considerations which involve activists necessarily in a process of translation such as framing their opposition according to land-use or legal criteria; and the recognition that the discourse of sustainability is often submerged within other, locally meaningful modes of expression. Let me examine each point briefly in turn with specific reference to the Corrib conflict.

First, the attainment of a point of view, of a political position in regards to an issue, may take time to construct. The initial reactions are often uncertain and confused. It takes time for what are often visceral and emotional reactions to form into language. A considered view is slowly formed. This construction of the community view may be the fruit of many factors – interlocutors, allies, administrative procedures, political opportunities and constraints, available media frames. For this reason, community views are often in a continual process of transformation. The longer the time involved in the dispute and the greater the complexity and density of the campaign field in regard to antagonists and allies, the more alterations and negotiations may be involved. The challenge for the researcher is how to get back to what is meant, to what truly animates mobilisation. This is because it must be recognised that what people say in the course of conflict is often not what they mean. It is the immense difficulty of addressing this challenge that suggests the importance of attentive dialogue as a helpful research methodology. Consider the progression in views indicated in the following two citations from *The Rossport Five: Our Story*, a text of interviews with the five local men jailed in 2005 for their opposition to Shell's project.

At first we were naïve. You wouldn't take a lot of notice of those things. We heard that there was gas found and it was coming in to Erris or Mayo somewhere (Corduff, W. In Garavan 2006: 19).

> I think the conclusion is that it is it is a banana republic at the end of the day. You saw that especially when the men were sent into prison. You don't know the sinking feeling I've had for the last six years about this country that had been fought and died for. It would leave you now lifeless almost. I loved history when I was going to school and I was nearly out there fighting the battles. And then to see what has happened! We were told for as long as I remember that there's nothing in Erris, there's nothing in Mayo. But now there's billions of euros worth of oil and gas just a couple of miles there off our shores here. And we're not going to benefit one bit except for a couple of jobs. They would take it and walk on us and take it through Erris and through Mayo without gain for the country or Erris or Mayo except that they will destroy this area. And whoever would live to see the day in thirty or forty years time there will be nobody living along Sruhwaddoccon and that area. If this happens and the big pipe goes in and the terminal in Ballinaboy, people will not be there. Number one, they won't get planning permission anyway for their house and two, they wouldn't want to live there. As a parent I wouldn't want to see my children building a house along Sruhwaddoccon or Glengad. This is not the country I thought it was. It's an awful shock and shattering experience. Life is gone from us (2006: 79).

These citations register a striking temporal transformation of views from a naïve passivity in the initial stages of the gas project to a deep opposition to the fundamental nature of the political system within which the community operated. For this reason, the researcher must be cautious here. At what point in this ongoing process is the 'community position' actually attained? The suggestion that I have made above is that this position is continually being modified and formed in light of new knowledge, new opportunities, the impact of new allies and the ongoing interaction with, and need to engage with, new interlocutors. This involves the community in a continual process of translation and articulation driven by the concern to make sense of what is happening and what their point of view actually is. The researcher must be alert to these nuances and to the reality that there are competing and varied views within the community. Often, in order to appear 'reasonable' and credible, activists rely on readily available frames and discourses, even though these may not fully accord with their position. Furthermore, who it is who speaks for the community shapes how the community represents itself.

Hence, politically committed or mobilised activists may in their representative role express views in a manner not quite rooted in the local perspective.

It is in light of all of these considerations that the researcher must engage in a deep process of listening and dialogue.

> To be an act of knowing the adult literacy process demands among teachers and students a relationship of authentic dialogue. True dialogue unites subjects together in the cognition of a knowable object which mediates between them. (Freire, 1974: 29)

The objective is to ensure that we are relating to the genuine view of the local people and not projecting onto them certain dominant perspectives. This is a difficult undertaking, often involving a slow articulation of otherwise taken-for-granted or unexpressed assumptions and conventions regarding sociality or culture.

Second, in the specific case of sustainability we must similarly exercise caution. The discourse of sustainability is often the product of a scientific-rational perspective which may not be expressed in quite those terms by local communities (see for example Moran 2011 for a study of rural communities in Connemara). Thus, local articulations of sustainability may be far more complex and outside the confines of conventional modes. This chapter began with an evocation of place names, both modern and ancient, in a communal time frame that appears seamless and continuous. Place names may represent archetypes of presence which vivify and personalise an otherwise inert landscape. Involved here is a perceptual transformation of landscape from being a collection of objects within geometrical observable and measurable space to a cultural–physical totality operating within a relational field. This mode of perception paradoxically brings local views which appear to be 'traditional' into the very cutting edge of contemporary deep ecological perspectives (see, for example, Naess, 1989: 54ff.). Thus, local descriptions of the area reveal sensibilities surprisingly consistent with images of ecological sustainability, though they may not be expressed precisely in those terms (Edmondson and Rau, 2008).

> I know this area will be destroyed if Shell's project comes through. The future of this area will be gone. I don't make any distinction between area and people or between people and environment. I don't see any sense in the area without people. There is continuity there from the Bronze Age or even earlier. To see that continuity destroyed for the sake of forty or fifty years. It affects me. For something so trivial as more money for already rich people. (O Seighin, M. in Garavan (2006) 93)

## Dialogic research methodology

Attaining this level of articulation, however, is not straightforward. In 11 years of conflict, modes of expression that reflect local people's culture-specific views and practices with regards to sustainability were very rarely heard, because the arena of conflict was structured in such a way that these formulations would literally have made very little sense to outside interlocutors. Thus the researcher must enter into the reality of local lives with great circumspection. This takes time and a commitment to build trust with local activists. Without a necessary level of empathy, real and deep listening is almost impossible. Communication (including research) is not a matter of extracting data from an object but is more effective when it occurs in the context of a relationship. This, of course, in turn imposes challenges and risks at both a personal level and in regards to the integrity of what might subsequently be claimed as empirical findings.

Let me illustrate this listening and formulation with citations from *Our Story*. It is not an academic book in any conventional sense. There are no interpretations, no grand theory, no proposals or considered argument presented. Instead, there are just voices left to speak on their own terms. However, the confidence and honesty of these voices have emerged through a prolonged process of dialogue over many years.

To examine the fruit of this methodological approach, we can investigate a number of key questions. Paying attention to how local activists address these questions permits the researcher to formulate some general ideas about the causes and course of their campaign. First, what exactly is the issue giving rise to the conflict?

> It's hard to pinpoint it. I saw harm in it from the word go. I don't know was it the fear of gas. I don't know if it was something like that that made us fear it ... Also, it probably was the love of the land and the love of the place. We loved the place so much and we were both from the area. (Garavan, 2006: 26–7)

> What was worrying me most was the safety aspect ... here we were being exposed to a high-risk, high-consequence project with little or no gain for Ireland. So it was the combination of a whole lot of factors that was motivating us, but safety was the main concern. (Garavan, 2006: 166)

> There was no doubt that for me the real issue was health. My main concern was the emissions from the terminal. (Garavan, 2006: 70)

Second, why did people decide to oppose the project despite the expensive and prolonged information campaigns designed to show that local fears were unfounded?

> Our attachment to place comes into it too. According as we were going on bit by bit and learning more it was obvious that it was the end of the place as somewhere to which the next generation could return whether visiting or otherwise. This was the end of it. It wasn't just a matter of new industry coming in – that alone is no problem – but that it would be the end of millennia of culture. For us, the cultural aspect was very simple. When people talk about culture it's a page in the *Times* that no one reads or the Sunday newspaper. But for us it's a different thing, it's all of living, every-day survival. (Garaven, 2006: 78)

> If you looked at the project ahead into the future you could see that it would mean the end of the community and the destruction of a beautiful part of the country. That's what has happened in other parts of the world so why would it be any different here? People would have to move out. Here in Rossport people would have had to leave because Shell would have made life intolerable. It was so wrong that in the next generation and in generations to come, our children and our grandchildren would say, 'This is awful. Look at that monstrosity over there, what did you do about it at the time'? We had to act, especially when we knew that it was wrong. It would be different if you didn't know. You'd have some justification. But when you did know you couldn't live with yourself if you did nothing. (Garavan, 2006: 170–1)

A third issue of interest is to enquire in what way did local activists oppose the project? What was their mode of activism?

> We took them on, not in the violent manner they were hoping for, but we confronted them in a way they hadn't expected. A Nigerian visitor said to me that this was the first time that an oil company had been challenged on an intellectual level … They were talking on the one hand about transparency and openness and consultation and yet when you wanted information and con-sultation they wouldn't divulge it. There was this inconsistency. We knew that they had a big, well-funded PR machine. We could only fight that by having the facts and by being upfront with the people and hoping they'd believe us. (Garavan, 2006: 166)

> I don't think though there was that much anger here. That was very important. I think it was controlled. In fact we were very

conscious that Shell would love to provoke us. This wasn't going to be won, we weren't going to make any headway, if we didn't pursue our campaign peacefully and through sound arguments. All we had to go on was our moral authority, our moral courage. We couldn't take them on physically. It was what they wanted. They could then portray us as thugs and as an unruly mob and so on. Then they would have footage that they would use as a propaganda weapon. (Garavan, 2006: 174–5)

A final issue that might be investigated is what response the local activists received to their opposition, particularly from outside actors or adversaries? How did their efforts proceed in light of events? A number of points need to be considered here, but the most outstanding feature of local activists' experiences was the complete refusal by any of their interlocutors to engage in meaningful dialogue with them.

But when you asked the questions you wouldn't be answered. You kind of know when there are people beginning to pull the wool over your eyes. That's one thing I cannot stand for. You have to be straight and clean with somebody. (Corduff, W. in Garavan, 2006: 27)

You asked questions and you were jailed. (Corduff, M. in Garavan, 2006: 56)

There was nobody asking questions. (Ni Sheighin, C. in Garavan, 2006: 65)

It was just a one-way sound. We talked but they didn't listen. (Corduff, W. in Garavan, 2006: 28)

They never wanted to meet those who weren't in favour. (Ni Sheighin, C. in Garavan, 2006: 72)

Efforts even to have an open, public meeting failed.

But they wouldn't hold a public meeting where all the people would meet. (Corduff, W. in Garavan, 2006: 25)

We tried to get them to have a public meeting. We tried them several times to get the people together and have a public meeting. They would meet private, no problem, any time you wanted them. I'd say no, we'd better get this out in the open. But they'd never have a public meeting. (Corduff, W. in Garavan, 2006: 35)

The public bodies didn't see it as their function to make decisions on their merits. Because of that it was not possible for them to listen. Their function was to do what they were told. The top authority had made a decision that this project was going through and that was that. There was to be no discussion. There was no sense of reality at all. They were not able – they were not allowed – to engage with the project at all. For example, the County Council admitted that they didn't have the expertise in-house to assess the project but they said that they would hire expertise and that it would all be done properly. They never did. (O Seighin, M. in Garavan, 2006: ·76)

This anti-dialogic approach was perceived as reducing the local community to passive objects to be manipulated and controlled.

But Shell would talk in those terms because to them money is the answer. Profit is all. People or environment doesn't come into the equation at all. Money for them is all and they'd nearly think how could it not be money. They can't understand the tie with the land and the ground and the community and your area. They don't understand that. (Corduff, M. in Garavan, 2006: 36)

We were never consulted about the route. There was not a word. It was as if we didn't exist. (McGrath, M. in Garavan, 2006: 164)

For this reason primarily, opposition to the project became more determined and resolute, and ultimately culminated in imprisonment for a number of community members.

It was a process. I knew from as soon as Shell got planning permission from An Bord Pleanala and as soon as they moved onto the pipeline that, bit by bit, prison was the next step. I could not avoid it. And I couldn't see beyond that because I couldn't see how we would get out of jail. (O Seighin, M. in Garavan, 2006: O Seighin, M. 82)

In the evolution of community opposition and views, might there be a point when the local campaign could be adjudged as becoming akin to a social movement?

It opened my eyes [being in prison]. I never will forget it. We didn't know that that kind of thing was happening. I mean we'd get up in the morning at home and do our jobs and you wouldn't think of anything like that. Ever since prison it never leaves my mind.

I had family myself, I had sons at the age of those lads in there, and I thought they belonged to some father and mother too. Society had let them down. They had nothing to do but steal. Putting them in jail wasn't going to correct them. It was going to ruin them. That's what I felt. If they were put somewhere where they could do something and be given some training. The majority of them were okay, they just needed someone to direct them. (Corduff, W. in Garavan, 2006: 47)

I feel let down by the system, let down by our politicians, let down by our county councillors. We were reared as children to obey the law and we did the same with our own children. And all of a sudden you feel you're out on your own, you've elected those people to look after us, and all of a sudden they're not looking after us. (Seighin, C. in Garavan, 2006: 75)

One result of our experience is that I look differently on people elsewhere who are fighting for causes. Before I wouldn't have taken any notice really. All we can do now though is offer our support. (McGrath, P. in Garavan, 2006: 131–2)

These citations do seem to suggest a transformation in views which bring local experiences into a wider political-analytical framework. In other words, the problems facing the community are recognised as systemic in nature and can occur, albeit in different forms, elsewhere.

## Assessment

Creating a dialogic bond between researcher and local community should, at a minimum, ensure that we can move beyond slogans and clichés in our understanding of local social reality. This is a methodology suggesting caution in projecting macro-theoretical frameworks in an uncritical manner onto local reality. The value of such a methodology is therefore its attentiveness to local reality, its democratic impulse, its responsiveness to the perceived lived reality of the people under study. This is an approach that reaches far beyond the 'case study' mentality, by which particular instances of conflict are often surveyed and served up as illustrations of general principles.

However, it is important to be modest and considered in our claims. No one methodology provides a privileged, or definitive, understanding of collective action. What I am choosing to designate as dialogic research is not novel. Sustained dialogue is implied within a number of longitudinal methodological approaches such as ethnography and feminist research. Any method, including that of dialogic research, illuminates aspects only of social reality. My proposal is simply that our understanding of the lived reality of sustainability, particularly as it becomes highlighted and visible among local lives in conflict over the immediate ecology, is enhanced by a process of engaged dialogue between researcher and local actors. This takes us beyond the case study only insofar as it involves the researcher in a temporal and empathic commitment to understanding that community's perspective in its own terms, rather than solely as a manifestation of broader social and political currents.

However, there are risks and disadvantages. In submerging ourselves into localist perspectives we may fail in the grand mission of sociology to explain the social world in its structural dimension. Sheer detail may blind us to the wider systemic forces ultimately shaping even local experiences. The limits of subjectivity may fatally undermine descriptive and critical rigour. Partisan engagement or empathy may of course be inimical to the academic enterprise. The researcher may become absorbed into a single local perspective and in effect co-opted. The requirement to observe critical distance may be compromised. In addition, communities cannot be essentialised. In this sense, there is never merely one community or cultural perspective, as there was not in the case of the Corrib conflict.

But there are always risks in our undertakings. There are always flaws. The researching of local lives in conflict through a methodology of dialogue is not of course necessarily a superior perspective upon which the researcher stakes a claim to greater insight into social reality. There can be no genuine human concern with sustainability without a deep regard for our earth. Nor can we encounter the specificity of human lives without a commitment to people in their struggles. However, as with all methodological approaches, empathic dialogue too must merely take its place in the diverse efforts of human beings to make sense of our sociality and our habitats. Its ultimate claim is simply to be a complement to the many qualitative and quantitative methods we must use in order to understand, in much the same way that the intimate human naming of a place can sit side by side with the geographical mapping of a physical coordinate.

## Notes

1   See Mac Graith, U. and Ní Ghearraigh, T. (eds) (2004) *Logainmneacha agus Oidhreacht Dhún Chaocháin: The Placenames and Heritage of Dún Chaocháin*. Ceathrú Thaidhg: Dun Chaocháin Teo.
2   Of course, it must be acknowledged that opposition was not supported by all of the local community. While a majority of the local parish directly affected by the proposed refinery and pipeline probably vaguely opposed it, only a small minority of the community became actively mobilised against it. There were many differing local views on the merits or otherwise of the project.
3   'Not in my backyard' – the assumption being made that local actors are only concerned with the local effect of an unwanted development but do not care about the wider systemic issues at stake once that development is located elsewhere.
4   The protest event research was conducted as part of a broader investigation into the patterns of Irish environmental activism, employing similar methodologies to the Transformation of

Environmental Activism project coordinated by Christopher Rootes, University of Kent, Canterbury. The Irish research was carried out under the aegis of the Environmental Change Institute, NUI Galway (Human Impact Cluster), under the supervision of Dr Ricca Edmondson, School of Political Science and sociology, NUI, Galway.

# References

Baker, S. (1990) 'The Evolution of the Irish Ecology Movement', in W. Rudig (ed.), *Green Politics One*. Edinburgh: Edinburgh University Press. pp.47–81.

Della Porta, D. and Diani, M. (1999) *Social Movements: An Introduction*. London: Blackwell Publishers.

Edmondson, R. and Rau, H. (eds) (2008) *Environmental Argument and Cultural Difference – Locations, Fractures and Deliberations*. Oxford: Peter Lang.

Eyerman, R. and Jamison, A. (1991) *Social Movements: A Cognitive Approach*. Cambridge: Polity Press.

Freire, P. (1974) *Cultural Action for Freedom*. Harmondsworth: Penguin Books.

Garavan, M. (2007) 'Resisting the costs of "development": local environmental activism in ireland', *Environmental Politics*, 16 (5): 844–63.

Garavan, M. (2006) *Our Story – The Rossport Five*. Dublin: Small World Media.

Leonard, L. (2006) *Green Nation*. Galway: Greenhouse Press in cooperation with Choice Publishing Ltd.

Mac Graith, U. and Ní Ghearraigh, T. (eds) (2004) *Logainmneacha agus Oidhreacht Dhún Chaocháin: The Placenames and Heritage of Dún Chaocháin*. Ceathru Thaidgh: Dun Chaocháin Teo.

Mayo, P. (2004) *Liberating Praxis: Paulo Freire's Legacy for Radical Education and Politics*. Rotterdam: Sense Publishers.

Melucci, A. (1988) 'Social movements and the democratisation of everyday life', in J. Keane (ed.), *Civil Society and the State: New European Perspectives*. London: Verso Press. pp. 245–60.

Moran, L. (2011) 'Tacit knowledge and resistance: the impact of rural knowledge-based cultures on the implementation of environmental policy in Connemara'. Ph.D. dissertation. NUI, Galway.

Naess, A. (1989) *Ecology, Community and Lifestyle*. Cambridge: Cambridge University Press.

Peires, J.B. (1989) *The Dead Will Arise – Nongqawuse and the Great Xhosa Cattle Killing Movement of 1856–7*. Johannesburg: Raven Press Ltd.

Rootes, C. (2003) *Environmental Protest in Western Europe*. Oxford: Oxford University Press.

Tovey, H. (2007) *Environmentalism in Ireland: Movement and activists*. Dublin: IPA Press.

Tovey, H. and Share, P. (2001) *A Sociology of Ireland*. Dublin: Gill and MacMillan.

Yearley, S. (1995) 'The social shaping of the environmental movement in Ireland', in Clancy, P., Drudy, S., Lynch, K. and O'Dowd, L. (eds), *Irish Society – Sociological Perspectives*. Dublin: Institute of Public Administration. pp. 652–74.

# PART III

Comparative Research on the
Sustainability Performance of Cities,
Regions and Nation-states

# 5

## Sustainable Development of What? Contesting global development concepts and measures

*Su-ming Khoo*

## Introduction

Whether we are trying to find out if a particular development situation is sustainable, assess a development trend for sustainability, or compare development performance of different countries or regions, we have inevitably to ask the question: sustainable development of *what*? This chapter explores efforts to define, measure and compare aspects of development at the global level. The starting point is the proposition that the meanings and definitions of sustainable development are neither static, nor given. Sustainable development has been called a *contestable* concept, containing competing interpretations and ideas (Jacobs, 1991). 'Sustainability' is a boundary term, signifying complex interactions between science, politics, policy making and development (Scoones, 2010: 153–4). 'Development' is similarly *emergent* and *contested*, with different understandings emerging over time and space. This fluidity has allowed different actors to redefine and manipulate the term 'sustainable development' to suit their own agendas (Krueger and Gibbs, 2007: 8). Sustainable development must gain intellectual clarity and rigour and give up politically expedient fuzziness, if it is to have an impact (Lélé, 1991: 607). The conceptual and empirical challenges converge in concerns with measurement – 'if sustainability is to mean anything, it must be measurable' (Hamilton and Atkinson, 2006: xi).

Debates about the meaning and measurement of sustainable development are usually situated within efforts to 'green' national accounting. These debates appear somewhat technical, but questions concerning what measures to choose and how to integrate different measures reflect profound, even radical efforts to redefine how societies think about, and value, social progress and wealth. This broader view encompasses factors such as poverty, inequality, welfare, basic needs, quality of life, ecology and resource limits – in a variety of combinations. The discussion in this chapter draws attention to the *global* character of these critiques and contestations. Taking a critical development perspective (e.g. Munck and O'Hearn, 1999; Kothari, 2005), this chapter emphasises the unevenness of global development. Historic claims for economic and political restructuring and global justice must be recognised as part and parcel of the sustainable development debates. The first three explain the roots of 'development' as a concept, the rise of national economic accounting and the search for alternative approaches. These early debates provided the foundations from which important new concepts emerged in the 1990s, including the *human development paradigm*, the concept of *environmental space*, and *the new economics*. The way we conceptualise and measure sustainability influences political decisions about the pathways that are taken towards sustainability. The fourth and fifth sections explore alternative measures as possible tools for re-routing future development thinking towards global sustainability, redirecting the meaning of 'development' away from 'unaimed opulence' (Drèze and Sen, 1989: 188) and towards sustained welfare and environmental prudence. The concluding discussion draws connections between the different alternative approaches, surveys a number of aggregate measures and considers their usefulness for shaping a future global 'development compact'.

## The roots of development: from colonial resource management to welfare

Current patterns of global development were shaped by a history of capitalist and colonial power relations which structured uneven and inequitable flows of resources, benefit and harm over centuries. 'Development' is conventionally understood as a post-Second World War concern with planned economic growth and structured international cooperation. However, current patterns of use and the conditions for access to land, water, forests and other natural resources in most developing countries are rooted in their colonial past and the continuation of such practices after independence. Imperial administration or colonial conquest, especially in the 'settled states', imposed new relationships between colonised people, nature and natural resources (Woodhouse and Chimhowu, 2005: 180).

Economic development referred to the *development of resources*, not people. In the nineteenth and early twentieth centuries, 'development' meant colonisation – 'opening up natural resources', promoting labour migration and developing infrastructure such as railways, ports and roads to facilitate their exploitation (Arndt, 1981: 462). Colonial law secured control of forests, water and minerals, often overturning traditional norms governing community access to critical livelihood resources (Randeria, 2003: 40–43). Conservation policies were colonial acts which often excluded, dispossessed and sometimes forcibly eliminated or displaced native populations as they enclosed 'wilderness' and valuable resources within 'conservation fortresses' (Haller *et al.*, 2008; Dowie, 2009).

Yet imperialists often perceived their activities to be humanitarian and benevolent. Social welfare became an explicit consideration with the advent of a new mode of colonialism, the '*dual mandate*', which cast the colonisers in a tutelary, protective role, even as they sought out resources and profits (Arndt, 1981: 463; Cooke, 2003). Cecil Rhodes thus famously defined imperialism as 'philanthropy plus a 5 percent dividend on investment' (Lawlor, 2000, cited in Kothari, 2005: 50), an ambiguous rationale which continued into the era of decolonisation under the term 'trusteeship'. The British Empire affirmed its colonial responsibility for 'minimum standards of nutrition, health and education' with the 1939 Colonial Development and Welfare Act (Hancock, 1947, cited in Arndt, 1981: 463). After the Second World War, 'development' became understood as the solution to a global problem of 'underdevelopment' in a new era of decolonisation and international cooperation. A 'New Deal' was promised to emerging nations as President Truman declared that '[t]he old imperialism – exploitation for foreign profit – has no place in our plans. What we envisage is a program of development based on the concepts of democratic fair-dealing' (quoted in Rist, 1997: 71).

The evidence that emerged suggested that unfair global economic structures persisted, perpetuating forms of neocolonialism (Frank, 1966; Chen and Sapsford, 1997). Developing countries criticised this neocolonial tendency and demanded global reforms. At the UN General Assembly in 1974, developing countries collectively demanded a New International Economic Order (NIEO), involving fairer financing and terms of trade; control over, and benefits from, multinational corporations and greater equality and influence within the United Nations. The likelihood of the NIEO demands being fulfilled declined from the moment they were announced, as global recession, debt crisis and neoliberal structural adjustment policies caused the 1980s to be known as the 'impasse' or 'lost decade' of development (Schuurman, 1993). After three decades of sustained economic progress with improving welfare, fiscal austerity, welfare cutbacks and militarisation set a pessimistic scene for de-development. By the 1990s, critical development thinkers took a 'post-development' turn, declaring development to be 'a ruin in the intellectual landscape' (Sachs, 1999). Development reformists, on the other hand, looked to alleviate suffering and protect the basic needs of the most vulnerable in the context of constrained development (Cornia, Jolly and Stewart, 1987).

## Measuring economies, critiques of economism and the rise of welfare measures

The 1940s to early 1970s period is sometimes described as the 'golden age' of welfare capitalism (Marglin and Schor, 1990). National accounting became established as the basis for planned development and advances in 'modernisation' and industrialisation were measured in terms of aggregate formal economic production, gross domestic product (GDP) and retained national income, gross national product (GNP) or gross national income (GNI). National accounting techniques developed in the US, UK, Netherlands and Sweden in response to major challenges and innovations – the Great Depression, the rise of Keynesian macroeconomics and the need to resource and finance major war efforts. Although increasingly sophisticated, national economic measurement also presented certain limitations. Critiques began to emerge as the tensions between differing social concerns, theoretical issues and data constraints became increasingly evident (Vanoli, 2008).

By the 1960s, some critics had begun to directly challenge the use of economic growth as a measure of development:

> Economic growth will not merely fail to solve social and political difficulties; certain types of growth can actually cause them. Now that the complexity of development problems is becoming increasingly obvious, the continued addiction to the use of a single aggregative indicator [economic growth] ... begins to look like a preference for avoiding the real problems. (Seers, 1963: 77)

The predominant 'modernisation school' of development theory assumed that the benefits of overall economic growth would trickle down to reach the poor (So, 1990). However, social statistics that were now being systematically collected showed that poverty, inequality and exclusion persisted and had even increased in many countries. Neo-Marxist critics of the 'dependency school' argued that unequal, neocolonial economic structures were the cause of economic dependency – 'the development of underdevelopment' (Frank, 1966).

---

### Box 5.1   The 'Brazilian Miracle'

In the 1960s Brazil's authoritarian government actively promoted industrial development, leading to a period of rapid economic growth dubbed 'Brazil's Economic Miracle' (1968–1975). However, these policies favoured upper- and middle-class industrialists and consumers, repressing workers' wages while marginalising the rural poor. Large income, health and educational inequalities prevailed. Commenting on the 'Brazilian Miracle', Brazil's then President, General Medici, remarked *'the economy does well, but the people do poorly'* (Goulet, 2002: 20). On another occasion, Medici commented that *'industry may be flourishing, but the people are not'* (Antoine, 1973, also cited in Goulet, 2002: 20). Increased resource extraction, industrial development and urbanisation also meant pollution, deforestation, inequality and repression. Davis (1977: xii) argued that there were many 'victims of the miracle' – Amazonian Indians, agricultural and highway workers, dispossessed rural migrants, especially in the poorest north-east, and millions of poor in the large cities. These marginalised groups failed to benefit from 'development' while the ecology of the Amazon and the earth itself came under threat. Eventually, the 'economic miracle' proved to be financially and socially unsustainable. Economic stagnation, hyperinflation and debt crisis characterised the 1980s, worsening unemployment and further widening inequality (Cardoso and Urani, 1995).

---

The later 1960s saw the appearance of major innovations in conceptualising and measuring development. Seers (1969: 3–4) argued that the three major problems of development were poverty, unemployment and inequality: 'if one or two of these central problems have been growing worse, especially if all three have, it would be strange to call the result "development," even if per capita income soared'. Another alternative measure was Morris's 'Physical Quality of Life Index' (PQLI), with three components: infant mortality rates, life expectancy at age one and literacy (Estes, 2003). The PQLI reflected the human results of development efforts rather than economic resources that were notionally available, but not necessarily mobilised for desired human outcomes. PQLI data showed that there was no automatic correlation between increasing aggregate income and welfare outcomes, suggesting that quality of life was only indirectly determined by high economic wealth, and more likely to be the outcome of wise government spending. Morris wanted the measure to avoid ethnocentric assumptions and be sensitive to a range of needs – not all countries might wish to develop in the same way. However, a measure still had to be internationally comparable and show how benefits were distributed. Survival and functioning were understood as basic conditions from which further forms of social satisfaction could be determined (Morris, 1978: 225, 230–1).

Human rights and development were connected through the 1972 'Right to Development' proposal to the United Nations, articulating the human right to 'a particular process of development, in which all human rights and fundamental freedoms can be fully realized'. The Right to Development was declared in 1986, announcing a humanist revolution in the meaning and purpose of development, by stating that 'the human person is the central subject of development and should be the active participant and beneficiary of the right to development' (United Nations, 1986). Governments were expected to empower citizens and guarantee them equal benefits from development as rights. In practice, the right to development was claimed not by individual citizens, but by developing country governments keen to assert their position in north–south bargaining. Tensions between north and south persisted as the proposed NIEO reforms failed to materialise. These tensions were made clear in Indira Gandhi's address to the 1972 UN Conference on the Human Environment at Stockholm. She asserted that poverty and need were 'the greatest polluters' while criticising the developed countries' route to affluence through their history of colonialism and oppression (Gandhi, 1972, cited in Vihma, 2011: 7, n. 9).

In 1976, the International Labour Organization (ILO) promoted the concept of 'basic needs' which integrated some of these emerging debates, arguing that 'it is no longer acceptable in human terms or responsible in political terms to wait several generations for the benefits of development to trickle down until they reach the poorest groups' (ILO, 1976). Basic needs defined a package of 'minimum food, shelter, clothing, access to essential services such as transport, education, sanitation, health care, an adequately paid job, healthy environment and popular participation in decision making' (Grindle, 1992). This expansive definition reflected the codification of the two major global human rights treaties in 1966 – the International Convention on Civil and Political Rights (ICCPR) and International Convention on Economic, Social and Cultural Rights (ICECSR). The basic needs idea was carried forward in attempts to define the 'minimum core' of socio-economic rights (Young, 2008).

## Sustainable development as a contested global concept

The concept of sustainable development can be understood as a response to two different global critiques of the dominant development paradigm that emerged in 1960s and 1970s. These were (i) the 'southern' critique of unequal, neocolonial and 'dependent' development discussed in the previous section, and (ii) growing concerns about population growth, pollution and ecological limits to growth that were global in scope, but largely northern in their origin.

Differing understandings of ecological sustainability and sustainable society began to emerge as counterpoints to the mainstream model of economic development, reflecting new concerns with population, pollution and food. The bestselling book *The Population Bomb* (Ehrlich, 1968) presented a pessimistic and controversial Malthusian view: 'that it can be a very bad thing to have more than a certain number of people alive at the same time, that Earth has finite *carrying capacity*, and that the future of civilization was in grave doubt' (Ehrlich and Ehrlich, 2009: 63, emphasis added). Malthus' *Essay on the Principle of Population* (1798) argued that population inevitably out-stripped food production, since food production grew at an 'arithmetic' rate (i.e. 1, 2, 3, 4...), while population grew at a 'geometric' rate (i.e. 1, 2, 4, 8...). Famine, war and disease functioned as 'natural checks' on population, hence Malthus opposed the provision of famine relief. Likewise, *The Population Bomb* suggested that civilisational collapse could only be prevented by mass birth control ('the birth rate solution') or allowing the poor to die ('the death rate solution') (Ehrlich and Ehrlich, 2009). The burden appeared to lie with the poorer countries, which had not yet undergone the demographic transition (Dyson, 2010). At its extremes, Malthusianism coincided with eugenicist views that the 'least fit' individuals must perish in order that the 'fitter' survive (Desrochers and Hoffbauer, 2009: 39). Malthusian pessimism was refuted by optimistic 'cornucopians' who viewed population growth as beneficial for development, providing labour and talent which compensated for the burden of food consumption (Desrochers and Hoffbauer, 2009: 39). This line of thinking would later be developed as the 'substitutability' argument by 'weak sustainability' theorists (Neumayer, 2003).

The poor have also been blamed for environmental degradation, although some political ecologists think this is unfair because the impact of poor people's activities on forests and soils is frequently exaggerated (Leach and Mearns, 1996), especially when compared with the environmental impacts of richer people's consumption. Early sustainability debates connected poverty, underdevelopment and environmental damage in ways that seemed to blame the victims, seeing the poor as destroyers of the environment due to necessity and ignorance. Environmental degradation in poorer countries and regions was explained as resulting from income poverty and the lack of development and modernisation. This was a very different explanation from the 'development of underdevelopment' critique of neocolonial economic and political structures (Frank, 1966), or a critical environmental political economy which saw environmental exploitation and damage as the result of modernisation, neocolonial dependence and uneven globalization (e.g. Yearley, 1991, 1996).

The early 1970s saw the introduction of systems thinking and computer-based modelling as tools for analysing population, environment, growth and sustainability questions. There was a new emphasis on interdependence and carrying capacity – distinctive features of an *ecological* perspective. *The Limits to Growth* (Meadows et al., 1972) was a research project commissioned by an elite business group, 'The Club of Rome' concerned with potential Malthusian global collapse. Computer modelling, pioneered at the Massachusetts Institute of Technology (MIT), enabled the development of systems thinking (Meadows, 2009) involving simulations of trends and interactions based upon data on global industrialisation, resource depletion, pollution, food production and population growth. The simulations demonstrated that different factors were highly interdependent, necessitating a holistic, interdisciplinary, globally cooperative and long-term approach (Martell, 1994: 24–33). Impending crises needed to be addressed by radically shifting the social systems and values that underpinned unsustainable growth.

Lélé (1991: 609–10) attributes sustainable development's rise to the International Union for the Conservation of Nature and Natural Resources' (IUCN) World Conservation Strategy (1980). He differentiates *ecological sustainability*, a concept that was broadly adopted by the environmental movement, from 'social interpretations of sustainability', asserting that social understandings are 'rarely used'. Dresner (2002) has a very different perspective, identifying a somewhat earlier point of origin in the arguments for a globally *sustainable society* that had been made at the World Council of Churches Conference on Science and Technology for Human Development in 1974. Barbier (1987) attempts to reconcile the ecological and social interpretations by associating sustainable development with basic needs strategies, which had to be

> environmentally sustainable over the long-term, consistent with social values and institutions, and encourage 'grassroots' participation in the development process ... there will be no sustained development of meaningful growth without a clear commitment at the same time to preserve the environment and promote the rational use of resources. (1987: 102)

The 1974 World Council of Churches conference revisited the difficulties raised by the 'southern' position, as articulated by Indira Gandhi at Stockholm in 1972. Poorer countries were characterised as being concerned with developmentalist priorities of economic growth and poverty alleviation, regarding environmentalism as a luxury. This presented a strong contrast against the anti-growth, population-controlling and conservationist concerns of 'Western' environmentalists:

> From the late 1960s, when the present-day environmentalist movement was starting, leftists and representatives of the developing countries had frequently accused environmentalists, with their concerns about 'the population bomb' and 'the limits to growth', of being unconcerned about the plight of the poor. They saw all this talk of 'limits' as a cover for traditional conservative arguments that wealth was too scarce for everyone to share in it – a thinly disguised justification for inequality. (Dresner, 2002: 2–3)

Thin (2002: 24) argues that the 'three pillars' conception of sustainable development as economic, environmental and social development could be more correctly depicted as two pins, representing environmental limitations and social inequality, pricking a balloon of naive expectations about economic growth (see also Douthwaite,1992). At the heart of this contention lies a question of 'carrying capacity'. Have world societies already moved from an 'empty world' scenario where there is still *environmental space* into which humanity can expand, to a 'full world' (Daly, 1996) with no environmental space left? How much (if any) total environmental space is left for human use, without diminishing future possibilities?

The concept of environmental space makes the sustainability question concrete (Bührs, 2009: 112). Defined as 'access to fair shares for all in the resources upon which a healthy quality of life depends' (McLaren, 2003: 19), the concept has influenced the measurement of sustainability in fundamental ways (see also Gaube et al., Chapter 6 in this volume). Recent estimates worryingly indicate that ecological overshoot has already been reached and humanity is now sinking deeper and deeper into ecological debt. Ecological footprint methods estimate that biocapacity is shrinking while global population continues to grow, to the extent that in the year 2010, 'Ecological Debt Day' was reached by 21 August. From then until the 31 December, humanity was living beyond sustainable limits (http://www.footprintnetwork.org/en/index.php/GFN/page/earth_overshoot_day/).

The 1987 World Commission on Environment and Development (WCED) popularised the definition of sustainable development as development that *'meets the needs of the present without compromising the ability of future generations to meet their own needs'* (WCED, 1987: 8). Fifteen years later, at the 2002 Johannesburg World Summit on Sustainable Development (WSSD), sustainable development was understood in terms of the need to '[improve] *the quality of life for all the world's people without increasing the use of our natural resources beyond the earth's carrying capacity'* (WSSD, 2002). The reference to 'quality of life for all the world's people' raised questions about how to determine quality of life, while implying the need for global justice, and introducing in the more specific ecological term carrying capacity to denote environmental limits to development.

Putting sustainability into practice depends on having appropriate and trustworthy data about the quality of life, needs and deprivations and the state of environmental carrying capacity. A useful and relevant conception of sustainable development requires adequate concepts and measures, but also adequate knowledge about development inputs, outcomes and the state of global ecology. However, there is considerable disagreement and insufficient data in every respect, not least in relation to ecological knowledge. May's recent assessment (2007) points to a basic lack of knowledge about species, impacts and dynamics, both in terms of data and conceptual/theoretical understanding. The eminent ecologist also notes that the most important unanswered questions – of ethics, economics and politics – are rarely addressed within ecological studies.

# The human development paradigm and sustainability

Amartya Sen, Mahbub ul-Haq and Martha Nussbaum are the key exponents of the human development paradigm. This approach, launched in 1990 under the auspices of the United Nations Development Programme (UNDP), incorporated aspects of the PQLI and responded to Seers' earlier question about the relationship between economic growth and other human needs or goals. Sen accepts that income is important, but regards it as a means and not an end – income is instrumental, not intrinsic. Sen's 'capabilities approach' (Box 5.2) formed the basis of the Human Development Index (HDI), a composite measure of welfare and income designed to integrate social and economic dimensions of well-being. The HDI components are: health, indicated by infant mortality and life expectancy; knowledge, indicated by school enrolment and adult literacy; and income, indicated by GNP. The HDI reunited welfare components with income measures, because the PQLI on its own 'misses the synergy between social and economic progress' (Ul-Haq, 1995: 128).

Ul-Haq admits that the HDI is a still a crude measure. Like Morris, Sen and Ul-Haq designed the HDI to displace the even cruder measures of GDP/ GNP, and to stimulate development policies that would build human capabilities, supporting investments in health and education, while recognising economic growth as a means for enabling human development. The human development approach aspired to be 'the most holistic model that exists today … a practical reflection of life itself' (Ul-Haq, 1995: 21). The door was left open to refine or expand the human development paradigm beyond the HDI. Two decades later, this has led to the evolution of new measures that expand and deepen the approach to include dimensions of poverty, gender and inequality. The translation of the capabilities idea into simple, replicable and comparable cross-country and within-country measures of human development has proved a challenging task, opening out a whole field of work on concept, measurement, theory and policy practice (e.g. Comim, Qizilbash and Alkire, 2008).

---

**Box 5.2   The capabilities approach – defining human development**

The philosopher and economist, Amartya Sen defined development in terms of *human capabilities* and *freedom*, taking freedom to be the ultimate goal of human development. 'Development' means the expansion of people's capabilities to lead the kinds of lives they have reason to value (Sen, 1999: 18), so policies should enhance capabilities, address deprivation and remove unfreedoms such as hunger, ill-health, illiteracy and gender discrimination. The human ability to choose and reason is valued in itself, as well as a democratic means of making decisions, hence development policies should be influenced by the exercise of public deliberation – 'the effective use of participatory capabilities by the public' (ibid.). Sen's capability approach strongly influenced the human development paradigm. The inaugural *Human Development Report* (UNDP, 1990) defined human development as

> *a process of enlarging people's choices. In principle, these choices can be infinite and change over time. But at all levels of development, the three essential ones are for people to lead a long and healthy life, to acquire knowledge and to have access to resources needed for a decent standard of living.*

These three essential elements were captured in the HDI. Since human development was defined in terms of 'enlarging people's choices', all additional options valued by people are also important, for example political, economic and social freedom, opportunities to be creative and productive, and enjoyment of personal self-respect and guaranteed human rights. Income remains important to the concept of human development, but human lives are seen in far broader terms than income alone. The human development approach therefore redefined development goals beyond income and wealth, to focus on human freedom. The wider 'human development paradigm' encompasses sociopolitical freedoms and self-respect – Adam Smith called this the ability to mix with others without being 'ashamed to appear in public'. Such subjective or dignitarian conceptions of human being and flourishing are also key to human rights.

*Sources:* UNDP *Human Development Report* (1990, 10; Sen, 1999).

The human development approach is impressive in terms of philosophical richness and openness to a diversity of human goals, but the question is whether such an open-ended and expansive conception of human freedom can be reconciled with ecological limits. Neumayer observes that the human development and sustainable development literatures have, for the most part, stayed separate. Understandings of sustainable economic development and sustainable human development remain too weak with respect to ecological limits (UNDP, 2010: 1).

Sustainability appeared as a prominent issue in only five out of eighteen annual *Human Development Reports* (HDR) published to date. The most significant of these was the 1994 HDR, which set an ambitious agenda for the 1995 World Summit on Social Development (Copenhagen Summit). Subsequent Human Development Reports have examined inter alia, the quality of economic growth, consumption, water scarcity and climate change; consistently highlighting the inequalities suffered by the poor and the responsibilities of the richer nations (Alkire, 2010). The 1994 Report

marked the fiftieth anniversary of the United Nations with a proposed
World Social Charter, presenting a renewed vision for global cooperation,
including a 'human development compact' to implement essential human
development targets by the year 2020. A new, post-cold war vision of collective 'human security' (UNDP, 1994: 5–6) was advanced, integrating
environmental protection and development goals with peace, human rights
and democratisation within a 'context of sustainable development that
leads to human security' (op. cit.: 1). The 1994 report called for a radical
global restructuring, combining peace and human development with an
understanding of limits and futurity:

> development patterns that perpetuate today's inequities are neither
> sustainable nor worth sustaining ... current consumption cannot be
> financed for long by incurring economic debts that others must
> repay. It also means that sufficient investment must be made in the
> education and health of today's population so as not to create a
> social debt for future generations. And it means that resources must
> be used in ways that do not create ecological debts by overexploiting
> the carrying and productive capacity of the earth. (UNDP, 1994: 18)

There are two basic options for linking sustainable development and human
development to yield a model of sustainable human development: combining
the HDI with (i) a weak sustainability measure, such as genuine savings, or
(ii) with a strong sustainability measure such as ecological footprint
(Neumayer, 2010: 10–11). Weak sustainability assumes that natural capital
is *substitutable* by other forms of capital such as human knowledge (e.g.
more education) or manufactured capital (improved technology and
machinery). Strong sustainability rejects the notion of substitutability,
regarding the planet's critical natural capital as finite. Sustainability cannot
be said to be present if natural capital declines below a certain level.

The key question for sustainable human development is how to balance long-
term, intergenerational sustainability with immediate demands for intragenera-
tional distribution, given the starting problems of existing human deprivation:
'human lives are battered and diminished in all kinds of different ways, and the
first task ... is to acknowledge that deprivations of very different kinds have to
be accommodated within a general overarching framework' (Sen, 2000: 18).
Low human development countries will find it difficult to achieve even optimistic weak sustainability scenarios. They cannot be expected to consume less and
they lack domestic means to invest in substitutes (Neumayer, 2010: 14). Low
human development countries need to gain sufficient initial investments to
achieve weak sustainability, before they can be expected to achieve stronger
sustainability. Over-consuming high human development populations have to
make a fundamental transformation towards strong sustainability (Neumayer,
2010: 16), but without lowering their welfare attainments.

## Environmental space, New Economics, and human development – can alternative aggregate measures shape a new global sustainable human development compact?

Environmental space is a helpful concept for conceptualising the necessary transition to sustainable human development. Environmental space analysis seeks to allocate resource consumption on geographical lines, setting rules for expanding or contracting resource use, to fit within ecological limits. Environmental space analysis links to concepts like the quality of life, the precautionary, proximity and subsidiarity principles and takes into account non-renewable resources (Bührs, 2009: 113). The technique for calculating fair shares and equity is disputed, but a per capita basis is regarded by many to be 'a moral and political necessity' (Bührs, 2009: 113, citing Carley and Spapens, 1998: 69). Environmental space analysis employs a range of indicators (Bührs, 2009), one well-known composite indicator being the *ecological footprint* (Wackernagel and Rees, 1996).

A survey of 155 countries (Neumayer, 2001) worryingly suggested that many low human development countries will find it difficult just to maintain their low levels of human development. Estimates show that resource use by the 'developed' north is broadly five times greater than that in the south (McLaren, 2003: 24), but the problem is not strictly geographical – the problem of inequality exists between countries and within them, since every country has a share of over-consuming wealthy individuals and a share of under-consuming poor. One major proposal for strong sustainability is to reduce the consumption of people with a larger than one-planet footprint, and try to prevent them from entering an increasingly burdensome 'consumption treadmill'. An alternative proposal is to promote forms of well-being and quality of life that can be achieved without intensifying resource depletion and attendant unfairness.

The 'New Economics' describes an alternative approach that reorients economics as a discipline, by emphasising well-being, not money, on the understanding that

> human happiness and well-being are not measured very well in terms of money wealth, and just as money is subservient to morality, spirituality and humanity, so economics is part of a wider ecosystem … It is an economics that broadens our definitions of wealth, rather than narrows them down to an abstraction that may or may not relate to human fulfilment. (Boyle and Simms, 2009: 18–19)

The origins of the new economics are diverse. Ruskin's (1862) statement that 'there is no wealth but life' and his critique of '*illth*' (the poverty, ill-health, pollution and despair that were the attendant downside of economic wealth) are cited as founding ideas. Mahatma Gandhi's ideas of self-restraint, self-reliance and voluntary simplicity, and E.F. Schumacher's 'Buddhist economics – economics as if people really mattered' are both influential. 'Happiness' entered the debate in the early 1970s when the ruler of Bhutan announced that 'Gross National Happiness is more important than Gross National Product' (Thinley, 1998; NEF, 2006, 13; Priesner, 1999). Boyle and Simms (2009: 22–5) note that the 'New Economics' came together at The Other Economic Summit (TOES), in London in 1984. The 'Happy Planet Index' is one alternative aggregate measure of progress developed by the New Economics Foundation (NEF). The Happy Planet Index combines available data about ecological footprint, life expectancy and subjective life satisfaction. Countries that score highly have managed to achieve relatively long and happy lives with smaller ecological footprints (see Box 5.3).

---

### Box 5.3   The Happy Planet Index 2.0 (NEF, 2009)

The HPI 2.0 provides data for 143 countries, covering 99 per cent of world population. Scores range from 0 to 100 – with high scores only achievable by meeting all three targets embodied in the index – high life expectancy, high life satisfaction (combined as 'Happy Life Years'), and a low ecological footprint. No country achieved high scores for all three criteria.

**Table 5.1**   Happy Planet Index (HPI) scores and ranking of selected countries

| Country | Life satisfaction | Life expectancy | Happy life years | Ecological footprint | HPI | HPI rank |
|---|---|---|---|---|---|---|
| Costa Rica | 8.5 | 78.5 | 66.7 | 2.3 | 76.1 | 1 |
| Netherlands | 7.7 | 79.2 | 61.1 | 4.4 | 50.6 | 43 |
| Ireland | 8.1 | 78.4 | 63.8 | 6.3 | 42.6 | 78 |
| Zimbabwe | 2.8 | 40.9 | 11.6 | 1.1 | 16.6 | 143 |

The countries where people enjoy the happiest and healthiest lives are mostly richer developed countries, but at an unsustainable ecological cost. The lowest scores were suffered by Sub-Saharan African countries, the bottom three achievers being Botswana, Tanzania and Zimbabwe. Some less wealthy countries in Latin America and the Caribbean have high levels of life expectancy and life satisfaction with smaller ecological footprints, the top three achievers being Costa Rica, the Dominican Republic and Jamaica. Europe and the rich 'developed' countries perform only averagely, due to their large ecological footprints.

*Source:* NEF (2009) http://www.happyplanetindex.org/public-data/files/happy-planet-index-2-0.pdf

The Happy Planet Index concurs with Neumayer's findings (2001), showing a global planet that is mainly 'unhappy', with most countries failing to deliver well-being at a sustainable rate of resource consumption. No country is presently achieving high life expectancy, high subjective satisfaction and one-planet ecological footprint. It is striking to note that rich OECD states saw a 15 per cent increase in life-satisfaction between 1961 and 2005, but at a cost of a 72 per cent increase in ecological footprints during the same period. The three largest countries in the world (China, India and the USA) saw their scores worsen between 1990 and 2005, although most other countries experienced marginal improvements (NEF, 2009).

A recent review of different aggregate sustainability measures (Pillarisetti and van den Bergh, 2010) cautions that the aggregate indexes they surveyed (Genuine Savings, Ecological Footprint, Environmental Sustainability Index, Genuine Progress Index and Index of Sustainable Welfare) suffer from major methodological limitations and weaknesses. Lawn (2006: 428) similarly criticises green national accounting measures, including genuine savings, green GDP, ecological footprint, Index of Sustainable Economic Welfare and Genuine Progress Indicator (see Table 5.2) for being under-theorised. There is weak comparability of values within as well as across indicators, which makes the evaluation and ranking of sustainability performance across nations deeply problematic. Care must be taken when choosing measures of sustainable development, as different measures yield very different results. Climate change – arguably the most serious threat currently faced by humanity – is not or only arbitrarily captured by most measures (Pillarisetti and van den Bergh, 2010: 50).

## Conclusion – sustainable human development and global justice

This chapter has discussed the emergence of different conceptions of development. The debates about the meanings, concept and measurement of sustainable development are not merely philosophical or semantic disagreements. They have a serious policy function: to concretely articulate and advocate shared common goals of human welfare and happiness without 'costing the earth'. Yet a lot more progress is needed in order for sustainable development to be a coherent concept that can be operationalised in a practical manner. A recurrent theme throughout the debates is the insufficiency of income measures and the turn to more humanistic alternatives. *Sustainable human development* has been proposed as the ultimate goal, however human development's expansive capability and freedom-based conceptions of justice, may come up against the limits of available environmental space. The tighter the limits, and

**Table 5.2** Comparison of major aggregate sustainable development measures*

| Aggregate SD measure and origins | Components | Benefits | Critiques |
|---|---|---|---|
| Genuine Savings (GS) World Bank (1997) | Domestic savings, depreciation of physical capital, education spending, natural capital depletion (energy, minerals, forest), $CO_2$ damage, willingness to pay to avoid pollution | Adjusts GNI to reflect welfare, resource depletion, pollution | Substitutability assumption unrealistic. Income biased. 'Erroneous and counterintuitive results' (Pillarisetti and van den Bergh, 2010: 60) |
| Environmental Sustainability Index (ESI) Yale Centre for Environmental Law and Policy (2005) | 76 data sets forming 21 indicators of (i) environmental systems, (ii) reducing environmental stress, (iii) reducing human vulnerability to environmental stress, (iv) societal/institutional capacity to respond to environmental challenges, (v) global stewardship | Many dimensions covered | Highly disparate indicators given equal weight. Income biased. |
| Index of Sustainable Economic Welfare (ISEW) Daly and Cobb (1989) Genuine Progress Indicator – variant of ISEW Redefining Progress (1995) | Personal consumption, public expenditures, private defensive expenditures, capital formation, domestic labour, environmental degradation, depreciation of natural capital | Accounts for welfare, defensive expenditures, social and environmental costs | Choice of welfare items questioned. Crude valuation methods, requiring 'heroic assumptions. Lawn (2006: 454) |
| Ecological Footprint Wackernagel and Rees (1996) | Cropland, pasture, forests, fisheries, built space, energy | Easy to understand ecological 'budget'/environmental space and estimate overshoot | Assumptions underlying land, energy criticised (*Ecological Economics*, 32: 341–89). Welfare not captured. |

| Aggregate SD measure and origins | Components | Benefits | Critiques |
|---|---|---|---|
| Happy Planet Index NEF (2006, 2009) | Ecological footprint, life expectancy, life satisfaction | Novel measure: eco-efficiency of human well-being<br><br>Objective and subjective data | No country performs well on all three criteria – unachievable? |
| Gross National Happiness<br><br>Centre for Bhutan Studies, Thimpu (2006) | Living standard, health, education, ecosystem diversity and resilience, time use and balance, good governance, community vitality, psychological well-being | Holistic, culturally rich, captured imagination<br><br>Indicators developed as part of national policy programme | 3 decades before concrete process to define goals, variables and indicators (2004–8). |

\* Full references for 'Commentary Forum: The Ecological Footprint', *Ecological Economics* 32 (3): 341–89: (Ayres, 2000; Costanza 2000, Deutsch et al 2000; Herendeen, 2000; Moffatt; 2000; Opschoor, 2000; Rapport, 2000; Rees, 2000; Simmons, Lewis and Barrett, 2000; Templet, 2000; van Kooten and Bulte 2000).

*Sources:* Pillarisetti and van den Bergh (2010); Centre for Bhutan Studies, Thimpu (2006); NEF (2006, 2009); Lawn (2006: 454); Daly and Cobb (1989); Redefining Progress (1995).

the more inequality there is, the more difficult we should expect the just redistribution of resources, benefits, costs and harms to be.

Human development was very much a concept seeking to push policy commitments, and the 1994 UNDP World Development Report and World Social Charter proposal suggested that human development and sustainability goals could be made to converge, since 'there is no tension between human development and sustainable development. Both are based on the universalism of life claims' (UNDP, 1994: 19). Yet attempts at convergence have been tentative and are some distance from the mainstream. Environmental concerns have not yet been systematically integrated into the human development agenda, despite the ubiquity of 'sustainable development' in every text. Some human rights scholars have made serious efforts to define the 'minimum core' of human needs or values, and sought to make these the subject of substantive, justiciable national and international responsibility (Young, 2008). Others have examined the connections between human rights and environmental protection and sought to clarify the scope and content of rights-based approaches to environmental protection (Boyle and Anderson, 1998; Anton and Shelton, 2011).

Advocates of sustainable human development hope that the divergence between economic and human development can be resolved by putting economic development 'back in its place' as a means of human development. However, economic growth remains a fundamental component of human development that may be impossible to sustain. From an ecological perspective, recognition for absolute carrying capacity is essential, but dealing with these limits requires more complicated questions that remain unanswered in ecology – of ethics, economics and politics. The concepts of environmental space and new economics try to bring together these concerns to inform and achieve more equitable and humanly satisfying ways of meeting our needs and developing, without costing the earth and incurring enormous injustice to the poor, the future generations and to the ecosystems and the life they sustain. Aggregate sustainable development measures provide governments, policy makers and citizens with tools to measure well-being and environmental impact in a consistent and regular way. Measures such as the Happy Planet Index set a fairly tough benchmark for future policy. Developed nations are required to set an HPI target of 89 by 2050, reducing per capita ecological footprint to 1.7 global hectares, increasing mean life satisfaction to 8 on a scale of 0–10, and increasing life expectancy to 87 years. Developed nations and the international community are expected to support developing nations to achieve the same target in the longer term, by 2070 (NEF, 2009: 6).

As Dresner notes (2002: 172), attempts to bring about sustainability will meet strong opposition from powerful vested interests favouring the continuation of unsustainability. Sustainability requires the present generation to rethink its own interests in well-being, but affluent consumers are likely to resist any changes. Meanwhile the poor and less economically developed continue to aspire to catch-up with northern levels of consumption, which would imply the requirement for anything between two and four planets at current rates. Both will try to ignore the long-term consequences. This is why sustainability efforts cling so optimistically to 'weak sustainability' hopes that new knowledge and technology can substitute for depleted resources and deliver cleaner, more efficient economic growth. Progress is lagging, even on agreed measures to achieve weak sustainability (see UNDP, 2010). Without global governance measures to minimise rebound effects and countermand a globalised environmental race to the bottom, it is more likely that unjust and unsustainable outcomes will dominate. Global limits have to be recognised and environmental space allocated more fairly, but this requires actually changing the rules of the game, redistributing the patterns of risk, responsibility and reward optimally not only in an economic sense, but in a more ethically optimal manner (Goulet, 1995).

Post-colonial demands for justice influence the north–south divide on sustainable development. Inequities caused by neocolonialism are issues of retribution for past injustice, as contrasted against appeals to achieve distributive justice within the present and with respect to future generations (Bührs, 2009: 122, citing Wissenburg, 2006). This demand underpins the Rio principle of 'common, but differentiated responsibility'. However, this principle cannot be employed by developing country governments to avoid taking a precautionary approach, or absolve them from the obligation to deliver distributive justice and basic needs to present and future citizens within their borders. Future approaches to sustainable human development might seek to integrate environmental space analysis with minimum core obligations for social, economic and cultural rights and the participatory, democratic and humanistic approach entailed by the Right to Development. In sum, what is called for is a new development compact based on north–south cooperation for fundamental social and economic change based on the principles of sustained welfare, greater equity and fairness.

## References

Alkire, S. (2010) 'Human development: definitions, critiques and related concepts', Human Development Research Paper 2010/01. Geneva: United Nations Development Programme.

Anton, D. and Shelton, D. (eds) (2011) *Environmental Protection and Human Rights*. Cambridge: Cambridge University Press.

Arndt, H. (1981) 'Economic development: a semantic history', *Economic Development and Cultural Change*, 29 (3): 457–66.

Ayres, R.U. (2000) 'Commentary on the utility of the ecological footprint concept', *Ecological Economics* 32 (3) : 346–49.

Barbier, S. (1987) 'The concept of sustainable economic development', *Environmental Conservation*, 14 (2): 101–10.

Boyle, A. and Anderson, M. (eds) (1998) *Human Rights Approaches to Environmental Protection*. Oxford: Oxford University Press.

Boyle, D. and Simms, A. (2009) *The New Economics: A Bigger Picture*. London: Earthscan.

Bührs, T. (2009) 'Environmental space as a basis for legitimating global governance of environmental limits', *Global Environmental Politics*, 9 (4): 111–35.

Cardoso, E. and Urani, A. (1995) 'Inflation and unemployment as determinants of inequality in Brazil: the 1980s', in R. Dornbusch and S. Edwards (eds), *Reform, Recovery, and Growth: Latin America and the Middle East*. Chicago and London: University of Chicago Press. pp. 151–76.

Centre for Bhutan Studies, Thimpu (2006) *GNH Index variables* http://www.grossnationalhappiness.com/gnhIndex/gnhIndexVariables.aspx

Chen, J.-R. and Sapsford, D. (1997) 'Economic development and policy: Professor Sir Hans Singer's contributions to development economics', *World Development*, 25 (11): 1853–56.

Comim, F., Qizilbash, M. and Alkire, S. (eds) (2008) *The Capability Approach: Concepts, Measures and Applications*. Cambridge: Cambridge University Press.

Cooke, B. (2003) 'A new continuity with colonial administration', *Third World Quarterly*, 24 (94): 47–61.

Cornia, A., Jolly, R. and Stewart, F. (1987) *Adjustment with a Human Face: Protecting the Vulnerable and Promoting Growth*. Oxford: Unicef/Oxford University Press.

Costanza, R. (2000) 'The dynamics of the ecological footprint concept', *Ecological Economics* 32 (3): 341–45.

Daly, H.E. (1996) *Beyond Growth: The Economics of Sustainable Development.* Boston, MA: Beacon Press.

Daly, H. and Cobb, J. (1989) *For the Common Good.* Boston, MA: Beacon Press.

Davis, S.H (1977) Victims of the Miracle: Development and the Indians of Brazil. Cambridge: Cambridge University Press.

Desrochers, P. and Hoffbauer, C. (2009) 'The post war intellectual roots of the population bomb. Fairfield Osborn's "Our Plundered Planet" and William Vogt's "Road to Survival" in retrospect', *Electronic Journal of Sustainable Development* 1, (3): 37–61.

Deutsch, L., Jansson, A., Troell, M., Rönnbäck, P., Folke, C. and Kautsky, N, (2000) 'The "ecological footprint": communicating human dependence on nature's work', *Ecological Economics* 32 (3) : 351–55.

Douthwaite, R. (1992) *The Growth Illusion.* Dublin: Lilliput Press.

Dowie, M. (2009) *Conservation Refugees.* Berkeley, CA: MIT Press.

Dresner, S. (2002) *The Principles of Sustainability.* London: Earthscan.

Drèze, J. and Sen, A. (1989) *Hunger and Public Action.* Oxford: Clarendon Press.

Dyson, T. (2010) *Population and Development: The Demographic Transition.* London: Zed Books.

Ehrlich, P.R. (1968) *The Population Bomb.* New York: Ballantine Books.

Ehrlich, P.R. and Ehrlich, A.H. (2009) 'The population bomb revisited', *Electronic Journal of Sustainable Development,* 1 (3): 63–71.

Estes, R.J. (2003) 'Global change and indicators of social development', in M. Weil (ed.), *The Handbook of Community Practice.* Thousand Oaks, CA: Sage Publications. pp 508–28.

Frank, A.G. (1966) 'The development of underdevelopment', *Monthly Review,* 18 (7): 27–37.

Goulet, D. (1995) *Development Ethics: A Guide to Theory and Practice.* New York: Apex Press.

Goulet, D. (2002) 'What is a just economy in a globalized world?', *International Journal of Social Economics,* 29 (1–2): 10–25.

Grindle, J. (1992) *Bread and Freedom.* Dublin: Gill and Macmillan/Trocaire.

Haller, T., Galvin, M., Meroka, P., Alca, J. and Alvarez, A.(2008) 'Who gains from community conservation? Intended and unintended consequences of participative approaches in Peru and Tanzania', *Journal of Environment and Development,* 17 (2): 118–44.

Hamilton, K. and Atkinson, G. (2006) *Wealth, Welfare and Sustainability: Advances in Measuring Sustainable Development.* Cheltenham: Edward Elgar.

Herendeen, R.A. (2000) 'Ecological footprint is a vivid indicator of indirect effects', *Ecological Economics* 32 (3): 357–358.

ILO (International Labour Organization) (1976) *Employment, Growth and Basic Needs: a One World Problem.* Geneva: ILO.

International Union for Conservation of Nature (IUCN) (1980) *World Conservation Strategy: Living Resource Conservation for Sustainable Development.* Gland, Switzerland: IUCN-UNEP-WWF.

Jacobs, M. (1991) *The Green Economy.* London: Pluto.

Kothari, U. (ed.) (2005) *A Radical History of Development Studies.* London: Zed Books.

Krueger, R. and Gibbs, D. (eds) (2007) *The Sustainable Development Paradox: Urban Political Economy in the United States and Europe*. New York and London: The Guilford Press.

Lawn, P. (2006) *Sustainable Development Indicators in Ecological Economics*. Cheltenham: Edward Elgar.

Leach, M. and Mearns, R. (1996) *The Lie of the Land: Challenging Received Wisdom on the African Environment*. Oxford and Portsmouth: James Currey/ Heinemann.

Lélé, S. (1991) '"Sustainable development": a critical review'. *World Development*, 19 (6): 607–21.

Malthus, T. (1798) An Essay on the Principle of Population. London: J.Johnson. Available from: : http://129.237.201.53/books/malthus/population/malthus.pdf

Marglin, S. and Schor, J. (1990) *The Golden Age of Capitalism: Reinterpreting the Post-war Experience*. Oxford, Clarendon Press.

Martell, L. (1994) *Ecology and Society*. Cambridge: Polity.

May, R. (2007) 'Unanswered questions and why they matter', in R. May and A. McLean (eds), *Theoretical Ecology: Principles and Practice*. Oxford: Oxford University Press. pp. 205–15.

McLaren, D. (2003) 'Environmental space, equity and ecological debt', in J. Agyeman, R.D. Bullard and B. Evans (eds), *Just Sustainabilities: Development in an Unequal World*. London: Earthscan. pp. 19–37.

Meadows, D. (2009) *Thinking in Systems: Primer*, edited by Diana Wright. River Junction, VT: Chelsea Green Publishing Co.

Meadows, D.H, Meadows, D., Randers, J. and Behrens, W.W. (1972) The Limits to Growth. A Report for the Club of Rome's Project on the Predicament of Mankind. New York: Universe Books.

Moffatt, I. (2000) 'Ecological footprints and sustainable development', *Ecological Economics* 32 (3): 359–62.

Morris, M.D. (1978) 'A physical quality of life index', *Urban Ecology*, 3: 225–40.

Munck, R. and O'Hearn, D (eds) (1999) *Critical Development Theory: Contributions to a New Paradigm*. London: Zed Books.

Neumayer, E. (2001) 'The human development index and sustainability – a constructive proposal', *Ecological Economics*, 39: 101–14.

Neumayer, E. (2003) *Weak Versus Strong Sustainability: Exploring the Limits of Two Opposing Paradigms*, 2nd edn. Cheltenham: Edward Elgar.

Neumayer, E. (2010) *Human Development and Sustainability, Human Development Research Paper 2010/05*. Geneva: United Nations Development Programme.

NEF (New Economics Foundation) (2006) *The Happy Planet Index*. London: New Economics Foundation.

NEF (New Economics Foundation) (2009) *The Happy Planet Index 2.0*. London: New Economics Foundation.

Opschoor, H. (2000) 'The ecological footprint: measuring rod or metaphor?', *Ecological Economics* 32 (3): 363–6.

Pillarisetti, J.R. and van den Bergh, J.C.J.M. (2010) 'Sustainable development: what do aggregate indexes tell us?', *Environment, Development, Sustainability*, 12: 49–62.

Priesner, S. (1999) 'Gross national happiness – Bhutan's vision of development and its challenges', in S. Kinga, K. Galay, P. Rapten and A. Pain (eds), *Gross National Happiness* pp1-29. Available at: http://www.bhutan2008.bt/ndlb/typescripts/10/ GNH_Ch3_Priesner.pdf

Randeria, S. (2003) 'Cunning states and unaccountable international institutions: legal plurality, social movements and rights of local communities to common property resources', *Archives of European Sociology*, XLIV (1): 27–60.

Rapport, D.J. (2000) 'Ecological footprints and ecosystem health: complementary approaches to a sustainable future', *Ecological Economics*, 32 (3): 367–70.

Redefining Progress (1995) 'Gross production vs genuine progress', in J. Cobb, T. Halstead and R. Rowe (eds), *The Genuine Progress Indicator: Summary of Data and Methodology*. San Francisco, CA: Redefining Progress.

Rees. W.E (2000) 'Eco-footprint analysis: merits and brickbats', *Ecological Economics*, 32 (3): 371–74.

Rist, G. (1997) *The History of Development: From Western Origins to Global Faith*. London: Zed Books.

Ruskin, J. (1862) 'Unto this last: four essays on the first principles of political economy', in E.T. Cook and A. Wedderburn (eds), *The Works of John Ruskin*, vol. 17. London: George Allen, 1903–1912.

Sachs, W. (1999) *Planet Dialectics: Explorations of Environment and Development*. London: Zed Press.

Schuurman, F. (ed.) (1993) *Beyond the Impasse: New Directions in Development Theory*. London: Zed Books.

Scoones, I. (2010) 'Sustainability', in A. Cornwall and D. Eade (eds), *Deconstructing Development Discourse: Buzzwords and Fuzzwords*. pp. 153–62. Rugby: Practical Action Publishing and Oxfam.

Seers, D. (1963) 'The limitations of the special case', *Bulletin of the Oxford Institute of Statistics and Economics*, 25 (2): 77–98.

Seers, D. (1969) 'The meaning of development', *International Development Review*, 11 (4): 3–4.

Sen, A. (1999) *Development as Freedom*. Oxford: Clarendon Press.

Sen, A. (2000) 'A decade of human development', *Journal of Human Development*, 1 (1): 17–23.

Simmons, C., Lewis, K. and Barrett, J (2000) 'Two feet - two approaches: a component-based model of ecological footprinting', *Ecological Economics*, 32 (3): 375–80.

So, A. (1990) *Social Change and Development*. London and New Delhi: Sage.

Templet, P.H. (2000) 'Externalities, subsidies and the ecological footprint: an empirical analysis', *Ecological Economics*, 32 (3): 381–3.

Thin, N. (2002) *Social Progress and Sustainable Development*. London: ITDG Publishing.

Thinley, J. (1998) Keynote Address to UNDP regional meeting for Asia and the Pacific October 1998.

Ul Haq, M. (1995) 'The birth of the Human Development Index', in S. Fukuda-Parr and A.K. Shiva Kumar (eds), reprinted 2003, *Readings in Human Development: Concepts, Measures and Policies for a Development Paradigm*. Oxford: Oxford University Press. pp. 127–37.

UNDP (United Nations Development Programme) (1990) *Human Development Report*. Oxford: Oxford University Press.

UNDP (United Nations Development Programme) (1994) *Human Development Report 1994: New Dimensions of Human Development*. Oxford: Oxford University Press/ UNDP.

UNDP (United Nations Development Programme) (2010) *Human Development Report 2010 The Real Wealth of Nations: Pathways to Human Development.* Oxford: Oxford University Press/ UNDP.

United Nations (1986) *Declaration on the Right to Development.* 4 December 1986 A/RES/41/128. Geneva: United Nations.

van Kooten, G.C. and Bulte, E.H. (2000) 'The ecological footprint: useful science or politics?', *Ecological Economics*, 32 (3): 385–9.

Vanoli, A. (2008) 'National accounting, history of', in S.N. Durlauf and L.E. Blume (eds), *The New Palgrave Dictionary of Economics*, 2nd edn. Available from http://www.dictionaryofeconomics.com/article?id=pde2008_N000160&edition=current&q=History%20of%20national%20accounting&topicid=&result_number=1

Vihma, A. (2011) 'India and the global climate governance: between principles and pragmatism', *Journal of Environment and Development*, 20 (1): 69–94.

Wackernagel, M. and Rees, W. (1996) *Our Ecological Footprint: Reducing Human Impact on the Earth.* Gabriola Island, British Columbia: New Society Publishers.

WCED (World Commission on Environment and Development) (1987) *Our Common Future, Report of the World Commission on Environment and Development.* Annex to General Assembly document A/42/427, 2 August 1987. Geneva: United Nations.

Woodhouse, P. and Chimhowu, A. (2005) 'Development studies, nature and natural resources: changing narratives and discursive practices', in U. Kothari (ed.), *A Radical History of Development Studies.* London: Zed Books. pp. 180–99.

World Bank (1997) *Expanding the Measure of Wealth: Indicators of Environmentally Sustainable Development.* Washington: The World Bank.

WSSD (World Summit on Sustainable Development) (2002) *Johannesburg Declaration on Sustainable Development: From our Origins to the Future.* Available from http://www.un.org/esa/sustdev/documents/WSSD_POI_PD/English/POI_PD.htm

Yale Centre for Environmental Law and Policy (2005) *2005 Environmental Sustainability Index: Benchmarking National Environmental Stewardship.* New Haven, CT and New York: Yale Center for Environmental Law and Policy, Yale University and Center for International Earth Science Information Network Columbia University.

Yearley, S. (1991) *The Green Case: A Sociology of Environmental Arguments, Issues and Politics.* London: Harper Collins.

Yearley, S. (1996) *Sociology, Environment, Globalization.* London: Sage.

Young, K. (2008) 'The minimum core of economic and social rights: a concept in search of content', *Yale Journal of International Law*, 33 (1): 113–75.

# 6

## Biophysical Indicators of Society–Nature Interaction: Material and energy flow analysis, human appropriation of net primary production and the ecological footprint

*Veronika Gaube, Helmut Haberl and Karl-Heinz Erb*

## Introduction

Societies depend on the availability of materials and energy. Above all, humans need food to stay alive, healthy and able to perform work. But there are many other socio-economic activities that require much more materials and energy. The production, distribution and consumption of goods and services both create and depend on buildings, infrastructure and machinery. These in turn require inputs of raw materials or manufactured goods as well as energy in several different forms, such as human or animal labour, electricity, fuels or heat. Extracting and harvesting materials like construction materials, metals, fossil fuels or biomass often lead to substantial impacts on ecosystems due to land-use changes, noxious substances, changes of biogeochemical cycles or other mechanisms. Changes in stocks and flows of carbon, water or nitrogen are a crucial aspect of global environmental change. For example, human activities such as transportation and industrial production cause greenhouse gas emissions (GHG), the most important being $CO_2$, $CH_4$ and $N_2O$, that accumulate in the atmosphere. Changes in GHG concentration in the atmosphere resulting from human activities are very likely responsible for most of the observed growth in global mean temperature since the mid-twentieth century (IPCC, 2007). Likewise, emissions of toxic substances into water bodies or the atmosphere influence ecosystems, including agro-ecosystems and forestry systems.

Human activities also affect biodiversity, e.g. through land-use change, hunting or poaching, or through human-induced changes in global biogeo-chemical cycles and climate change. For instance, nitrogen enrichment has been shown to reduce species diversity in many environments (Vitousek et al., 1997). There is evidence that biodiversity is positively related to bio-mass stocks in ecosystems (Hatanaka et al., 2011), implying that a reduction in biomass stocks (e.g. through deforestation or harvest) may contribute to species loss. Empirical studies show that species richness is lower in ecosys-tems where human activities reduce biomass availability (Haberl et al., 2004b, 2005).

In this contribution, we outline some of the available methods that are suitable for analysing biophysical aspects of society–nature inter-action; in particular, we cover methods that can be used to analyse the consumption of natural resources such as land, raw materials, energy and others. We discuss concepts to investigate different types of eco-logical impact that accordingly provide different insights into sustain-ability. The remainder of this chapter is divided into five principal sections. Section two covers the main aspects of socio-economic and socio-ecological metabolism and the related methodology of material and energy flow analysis (MEFA). Sections three and four offer a com-parison of two key methods for analysing the connections between biophysical stocks and flows and land use: the human appropriation of net primary production (HANPP) and the ecological footprint (EF). In section five we then draw on case studies from Austria to demonstrate how these three methods can be used to analyse and better understand socio-ecological transitions. Finally, we offer some concluding remarks on the usefulness, limitations and comparability of the presented socio-ecological indicators.

## Socio-economic and socio-ecological metabolism

The heuristic concept of socio-ecological systems contributes to current sustainability science by taking the emergent character of biophysical, sym-bolic and social systems and the interactions of these systems into account. Figure 6.1 illustrates this concept by showing two overlapping spheres, one depicting a 'natural' or 'biophysical' sphere of causation governed by natu-ral laws and a second representing a 'cultural' or 'symbolic' sphere of causa-tion reproduced by symbolic communication. The overlap between the two spheres constitutes the 'biophysical structures of society' that are part of both the cultural and the natural sphere of causation. According to this model – discussed elsewhere in more detail (Fischer-Kowalski and Weisz, 1999) – society continuously reproduces its symbolic as well as its bio-physical structures by interacting with its biophysical environment (Weisz et al., 2001: 121).

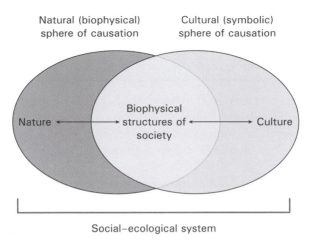

**Figure 6.1** A conceptual model of society–nature interaction.

*Source:* redrawn after Haberl et al. (2004).

The metabolism approach views society as a physical input–output system that extracts material and energy from its environment, maintains internal physical processes and finally dissipates wastes, emissions and low-quality energy back to the environment. For instance, humans have harvested wood from the environment for centuries, either as a source of energy or as a means to build artefacts such as houses, furniture, machinery and so on. While a part of the wood serves to build up long-lasting stocks of bio mass within the socio-economic system, another part is used quickly (i.e. represents a flow). Any use of wood of course entails losses, in the form of unused pieces of wood or waste heat that goes back into the environment sooner or later as waste or emissions.

If one wishes to trace these processes in a consistent manner, thereby building up reporting systems capable of monitoring socio-economic resource use, the essential question is how to define the system's boundaries. The metabolism approach focuses on three main elements of society's bio-physical structures (Fischer-Kowalski and Weisz, 1999): humans, livestock (all animals kept and used by humans) and artefacts (all non-living structures constructed and used by humans, such as buildings and infrastructure, machinery and all products that are used by humans).

Analyses of socio-economic metabolism account for the flows of materials (material flow analysis or MFA), individual substances (substance flow analysis or SFA) or energy (energy flow analysis or EFA). These analysis frameworks aim at establishing comprehensive accounts of the throughput of materials, one or several substances, or energy of a defined societal subsystem, e.g. a national economy, a city or village, a household or an economic sector. Figure 6.2 shows a set of indicators that can be derived

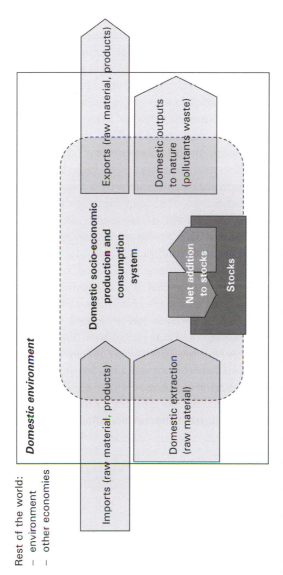

Rest of the world:
— environment
— other economies

**Domestic environment**

Exports (raw material, products)

Domestic outputs
to nature
(pollutants waste)

**Domestic socio-economic
production and
consumption
system**

Net addition
to stocks

Stocks

Imports (raw material, products)

Domestic extraction
(raw material)

**Figure 6.2** Scheme of national-level material and energy flow (MEFA) accounts.

*Source:* adapted from OECD (2008).

from the MFA framework. The accounting framework distinguishes two sources of inputs of material as well as energy, the domestic extraction of raw material and trade imports. On the output side, wastes and emissions as well as exports are accounted for. Important indicators analysed by the MFA framework include the direct material input (imports plus domestic extraction of used materials) and domestic material consumption (direct material input minus exports) (Eurostat, 2007; OECD, 2008). While the domestic material input is an indicator for overall materials mobilisation, domestic material consumption is a rough proxy for apparent domestic consumption calculated by deducting exports from the material input. Domestic material consumption includes both final consumption and intermediate consumption for the production of domestic and foreign final goods. Overall, the quantification of socio-economic material stocks and stock changes is still in its infancy (but see Matthews et al., 2000; Kovanda et al., 2007).

The same concept can be used to measure and illustrate the energetic metabolism of societies (Haberl, 2001). In terms of energy, industrial society managed to overcome this limitation because of the availability of fossil fuels. Fossil fuels release stocks of energy that have been accumulated for thousands of years. For example, the agricultural system of industrialised societies is characterised by the production of many food products with the application of highly energy-intensive techniques (e.g. through fertilisers, manufacturing machines, etc.); the amount of energy invested may eventually surpass the amount of energy contained in the product (e.g. vegetables, cereals, corn, etc.). By contrast, agrarian societies depend on the energy content of products from the agricultural sector being substantially larger than the energy that is used for their production because it is their most important source of net energy. Several empirical studies are available that support these assumptions (e.g., Krausmann, 2004; Sieferle et al., 2006).

The socio-economic metabolism accounting framework is important for sustainability science for several reasons (Haberl et al., 2004a). In our view, one of the most important of these is the ability of the metabolism approach to provide a framework for linking socio-economic drivers, such as decisions of actors, policies, institutions, prices or technology, to biophysical flows that are ecologically significant. For example, one might use metabolism-based accounts of energy or material flows to analyse changes in resource use induced by events such as an economic crisis or by policies such as a socio-ecological tax reform (shifting tax burdens from labour to resource use).

However, the socio-economic metabolism approach is not sufficient to cover all relevant aspects of socio-economic use of natural resources. For example, land use is an activity that is only incompletely addressed by the metabolism approach, despite its importance as a pervasive driver of global environmental change (Foley et al., 2005). Human land use for agriculture and forestry, infrastructure and the deposition or absorption of waste almost always results in changes in stocks and flows of materials and energy in ecosystems. For example, converting natural ecosystems to cropland or managed grasslands affects not only the species composition of the ecosystem but also water and nutrient flows, stocks and flows of carbon, water flows and retention capacity (Haberl et al., 2001; Hoekstra and Chapagain, 2008).

Land use is related to biological productivity in two ways:

1  Many human uses of the land essentially seek to harness biological productivity of ecosystems for human purposes – therefore, the productivity of the land is decisive for its suitability for different uses;
2  Land use affects biological productivity, as humans replace natural ecosystems with more or less intensively managed ones.

Biological productivity is a central parameter of ecosystem functioning and encompasses biomass production of green plants through photosynthesis (Lindeman, 1942; Whittaker and Likens, 1973). Photosynthesis is the process by which plants capture sunlight energy and transform it into the energy of chemical bonds in carbohydrates. It can be measured by primary production. One can distinguish two measures of assimilated energy. Gross primary production is the total energy assimilated by photosynthesis. Plants need a certain proportion of this total assimilated energy for their own respiration, which is energy utilised by the plant for maintenance and for the plant's metabolism. Net primary production (NPP) is the amount of energy that is finally accumulated in plant biomass – that is, plant growth and reproduction. As biomass contains approximately 50 per cent carbon NPP can also be expressed as carbon flow. Annual NPP equals the amount of biomass produced per year and it is the upper limit of the amount of biomass that could in theory be used by humans sustainably (one may also harvest long-accumulated stocks, e.g. in forestry; but sustainable forestry must stay far below NPP over larger areas). In practice much less biomass can be used because aggregate NPP includes below-ground NPP. Terrestrial plants are rooted in soil, which contains micro-organisms and other organisms that decompose dead plant and animal material. The energy used by these soil organisms is unavailable to consumers of plants. Therefore it is important to differ between above-ground and below-ground NPP. Above-ground NPP represents an upper limit to the amount of biomass which can be harvested each year without exceeding renewal rates; in practice, however, there will inevitably be some losses, e.g. through herbivory or during harvest.

NPP varies between almost nil in deserts or arctic zones, around 15–25 $MJ/m^2/yr$ in humid, temperate regions, and more than 30 $MJ/m^2/yr$ in most tropical forests (Saugier et al., 2001). Moreover, photosynthetically fixed energy in plants is consumed by wild-living animals, fungi and microorganisms, and is thus essential for ecosystem functioning. Human harvest of biomass often leads to a reduction in vegetation's carbon uptake (Schlamadinger et al., 1997). Many important processes such as nutrient cycling (carbon, nitrogen, phosphorus, etc.), build-up of organic material in soils or in aboveground biomass stocks by plant growing, vitally depend on NPP. NPP is related to the capacity of ecosystems to provide services, such as biomass supply through agriculture and forestry, but also the buffering capacity or the absorption capacity for wastes and emissions (Millennium Ecosystem Assessment, 2005).

A variant of the MEFA approach traces carbon flows through the economy. Many materials contain carbon as dominant element. For example, fossil energy consists of approximately 80–95 per cent of carbon, biomass of approximately 50 per cent carbon. This Carbon Flow Accounting (CFA) variant provides a consistent link between socio-economic and natural carbon flows, and provides a valuable tool for analysing anthropogenic pressures on the global climate system (Erb et al., 2008; Gingrich et al., 2007).

Overall, changes in the availability of energy in the ecosystem can be analysed using different approaches to accounting for socio-ecological metabolism. The research question to be addressed plays a key role in the selection of an appropriate approach. If the question is how much land is required and does this land compete with others, such as land required for agriculture, the ecological footprint (EF) approach can aid analysis. If the question focuses on the intensity of land use, then the HANPP can be used. These two approaches are discussed in the following sections.

## The human appropriation of net primary production approach

One useful indicator of land-use intensity is the human appropriation of net primary production (HANPP). HANPP measures changes in biomass flows in ecosystems resulting from land use (Vitousek et al., 1986; Wright, 1990; Haberl et al., 2007). There are several different definitions of HANPP. In this chapter we focus on a more socio-economic definition of HANPP:

$$HANPP = \Delta NPP_{LC} + NPP_h \text{ with } \Delta NPP_{LC} = NPP_0 - NPP_{act}$$

According to this definition, HANPP is defined as the difference between the NPP of potential vegetation (Tüxen, 1956) and the actually prevailing vegetation in the same ecosystem after accounting for the part of the actual NPP harvested by humans or destroyed during harvest ($NPP_h$). Potential vegetation ($NPP_0$) is the amount of biomass that would be available in an ecosystem without human intervention under current climate conditions. Estimates of $NPP_0$

can be obtained by applying literature values on the productivity of the type of vegetation under similar climatic and soil conditions (e.g. Cannell, 1982, http://daac.ornl.gov/NPP/npp_home.shtml). Another possibility would be to use suitable models, such as DGVMs (Dynamic Global Vegetation Models). A first and rough estimate can be obtained by using Lieth's Miami Model (Lieth and Whittaker, 1975) which requires only annual mean temperature and precipitation as inputs. In the meantime more elaborate and perhaps also more precise calculations may be used, which of course require more detailed modelling efforts (e.g. McGuire et al., 2001; Stich et al., 2003). Nevertheless, in principle all model approaches – also more detailed DGVM's – consider temperature and precipitation as major factors affecting NPP; newer models of course take more parameters into account (e.g. soil type and atmospheric carbon concentration).

HANPP considers changes in the availability of NPP in ecosystems resulting from two processes. First, land use alters the NPP by supplanting the potential natural vegetation (the productivity of which is denoted as $NPP_0$) with another form of vegetation denoted as 'actual vegetation' (with a productivity called $NPP_{act}$). One example is deforestation to create new agricultural production areas. Clearing of forests to use the land for farming considerably affects (and predominantly decreases) NPP. The difference between $NPP_0$ and $NPP_{act}$ is denoted as $\Delta NPP_{LC}$. Second, harvest ($NPP_h$) removes NPP from the ecosystem, thereby reducing the amount of available biomass remaining in the ecosystem for all heterotrophic food chains or for biomass accumulation ($NPP_h$ also includes biomass destroyed during harvest, e.g. roots or biomass burned in human-induced fires). The amount of NPP remaining in the ecosystem is denoted as $NPP_t$ (see Figure 6.3).

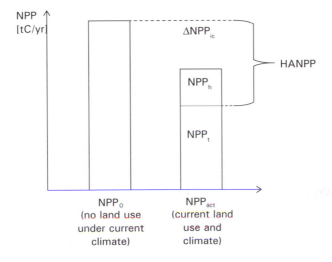

**Figure 6.3**   Definition of HANPP.

*Source:* adapted from Krausmann et al. (2009).

HANPP expresses the land-use intensity of a defined area in terms of ecosystem energetics. With reference to a given territory, it reveals how much energy is diverted by humans compared with all other heterotrophic organisms (e.g. animals, fungi, some bacteria) in the ecosystem. HANPP is thus a measure of how intensively humans use a particular land area. HANPP is related to a series of sustainability issues, such as the undernourishment of a substantial proportion of the global population (FAO, 2005) or the conversion of valuable ecosystems (e.g. forests) into infrastructure, cropland or grazing land (Millennium Ecosystem Assessment, 2005; Lambin and Geist 2006), with detrimental consequences for biodiversity (Haberl et al., 2005). HANPP is connected to changes in global water flows (Gerten et al., 2005), carbon flows (McGuire et al., 2001) and nitrogen (N) flows, all of which are vitally important for agricultural productivity. In fact, human activities now dominate many aspects of the biophysical world, thereby driving the earth system into a new geological era – the 'anthropocene' (Steffen et al., 2007).

Recent research has demonstrated that HANPP can be assessed with reasonable effort and precision at many spatial and temporal levels. For example, global maps of terrestrial HANPP in the year 2000 at a resolution of approximately 10 kilometres are readily available (Haberl et al., 2007; a free download of gridded HANPP data can be found at http://www.uni-klu. ac.at/socec/inhalt/1191.htm). Figure 6.4 shows one of these maps of land use and human appropriation of NPP on a global scale. The map reveals the locations and intensity of anthropogenic changes in ecological energy flows caused by the appropriation of NPP through human land use and harvest. This map thus attempts to localise the intensity of human pressures on ecosystems on a global scale.

There are several reasons why HANPP should be considered in sustainability assessments. It not only assesses the amount of land use in terms of square metres or hectares, as other indicators such as the ecological footprint do; it also focuses on the intensity with which land is used in producing biomass. Another reason for applying HANPP is connected with the issue of biodiversity. In ecology, a central concept exists (known as the species–energy hypothesis: Brown, 1981; Hutchinson, 1959; Wright, 1983) which relates species numbers in ecosystems to the availability of trophic energy. If humans remove energy from the ecosystem, the availability of energy for other species decreases and the number of species will, in turn, decline (Wright 1990), according to this hypothesis.

Then again, there are of course shortcomings of the HANPP indicator (Haberl et al., 2004c). First, there is no unambiguous 'sustainability threshold'. It is clear that 100 per cent HANPP would be destructive because this would leave no resources for other species than those needed for human purposes, but the crucial question is how to set a meaningful lower threshold. Second, HANPP refers to land use on a given territory. Demands of this

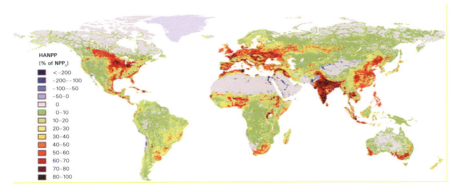

**Figure 6.4** Map of the human appropriation of net primary production (HANPP): Total HANPP represented as a percentage of NPPO. Blue (negative values) indicates increases of NPPt over NPPO. Green and yellow indicate low HANPP and red indicates medium to high HANPP.

*Source:* reprinted from Haberl et al. (2007) with permission based on the PNAS copyright policy.

territory's people on ecosystems outside the territory are ignored and demands on the territory's ecosystem by people from outside the territory are not treated separately. Altogether, the extent to which HANPP tracks the maintenance of the biosphere's capacity is not straightforward. In terms of calculating the maintenance of the biosphere's capacity, a more appropriate approach is provided by the ecological footprint indicator, which is discussed in the following section.

## The ecological footprint approach

The term 'ecological footprint' (EF) denotes approaches which aim to assess the total area required for sustaining socio-economic processes. The concept of the ecological footprint was originally developed in the early 1990s by William Rees and Mathis Wackernagel (Wackernagel and Rees, 1996; Wackernagel et al., 2002). The basic methodology has been subject to a variety of adaptations, extensions and modifications by several authors since then. In principle, the ecological footprint of a specified population (e.g. the population of a city, municipality, region or nation) can be defined as the area of ecologically productive land needed to maintain the population's current consumption patterns. The biologically productive area is necessary to provide humans with three core ecosystem functions: (1) producing resources, (2) hosting buildings and infrastructure and (3) absorbing wastes (Wackernagel and Rees, 1996; Erb, 2004; Kitzes et al., 2009).

| Land for resource extraction | + | Land needed as living space | + | Land needed to absorb wastes | = | Hectares of bioproductive area "appropriated" anywhere on earth |
|---|---|---|---|---|---|---|

**Figure 6.5** Calculating ecological footprints.

There are two principal approaches to calculating ecological footprints. The more popular 'systems approach' calculates footprints for socio-economic units such as nations, cities, regions or households. The second approach calculates footprints for (industrial) processes, products and services. In the systems approach, the EF assesses how much biologically productive area is needed to sustain the socio-economic metabolism of a country or other politically defined entity. This overall demand is compared in a second step with 'biocapacity', that is, the amount of bioproductive area available. An ecological deficit (or 'overshoot') occurs whenever human consumption exceeds ecological limits, that is, when area demand exceeds the available biocapacity. Overall, the EF constitutes a measure of strong sustainability because it assesses the utilisation of the environment in absolute terms and compares the extent of resource use with the availability of resources.

In its 'classical' version, the ecological footprint is expressed in normalised or 'global hectares'. Each global hectare represents an equal proportion of a given year's biocapacity. In order to convert physical hectares into global hectares (gha), the area of each category of land used is scaled up or down in proportion to its maximum potential crop yield using equivalence factors (Monfreda et al., 2004; Wackernagel et al., 2002). These equivalence factors weigh the utility of the land according to its potential for a specific human use, which is growing crops. This assumption allows analysts to determine a given population's appropriation of the world's biocapacity. The earth's total number of global hectares equals its total number of biologically productive hectares. These global hectares are the standardised currency of EF accounts. Usable bioproductivity refers to the capacity to support the primary ecosystem function derived from a specific type of bioproductive area. For example, timber is included; the ivy of the forest is not. EF analyses reflect the prevailing technology of the year to which the assessment refers. More efficient technology and more productive ecosystems reduce the EF of a given consumption pattern.

In practice, footprint calculations include only a limited range of environmental concerns which are directly related to land use on a large scale ('conservative approach'). Area demand – typically consisting of the land-use classes arable land, grassland, forests, fishing ground area, built up area and (hypothetical) $CO_2$-absorption land – is calculated from the quantity of domestic production plus imports minus exports; hence, the footprint focuses on what is usually called the 'apparent consumption' of resources. In its original version, EF assessments rely on globally average productivities, i.e. EF assessments appraise the area with global average productivity that would be required to sustainably produce the goods and services consumed in a country. Also biocapacity is calculated as global average area equivalent. This global average approach renders comparable different consumption levels of different countries, regardless of local or regional differences in production conditions like climate, soil characteristics or technology, thereby opening up new opportunities for cross-national sustainability research.

Ecological footprinting has attracted criticism and praise in equal measure. Advantages include its comprehensiveness, its strength as a communication tool and its usefulness in comparing resource consumption levels across different countries. Its ability to demonstrate to what extent human consumption already exceeds ecological limits, and which regions contribute most to this state of affairs, has attracted considerable attention among both scientists and the general public. Moreover, studies of the global distribution of access to natural resources and of the consequences of trade in reallocating environmental pressures between world regions have benefited from the EF methodology.

On the other hand, the EF has among other things been criticised for oversimplifying the sustainability question (e.g. by failing to acknowledge the multifaceted nature of human welfare), for its narrow focus on a small number of environmental concerns, for how it addresses issues of greenhouse gas emissions, for not distinguishing between sustainable and non-sustainable land use, for methodological problems related to grazing land and for ignoring the possibility of multifunctional use of ecosystems. The application of world average yields (or productivity) has also attracted criticism because it results in global average areas which cannot directly be related to actual land use. Therefore, variants of the ecological footprint have been proposed that calculate the 'actual land demand' expressed in physical hectares, and so provide consistent links to land use accounts (Erb, 2004; Kitzes et al., 2009). Despite its rather specific definition, the term 'ecological footprint' is sometimes used synonymously with other indicators of human impacts on terrestrial ecosystems, especially the above-described human appropriation of NPP, although the two concepts differ considerably (Haberl et al., 2004c).

Comparing EF with HANPP, one can conclude that these two approaches start from different perspectives, examine different aspects of ecological impact and consequently provide different insights. Ecological footprint assesses how much bioproductive area is needed exclusively to sustain the activities of a given society and compares this area with the amount of bioproductive area available, thereby facilitating the assessment of overshoot. In contrast, HANPP asks how intensively humans use a specific area, for example, a national territory. HANPP calculates how intensively and efficiently societies use their territories and what this means for ecological processes such as carbon budgets and biodiversity. Nevertheless, HANPP calculations do not provide a comprehensive judgement on whether a society is sustainable or not. To show empirically the overlaps as well as complementarities of the above-presented approaches, the next section shows the results of different studies using all three methods – MEFA, HANPP and EF – in order to analyse Austria's transition from an agrarian to an industrialised country from 1830–2000.

## Using socio-ecological indicators for empirical analysis

This section reviews recent research on the flows of carbon in Austria from 1830–2000, focusing in particular on evidence for the intensification of land use from 1920–2000. During the period 1830–2000, Austria underwent an almost complete socio-metabolic transition from a predominantly agrarian to an industrial society. Population more than doubled from 3.6 to 8.1 million. At the same time, the country's agrarian population (farmers and their families) dropped from 75 to 5 per cent of the total. The contribution of agriculture to GDP declined to 1.4 per cent in the year 2000, while total GDP rose by a factor of 28 and per-capita GDP by a factor of 12 (Krausmann and Haberl, 2007).

In 1830, biomass accounted for 99 per cent of the socio-economic energy input for food, feed, fibre but also mechanical work, light and heat. The first wave of Austria's industrialisation until the First World War was largely powered by coal. This changed abruptly with the First World War, after which most coal had to be imported from now independent countries. This in effect resulted in a restructuring of the Austrian industry, with much less emphasis on heavy industry. After the Second World War, Austria's rapid economic growth was mostly powered by oil products, later by natural gas and by a large-scale hydropower programme that lead to the utilisation of approximately three-quarters of economic potential of energy-relevant water resources (for detail see Krausmann and Haberl, 2002, 2007).

An EF analysis over a 75-year time series based on the actual land demand approach (Erb, 2004) quantifies the size and location of the area needed to sustain the country's metabolism. The results of this study show a substantial ecological deficit that is attributable to the consumption of fossil fuels. The area demand directly related to land use (agriculture, forestry and built-up land), on the other hand, is comparatively small and averages only 30 per cent of the total area. Austria's area demand is considerably larger than its biologically productive area during the entire time period. The area demand shows a fast growth between 1926 and 1970 and levels off between 1980 and 2000. Consequently, according to the footprint approach Austria used an area between 1.6 and 1.7 times of its own biologically productive area in 1926 and around 3.1 times in 2000.

The reduction in farmland was made possible by massive technological change in agriculture that helped to increase yields and large-scale conversion efficiencies in the livestock sector (e.g. feed to meat ratios). These changes were significant enough to allow for a 70 per cent increase in primary biomass harvests on Austrian territory from 1830 to 2000 without increasing HANPP. This was possible because $NPP_{act}$ increased more than $NPP_h$ and because the fraction of $NPP_h$ that could be used commercially increased significantly too (Krausmann, 2001). These technological improvements were only possible due to large-scale inputs of fossil fuels into agriculture (e.g. fuel for tractors, artificial fertiliser). These changes massively increased agricultural yields per hectare and consequently allowed for a substantial reduction of land area to produce the same yield as before the use of fossil fuels (Krausmann, 2004). An analysis of the socio-ecological carbon metabolism allows linking these developments to carbon flows (and stocks) in Austria's ecosystems and so to investigate into the underlying mechanisms of the currently ongoing 'forest transition' in Austria (Erb et al., 2008, Gingrich et al., 2007): The reason for this phenomenon is that cropland and grassland areas are shrinking and that forests are regrowing, both in terms of area as well in terms of stocking density, i.e. in carbon stocks per unit area. The very same input of fossil fuels that results in the massive increases in total GHG emissions allowed for increased production on shrinking areas and so also helped to turn Austria's biota and soils into a carbon sink – it is therefore fully justified to speak of a 'fossil-fuel powered carbon sink' (Erb et al., 2007).

All three methods were used to analyse the same phenomenon: the transition of Austria's society from an agrarian to a fossil fuel-dependent industrial society. The results show how much the foci of the three methods differ from each other. The MEFA addresses society's metabolism in terms of changes in inputs and outputs of material and energy for the production and consumption system of Austria's society 1830–2000. This metabolism represents the underlying driver for land-use change which, in turn, can be analysed by the two land-use indicators HANPP and EF. In the case of Austria, HANPP has barely changed because of the massive intensification of the agricultural sector that allows for an immense increase of biomass yields per hectare, which again facilitates a reduction of agricultural land. This intensification is based on a massive increase in the input of fossil fuels. This increase of fossil fuels leads to a clear increase of the EF due to the greater quantity of land needed for the absorption of the increasing GHG emissions.

## Conclusions

This chapter has shown that the application of complex socio-ecological indicators requires careful conceptual and methodological consideration as well as an integrated scientific perspective of society–nature interactions. These should serve as tools for assessing and monitoring socio-ecological interactions and provide insights into the cumulative effects of human activities across different scales. Insights into these dynamics are highly relevant not only in terms of mapping biophysical flows, but also to understand feedback loops between these and other social, cultural, economic and political variables.

The three presented methods – MEFA, HANPP and EF – ask questions about different facets of sustainability. MEFA asks for the amount of inputs (imports and domestic extraction) of materials and energy on the one side and for the amount of outputs of these materials and energy (exports, wastes and emissions) on the other side. In order to maintain this societal metabolism HANPP measures the intensity of land use, while EF measures exclusivity of land use. EF is an efficient tool to evaluate overshoot and communicate the results to a broad audience. It calculates the amount of bioproductive area needed to sustain the activities of a defined human population. Therefore, EF is directly linked with – at least specific – socio-economic activities. HANPP measures the extent of human domination of a given terrestrial ecosystem, but it includes a more limited subset of resources than EF. MEFA can be considered as a set of indicators analysing the biophysical requirements of a society, while the other two approaches focus on land-use change caused by societal metabolism. Consequently, the most promising approach is to link the analytical tool of MEFA with land-use indicators in order to relate societies' metabolism to humans impacts on ecosystem functioning.

Such efforts require an interdisciplinary approach that is able to bring together at least the social and natural sciences, but also civil society and policy makers. This chapter offers promising perspectives in dealing with some of the conceptual and methodological challenges in socio-ecological research. However, the indicators presented are biased towards understanding the biophysical aspects of society–nature interactions. In light of this, there is an urgent need for more social science input and integrative research in order to effectively influence policy and human behaviour in terms of the choices we make. The success or otherwise of global sustainability efforts hinges on the equitable distribution of resources among current and future generations both in quantitative and qualitative terms. Attempts to understand and measure levels of sustainability thus have to move beyond mere ecological considerations to include social considerations too.

## Acknowledgements

This chapter draws on research funded by the Austrian Science Fund (FWF), project P20812-G11, by the Austrian Ministry of Science under the research programme proVISION, and from the FP7 project Volante. Karlheinz Erb gratefully acknowledges funding from the ERC, Grant 263522, LUISE. Research for this chapter also contributes to the Global Land Project (http://www.globallandproject.org) and to long-term socio-ecological research (LTSER) initiatives within LTER Europe (http://www. lter-europe.ceh.ac.uk/).

## References

Brown, J.H. (1981) 'Two decades of homage to Santa Rosalia: toward a general theory of diversity', *American Zoologist*, 21: 877–88.

Cannell, M.G.R. (ed.) (1982) *World Forest Biomass and Primary Production Data.* London: Academic Press.

Erb, K.-H. (2004) 'Actual land demand of Austria 1926–2000: a variation on ecological footprint assessments', *Land Use Policy*, 21: 247–59.

Erb, K.-H., Gingrich, S., Krausmann, F. and Haberl, H. (2008) 'Industrialization, fossil fuels and the transformation of land use: an integrated analysis of carbon flows in Austria 1830–2000', *Journal of Industrial Ecology*, 12: 686–703.

Erb, K.-H., Haberl, H. and Krausmann, F. (2007) 'The fossil-fuel powered carbon sink. Carbon flows and Austria's energetic metabolism in a long-term perspective', in M. Fischer-Kowalski and H. Haberl (eds), *Socioecological Transitions and Global Change: Trajectories of Social Metabolism and Land Use*. Cheltenham, UK, Northampton, MA: Edward Elgar. pp. 60–82.

Eurostat (eds) (2007) *Economy-wide Material Flow Accounting. A Compilation Guide*. Luxembourg: European Statistical Office.

FAO (2005) *The State of Food Insecurity in the World 2005. Eradicating World Hunger – Key to Achieving the Millennium Development Goals*. Rome: Food and Agriculture Organization of the United Nations.

Fischer-Kowalski, M. and Weisz, H. (1999) 'Society as a hybrid between material and symbolic realms. Toward a theoretical framework of society–nature interaction', *Advances in Human Ecology*, 8: 215–51.

Foley, J.A., DeFries, R., Asner, G.P., Barford, C., Bonan, G., Carpenter, S.R., Chapin, F.S., Coe, M.T., Daily, G.C., Gibbs, H.K., Helkowski, J.H., Holloway, T., Howard, E.A., Kucharik, C.J., Monfreda, C., Patz, J.A., Prentice, I.C., Ramankutty, N. and Snyder, P.K. (2005) 'Global consequences of land use', *Science*, 309: 570–74.

Gerten, D., Hoff, H., Bondeau, A., Lucht, W., Smith, P. and Zaehle, S. (2005) 'Contemporary "green" water flows: Simulations with a dynamic global vegetation and water balance model', *Physics and Chemistry of the Earth, Parts A/B/C*, 30: 334–8.

Gingrich, S., Erb, K.-H., Krausmann, F., Gaube, V. and Haberl, H. (2007) 'Long-term dynamics of terrestrial carbon stocks in Austria. A comprehensive assessment of the time period from 1830 to 2000', *Regional Environmental Change*, 7: 37–47.

Haberl, H. (2001) 'The energetic metabolism of societies, part I: accounting concepts', *Journal of Industrial Ecology*, 5: 11–33.

Haberl, H., Erb, K.-H., Krausmann, F., Gaube, V., Bondeau, A., Plutzar, C., Gingrich, S., Lucht, W. and Fischer-Kowalski, M. (2007) 'Quantifying and mapping the human appropriation of net primary production in earth's terrestrial ecosystems', *Proceedings of the National Academy of Sciences of the United States of America*, 104: 12942–7.

Haberl, H., Erb, K.-H., Krausmann, F., Loibl, W., Schulz, N.B. and Weisz, H. (2001) 'Changes in ecosystem processes induced by land use: human appropriation of net primary production and its influence on standing crop in Austria', *Global Biogeochemical Cycles*, 15: 929–42.

Haberl, H., Fischer-Kowalski, M., Krausmann, F., Weisz, H. and Winiwarter, V. (2004a) 'Progress towards sustainability? What the conceptual framework of material and energy flow accounting (MEFA) can offer', *Land Use Policy*, 21: 199–213.

Haberl, H., Plutzar, C., Erb, K.-H., Gaube, V., Pollheimer, M. and Schulz, N.B. (2005) 'Human appropriation of net primary production as determinant of avifauna diversity in Austria', *Agriculture, Ecosystems and Environment*, 110: 119–31.

Haberl, H., Schulz, N.B., Plutzar, C., Erb, K.-H., Krausmann, F., Loibl, W., Moser, D., Sauberer, N., Weisz, H., Zechmeister, H.G. and Zulka, P. (2004b) 'Human appropriation of net primary production and species diversity in agricultural landscapes', *Agriculture, Ecosystems and Environment*, 102: 213–18.

Haberl, H., Wackernagel, M., Krausmann, F., Erb, K.-H. and Monfreda, C. (2004c) 'Ecological footprints and human appropriation of net primary production: a comparison', *Land Use Policy*, 21: 279–88.

Hatanaka, N., Wright, W., Loyin, R.H. and MacNally, R. (2011) '"Ecologically complex carbon" – linking biodiversity values, carbon storage and habitat structure in some austral temperate forests', *Global Ecology and Biogeography*, 20: 260–71.

Hoekstra, A.Y. and Chapagain, A.K. (eds) (2008) *Globalization of Water. Sharing the Planet's Freshwater Resources*. Malden, MA: Blackwell Publishing.

Hutchinson, G.E. (1959) 'Homage to Santa Rosalia, or why are there so many kinds of animals?', *The American Naturalist*, 93: 145–59.

IPCC (eds) (2007) *Climate Change 2007. Synthesis Report. Contribution of Working Groups I, II and III to the Fourth Assessment Report of the Intergovernmental Panel on Climate Change*. Cambridge, UK and New York: Cambridge University Press.

Kitzes, J.A., Galli, A., Bagliani, M., Barrett, J., Dige, G., Ede, S., Erb, K.-H., Giljum, S., Haberl, H., Hails, C., Jolia-Ferrier, L., Jungwirth, S., Lenzen, M., Lewis, K., Loh, J., Marchettini, N., Messinger, H., Milne, K., Moles, R., Monfreda, C., Moran, D., Nakano, K., Pyhälä, A., Rees, W., Simmons, C., Wackernagel, M., Wada, Y., Walsh, C. and Wiedmann, T. (2009) 'A research agenda for improving national ecological footprint accounts', *Ecological Economics*, 68: 1991–2007.

Kovanda, J., Havranek, M. and Hak, T. (2007) 'Calculation of the "net additions to stock" ondicator for the Czech Republic using a direct method', *Journal of Industrial Ecology*, 11: 140–54.

Krausmann, F. (2001) 'Land use and industrial modernization: an empirical analysis of human influence on the functioning of ecosystems in Austria 1830–1995', *Land Use Policy*, 18: 17–26.

Krausmann, F. (2004) 'Milk, manure and muscular power. Livestock and the industrialization of agriculture', *Human Ecology*, 32: 735–73.

Krausmann, F. and Haberl, H. (2002) 'The process of industrialization from the perspective of energetic metabolism. Socioeconomic energy flows in Austria 1830–1995', *Ecological Economics*, 41: 177–201.

Krausmann, F. and Haberl, H. (2007) 'Land-use change and socio-economic metabolism. A macro view of Austria 1830–2000', in M. Fischer-Kowalski and H. Haberl (eds), *Socioecological Transitions and Global Change: Trajectories of Social Metabolism and Land Use*. Cheltenham, UK, Northampton, MA: Edward Elgar. pp. 31–59.

Krausmann, F., Haberl, H., Erb, K.-H., Wiesinger, M., Gaube, V. and Gingrich, S. (2009) 'What determines spatial patterns of the global human appropriation of net primary production?', *Journal of Land Use Science*, 4: 15–34.

Lambin, E.F. and Geist, H.J. (eds) (2006) *Land-Use and Land-Cover Change. Local Processes and Global Impacts*. Berlin: Springer.

Lieth, H. and Whittaker, R.H. (eds) (1975) *Primary Productivity of the Biosphere*. Berlin, Heidelberg, New York: Springer.

Lindeman, R.L. (1942) 'The trophic–dynamic aspect of ecology', *Ecology*, 23: 399–417.

Matthews, E., Amann, C., Fischer-Kowalski, M., Bringezu, S., Hüttler, W., Kleijn, R., Moriguchi, Y., Ottke, C., Rodenburg, E., Rogich, D., Schandl, H., Schütz, H., van der Voet, E. and Weisz, H. (eds) (2000) *The Weight of Nations: Material Outflows from Industrial Economies*. Washington, DC: World Resources Institute.

McGuire, A.D., Sitch, S., Clein, J.S., Dargaville, R., Esser, G., Foley, J.A., Heimann, M., Joos, F., Kaplan, J., Kicklighter, D.W., Meier, R.A., Melillo, J.M., Moore III, B., Prentice, I.C., Ramankutty, N., Reichenau, T., Schloss, A., Tian, H., Williams, L.J. and Wittenberg, U. (2001) 'Carbon balance of the terrestrial biosphere in the twentieth century: analyses of $CO_2$, climate and land-use effects with four process-based ecosystem models', *Global Biogeochemical Cycles*, 15: 183–206.

Millennium Ecosystem Assessment (eds) (2005) *Ecosystems and Human Well-Being – Our Human Planet. Summary for Decision Makers*. Washington, DC: Island Press.

Monfreda, C., Wackernagel, M. and Deumling, D. (2004) 'Establishing national natural capital accounts based on detailed ecological footprint and biological capacity accounts', *Land Use Policy*, 21: 231–46.

OECD (eds) (2008) *Measuring Material Flows and Resource Productivity. Synthesis Report*. Paris: Organisation for Economic Co-operation and Development.

Saugier, B., Roy, J. and Mooney, H.A. (2001) 'Estimations of global terrestrial productivity: converging toward a single number?', in J. Roy, B. Saugier and H.A. Mooney (eds), *Terrestrial Global Productivity*. San Diego, CA: Academic Press. pp. 543–57.

Schlamadinger, B., Apps, M. J., Bohlin, F., Gustavsson, L., Jungmeier, G., Marland, K., Pingoud, K. and Savolainen, I. (1997) 'Towards a standard methodology for greenhouse gas balances of bioenergy systems and comparison with fossil energy systems', *Biomass and Bioenergy*, 13: 359–75.

Sieferle, R.P., Krausmann, F., Schandl, H. and Winiwarter, V. (eds) (2006) *Das Ende der Fläche. Zum gesellschaftlichen Stoffwechsel der Industrialisierung*. Köln: Böhlau.

Steffen, W., Crutzen, P.J. and McNeill, J.R. (2007) 'The anthropocene: are humans now overwhelming the great forces of nature?', *Ambio*, 36: 614–21.

Stich, S., Smith, B., Prentice, C. I., Arneth, A., Bondeau, A. and coauthors (2003) 'Evaluation of ecosystem dynamics, plant geography, and terrestrial carbon cycling in the LPJ dynamic global vegetation model', *Global Change Biology*. 9: 161–85.

Tüxen, R. (1956) 'Die heutige potentielle natürliche Vegetation als Gegenstand der Vegetationskartierung', *Angewandte Pflanzensoziologie*, 13: 5–42.

Vitousek, P.M., Aber, J.D., Howarth, R.W., Likens, G.E., Matson, P.A., Schindler, D.W., Schlesinger, W.H. and Tilman, D.G. (1997) 'Human alteration of the global nitrogen cycle: causes and consequences', *Issues in Ecology*, 1: 1–15.

Vitousek, P.M., Ehrlich, P.R., Ehrlich, A.H. and Matson, P.A. (1986) 'Human appropriation of the products of photosynthesis', *BioScience*, 36: 363–73.

Wackernagel, M. and Rees, W.E. (eds) (1996) *Our Ecological Footprint, Reducing Human Impact on the Earth*. Gabriola Island, BC; Philadelphia, PA: New Society Publishers.

Wackernagel, M., Schulz, N.B., Deumling, D., Linares, A.C., Jenkins, M., Kapos, V., Monfreda, C., Loh, J., Myers, N., Norgaard, R.B. and Randers, J. (2002) 'Tracking the ecological overshoot of the human economy', *Proceedings of the National Academy of Sciences of the United States of America*, 99: 9266–71.

Weisz, H., Fischer-Kowalski, M., Grünbühel, C.M., Haberl, H., Krausmann, F. and Winiwarter, V. (2001) 'Global environmental change and historical transitions', *Innovation – The European Journal of Social Sciences*, 14: 117–42.

Whittaker, R.H. and Likens, G.E. (1973) 'Primary production: the biosphere and man', *Human Ecology*, 1: 357–69.

Wright, D.H. (1983) 'Species–energy theorie: an extension of the species–area theory', *Oikos*, 41: 495–506.

Wright, D.H. (1990) 'Human impacts on the energy flow through natural ecosystems, and implications for species endangerment', *Ambio*, 19: 189–94.

# 7

# Mapping for Sustainability: Environmental noise and the city

*Enda Murphy and Eoin A. King*

## Introduction

In the last decade or so, the term sustainability has become fashionable not only among scientists but also among the general public. While this undoubtedly demonstrates that public awareness of environmental issues is increasing, it is also the case that the meaning of the concept can be elusive for many. As has been highlighted earlier in this volume, the notion of sustainability is something of a contested term quite aside from the idea of environmental sustainability, which is a more specific component of the broader concept.

The concept of environmental sustainability is somewhat different to the general concept of sustainability alluded to earlier. To a large extent, environmental sustainability is defined differently to social and economic sustainability (see Goodland and Daly, 1996). Goodland's seminal paper (1995: 10) defines environmental sustainability as 'a set of constraints on the four major activities regulating the scale of the human economic subsystem: the use of renewable and non-renewable resources on the source side, and pollution and waste assimilation on the sink side'. He argues convincingly that the concept of environmental sustainability does not allow for economic growth, quite aside from the idea of sustainable economic growth. His rationale is that environmentally sustainable development 'implies sustainable levels of production (sources), and consumption (sinks), rather than sustained economic growth' (Goodland, 1995: 5). And he is not alone in this assertion; other scholars hold similar views (Meadows et al., 1972, 1992; Daly, 1993). Yet these views are certainly not adhered to in any practical manner, and while they are highly controversial, they deserve attention as a potential alternative and radical solution to our environmental problems. Nevertheless, there is no debating that environmental sustainability is fundamentally important for human well-being, because it allows for the maintenance of human life-support systems which are under considerable threat from the economic growth imperative.

The primary focus of this chapter is demonstrating the importance of mapping as a method for environmental sustainability, using the issue of noise pollution in cities as an illustrative example. The relationship between noise pollution and environmental sustainability is considerable. What is not quite as well-developed is the link between noise pollution and public health sustainability – this will be outlined later. However, numerous studies have demonstrated that preservation of a good sound environment is important for the maintenance of public health well-being and overall quality of life. Any serious threat to this environment is a threat to broader environmental sustainability. This is so because the continued deterioration of the sound quality of our cities directly affects the public health conditions of city inhabitants in a highly negative fashion.

The next section of this chapter focuses on highlighting the general importance of mapping as a sustainability tool in the social sciences and specifically for environmental sustainability. Then, section three details the role of noise mapping for future environmental and public health sustainability. In section four, the methodological approach used for noise mapping and population exposure estimation is presented together with results from a recent case study of Dublin, Ireland. Section five offers some limitations associated with the noise mapping approach before some critical concluding comments are offered in the final section.


## Mapping as a sustainability tool

The role of mapping in sustainability is something that is given relatively little attention, despite the fact that maps are used very frequently for informing sustainability research and associated policy decisions. In fact, throughout history, maps have been used repeatedly to understand and represent the surrounding environment. As a discipline, cartography is primarily concerned with the making and use of maps, but it is also concerned heavily with the entire process of mapping 'from data collection, transformation and simplification through to symbolisation ... map reading, analysis and interpretation' (Visvalingam, 1989: 26). Lydon (2003: 133) suggests that 'all maps represent and reflect how an individual or society names and projects themselves onto nature, literally and symbolically'. Indeed, they can be regarded as a conduit for the understanding, recording and communication of spatial relationships and forms. In this regard, much environmental research is inherently spatial in nature and as a result the contribution of mapping to the display, analysis and interpretation of environmental data has become increasingly important in recent years, particularly in light of the enhanced interdisciplinary nature of environmental research.

The first known use of maps can be traced to the gold mines of ancient Egypt; it was the ancient Greeks who combined basic maps with the mathematics of space to develop the first coordinate system (Burrough and McDonnell, 1998) while, in more modern times, the first explorers used maps to document new coastlines and land masses (Bernhardsen, 1999). However, the first known utilisation of maps for informing public health issues was not until 1854 when Dr John Snow plotted the location of cholera outbreaks in Soho, London and was able to trace the outbreak very accurately to a public water pump in the area as a result of this basic mapping exercise (Bernhardsen, 1999). This single case demonstrated the merit of mapping public health information spatially to inform policy responses on the ground.

The role of mapping in understanding environmental sustainability issues has increased considerably in recent years with the emergence of digital mapping in the form of Geographic Information Systems (GIS). GIS has transformed the nature and range of the applicability of mapping techniques in a variety of contexts. Although defining the exact role and meaning of a GIS can be difficult (see Chrisman, 1999), it is generally accepted that it is a digital cartographic system for storing, organising, analysing, managing and presenting spatial data (Murphy and Killen, 2010). In an environmental context, the real strength of a GIS is its versatility in terms of its ability to deal with a huge range of spatial data from a wide variety of contexts. In this sense, GIS have been used to inform many environmental research activities over the past decade and beyond. It has been utilised in community based management of wildlife (Lewis, 1995), for assessing the environmental impact of land cover change (Yuan, 2008), for flood risk mapping (Tran et al., 2009), water pollution detection (Shaban et al., 2010), understanding climate change impacts on the environment (Alijani et al., 2008; Jarnevich et al., 2010; Linsbauer et al., 2009; Mo et al., 2009) and for the sustainable management of forestry (Chertov et al., 2005), among many others. However, the use of maps for environmental sustainability research is by no means confined to the realm of GIS. More recently, community mapping techniques have been used as an innovative approach for informing locally derived sustainability indicators and practices (Fahy and O'Cinneide, 2009; Lydon, 2003).

One important consequence of the emergence of GIS and related digital mapping technology is the role that these technological improvements have played in enhancing visualisation of the results of environmental research. Enhanced visualisation may take a number of forms including improved photorealism, 3D visualisations and even the incorporation of results into virtual multimedia gaming environments (Ball, 2002; Drettakis et al., 2007; Sheppard, 2006). Together these approaches have the potential to play an important and more effective role in the dissemination of various forms of environmental sustainability research and related information, in a manner that is both intuitive and easy for the general public and local communities to understand. This is particularly important due to the increasing emphasis being placed on effective public communication of the results emerging from environmental research in recent years.

To summarise, it is clear that the role of mapping in informing environmental research is considerable. In particular, the emergence of digital mapping technologies has allowed for a wide variety of spatial data to be assimilated, analysed and represented graphically in a manner which aids understanding of issues that are pertinent to environmental sustainability. Noise pollution is one of the environmental sustainability issues where mapping has been of considerable importance in the recent past, and this will now be discussed in detail.

## Noise mapping and environmental sustainability

### Noise and public health: A sustainability issue?

Environmental noise is any unwanted or harmful sound created by human activities that is considered detrimental to health and quality of life (Murphy et al., 2009). In urban areas these unwanted sounds come primarily from road-based transportation but also from rail and airport transportation and various sources of industrial noise. In the European Union (EU), problems with noise pollution, and particularly night-time noise, have often been given similar concern ratings as those for global warming (CALM, 2007). In fact, preliminary results from the Environmental Burden of Disease (EBD) in Europe show that traffic noise was ranked second among the selected environmental stressors evaluated in terms of their public health impact in six European countries (WHO, 2011). The World Health Organisation (WHO) (2011) has recently acknowledged that contrary to the trend for other environmental stressors (e.g. second-hand smoke, dioxins and benzene), noise exposure is increasing in Europe. In other words, it is one of the only major environmental problems (with the exception of anthropogenic climate change) that is deteriorating rather than improving.

It is important to note, however, that discussions concerning noise pollution imply and perhaps overemphasise the negative aspects of the sound environment (Papadimitriou et al., 2009). We are all aware and have experiences of sounds that are not only associated with negative feelings and emotions but also with positive feelings and emotions, e.g., birds, music, etc. In this context, recent research around the sonic dimension of the landscape has started to receive more attention in the academic literature (Mazaris et al., 2009). Here, this research is often referred to within the context of the concept of 'soundscape', a term coined by Schafer (1977, 1994) to describe perceptions of the acoustic environment in a landscape setting. Thus, while there are other more positive aspects of the sound environment being researched, it is clear that it is the negative aspects that have the greatest need for attention given their ability to impact detrimentally on public health, quality of life and related environmental sustainability issues.

The relationship between noise pollution and human health has been the subject of much research over the last two decades. To a large degree, the primary focus of this research has analysed the impact of noise on the auditory system, with the result that it is now well established that prolonged exposure to excessive noise levels can lead to direct hearing loss and/or hearing impairment (see Prasher, 2003; Ingle et al., 2005). However, the bulk of the most recent research has tended to concentrate on the non-auditory effects of prolonged noise exposure. A considerable amount of social survey data has demonstrated that the most important non-auditory effects of environmental noise exposure are annoyance and sleep disturbance. In fact, studies have shown that annoyance from transportation noise produces a series of negative emotions some of which include anger, disappointment, unhappiness, anxiety and clinical depression (Fidell et al., 1991; Fields, 1998; Miedema, 2003; Michaud et al., 2005).

Perhaps a more serious concern from a public health perspective is the unmasking of a link between excessive noise exposure and negative cardiovascular outcomes (Babisch 2006; Belojevic et al., 2008). Through a series of recent studies, Babisch et al. (2003, 2005) have provided demonstrable causal evidence that annoyance and sleep disturbance resulting from road traffic noise is associated with a higher incidence of heart disease in middle-aged men. In a recent WHO report, it is estimated that 'the burden of disease from environmental noise is approximately 61,000 years for ischaemic heart disease in high-income European countries' (WHO, 2011: xv). However, this is not the only population cohort at risk; children appear to be particularly susceptible to excessive noise exposure. The most consistent impacts on children exposed to excessive noise levels are considered to be in the arena of cognitive impairments. In particular, tasks involving central processing and language comprehension, including reading, attention span, problem solving and memory appear to be most negatively affected from exposure (Evans and Lepore, 1993; Evans et al., 1995; Evans and Maxwell, 1997). Adding to this, the reduced motivation of children inside and outside learning settings is also a considerable problem (Evans et al., 2001).

Research conducted by Carter (1996) has shown that exposure to noise during the night can lead to considerable disruption in the stages of the sleep cycle, and particularly deep sleep stages which are considered essential for physical recuperation (Naitoh et al., 1975; Thiessen, 1988) while Ohrstrom and Skanberg (2004) have shown that the quality of sleep at home is reduced considerably after exposure to traffic noise when compared to a quiet reference night. The problem with over-exposure to night-time noise is that it produces a number of secondary effects as a result of sleep disturbance including affecting deep sleep stages, arousals and awakenings and this produces a number of secondary effects (i.e. those that can be measured the day after the individual is exposed to night-time noise) including psychological and physiological symptoms as well as reduced performance in adults (Ohrstrom et al., 2006).

Table 7.1 shows a summary of the results from a recent WHO study investigating the burden of disease resulting from environmental noise in Europe (WHO, 2011). The results of the study are the first comprehensive effort at identifying the impact of excessive environmental noise on public health. In many instances, the calculations are based on data taken from environmental noise maps constructed as part of EU member state requirements under the terms of the EU Environmental Noise Directive (END). As can be seen, the impacts are highly significant and demonstrate the detrimental impacts of excessive environmental noise exposure on public health and overall quality of life.

**Table 7.1**   Burden of disease from environmental noise in Europe

| Noise-induced exposure | Public health impact |
| --- | --- |
| Annoyance | 587,000 DALYs* lost for inhabitants in towns >50,000 population |
| Sleep disturbance | 90,3000 DALYs for EUR-A[†] inhabitants in towns >50,000 population |
| Cardiovascular diseases | 61,000 years for ischaemic heart disease in high-income European countries |
| Tinnitus[‡] | 22,000 DALYs for the EUR-A adult population |
| Cognitive impairment in children | 45,000 DALYs for EUR-A countries for children aged 7–19 years |

*Source:* Adapted from WHO (2011).

* DALYs are disability adjusted life years, the sum of the potential years of life lost due to premature death and the equivalent years of 'healthy' life lost by virtue of being in states of poor health or disability (WHO, 2011).

[†]EUR-A is a WHO epidemiological sub-region in Europe comprising Andorra, Austria, Belgium, Croatia, Cyprus, the Czech Republic, Denmark, Finland, France, Germany, Greece, Iceland, Ireland, Israel, Italy, Luxembourg, Malta, Monaco, the Netherlands, Norway, Portugal, San Marino, Slovenia, Spain, Sweden, Switzerland and the UK.

[‡]Tinnitus is defined as the sensation of sound in the absence of an external sound source (WHO, 2011).

In summary, the previous discussion points towards a growing body of evidence linking excessive environmental noise exposure to detrimental impacts on public health. If we are to take the previously outlined concept of environmental sustainability seriously, it is clear that current level of exposure poses a considerable threat to public health and the general welfare of existing and future generations in cities. Thus, in order to maintain environmentally sustainable cities, it is important to implement policies that attempt to mitigate the worst impacts on these and other serious environmental concerns.

## Environmental noise policy evolution and the EU Environmental Noise Directive

Within the context of an emerging evidence base suggesting links between exposure to environmental noise and public health concerns, noise policy gained greater prominence in EU environmental policy throughout the 1990s. In 1993, the Fifth Environmental Action Programme of the European Community established as a basic objective that individuals should not be exposed to noise levels which may endanger their health and quality of life (European Community, 1993) and established a number of targets for mitigating exposure by the year 2000. Later, the EU Green Paper on Future Noise Policy was published (European Commission, 1996). It focused on stimulating public discussion on a future approach for EU environmental noise policy as well as outlining a framework for the assessment and reduction of noise exposure and the future actions for noise mitigation.

The key document linking noise exposure to public health concerns was produced by the WHO – *Guidelines for Community Noise* (Berglund et al., 1999). According to the document, 40 per cent of the population of European Union (EU) countries were exposed to road traffic noise with an equivalent sound pressure level exceeding 55 dB(A) during daytime, the level above which they considered prolonged exposure to have adverse health effects; the corresponding figure for night-time was 30 per cent. Taking all exposure to transportation together, the WHO estimated that approximately 50 per cent of EU citizens lived in zones of acoustical discomfort. Just a few years later, the Sixth Environmental Action Programme of the European Community was adopted by the Council and the European Parliament and specifically targeted the problem of environmental noise. The Programme stipulated that future environmental noise policy should aim at 'substantially reducing the number of people regularly affected by long-term average levels of noise, in particular from traffic' as well as 'developing and implementing instruments to mitigate traffic noise' (European Commission, 2002: 10, 12).

At the EU level, these policy documents, together with academic research on noise and health dose–effect relationships, have been instrumental in the development of a legislative framework for the management of environmental noise in Europe. As a result, the EU passed Directive 2002/49/EC, also known as the Environmental Noise Directive (END) (European Union, 2002). Recognising the potential public health concerns, it seeks to develop a common approach towards the avoidance, prevention and reduction of the harmful effects of exposure to environmental noise using a strategic noise mapping process. This highlights the importance of mapping approaches to issues of environmental sustainability.

The 'global assessment' of noise exposure is to be achieved using strategic noise maps for major roads, railways, airports and agglomerations using the harmonised noise indicators $L_{den}$ (day–evening–night equivalent sound pressure levels) and $L_{night}$ (night-time equivalent sound pressure levels). A noise map is simply a means of presenting calculated and/or measured noise levels in a representative manner for a particular geographic area (Murphy and King, 2010) while strategic noise maps are defined within the Directive as maps 'designed for the global assessment of noise exposure in a given area due to different noise sources for overall predictions for such an area' (European Union, 2002: 14). Strategic noise maps are to be used as a basis for identifying levels of population exposure within agglomerations. In this regard, the Directive requires competent authorities in each member state to provide estimates of the number of people living in dwellings or individual buildings that are exposed to various noise categories at the most exposed building façade and separately for different modes of transport (European Union, 2002: 24). Thus strategic noise maps must be accompanied by relevant assessment data detailing the level of noise exposure for each area under consideration.

Noise action planning is also a major concern, notably within the context of noise mitigation and the preservation of areas of good sound quality. In the Directive, action plans are 'designed to manage noise issues and effects, including noise reduction if necessary' (European Union, 2002: 14). In fact, it is a requirement that competent authorities draw up action plans for the major roads, railways and agglomerations within their remit, and that these plans are reviewed every five years once adopted and on an ongoing basis by accounting for major new developments.

A final area of concern is in terms of dissemination of information to the public. One of the core objectives of the END is to raise awareness of noise issues, and particularly of noise as a potential public health concern. As a result, the importance of dissemination of information to the general public is a major area of concern. It can be achieved in a variety of ways from using enhanced visualisation techniques, to holding public meetings regarding results, to placing noise maps and associated data on display in local libraries and associated citizen information centres, to news reports in various media outlets.

## Environmental noise and sustainability: mapping public exposure to noise

### Methodological approach: the case of Dublin, Ireland

The methodological approach used for estimating human exposure to noise involves a series of steps where either a GIS mapping environment or similar is used as a basis for housing the data necessary to undertake the analysis. This procedure involves four main components: strategic noise mapping, estimating population exposure, noise action planning and dissemination of information to the general public. A representation of the steps in the approach is illustrated in Figure 7.1. In order to outline the process a case study of Dublin, Ireland will be examined to assess the extent of population exposure to noise and to assess the impact of various mitigation measures on reducing exposure and improving the sustainability of public health in the city with respect to environmental noise reduction (see Murphy and King, 2011).

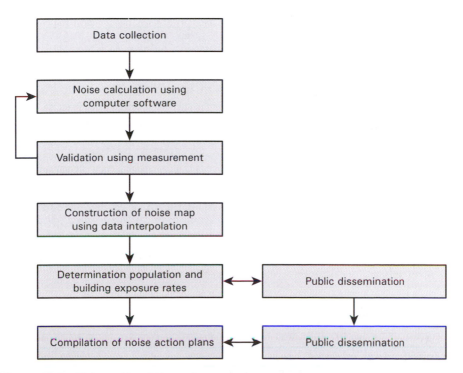

**Figure 7.1** Schematic of the noise mapping process.

## Study area and data acquisition

Dublin is Ireland's primary city and is located on the east coast of the island. Until the global economic recession in 2007, the city witnessed rapid economic and population growth. The population of the city region[1] now stands at 1.8 million (Central Statistics Office, 2011). The city centre is the main destination in the region for employment, shopping, entertainment and education (Dublin City Council Traffic and Transportation Strategic Policy Committee, 2009). Moreover, major road and rail infrastructure converges at the central area and most of the travel is dominated by the private car, which means that the volume of traffic in the city centre and the surrounding area is high relative to outer locations (King et al., 2009). Given that road transport is the major source of environmental noise in cities, Dublin city is particularly susceptible to high levels of environmental noise exposure.

The data required for noise mapping is primarily information relating to road traffic flows on the links within the study area which are representative of (say) a three- to six-month period for the year being studied. Traffic composition as well as traffic speed data along road links is also required. Building height and geometry information is also needed as this affects the path of sound waves in the built environment. In addition, depending on the calculation method being utilised, local meteorological and topographical information may be needed.

The data for the case study was provided by Dublin City Council including 24-hour traffic flow information along the road links in the study area for a six-month period from January to June 2007. The traffic flow data was derived using Dublin City Council's traffic monitoring system, which provides hourly traffic counts at junctions within the study area. Traffic composition data was unavailable on all links and was assumed to be 90 per cent light vehicle and 10 per cent heavy vehicles. This is in keeping with the Good Practice Guide for Noise Mapping (WGAEN, 2006). Building geometry, building height information and road network information were provided by Dublin City Council in the form of Geographic Information System (GIS) shapefiles. Annualised meteorological information was acquired from the closest weather station to the study area – Dublin Airport. Data such as mean temperature, mean relative humidity and mean atmospheric pressure were included in the noise calculations.

## Noise modelling

As part of the development of the END, the EU developed two harmonised noise indicators, $L_{den}$ and $L_{night}$. $L_{den}$ is an annual noise indicator which describes the average day–evening–night-time equivalent sound pressure level over a complete year while $L_{night}$ describes the night-time equivalent sound pressure level over a complete year. These harmonised noise indicators were used to gauge average noise emission levels in the study area. Both $L_{den}$ and $L_{night}$ represent the annual A-weighted long-term average sound pressure level determined over the entire day and night periods respectively. The day period varies slightly across the EU, but is generally taken to be from 07.00 to 19.00 while evening and night-time periods are taken to be from 19.00 to 23.00 and 23.00 to 07.00 respectively. It is worth noting also that the night-time period is given additional weighting over the day and evening periods in calculations due to the fact that night-time noise is associated with the greatest array of associated public health concerns.

In order to fulfil the requirements of the END, many different calculation approaches have been used in the first phase of noise mapping.[2] Murphy and King (2011) have identified a total of 25 different calculation methods used across Europe for estimating noise levels from road transport, rail transport, industry and air transport. However, work is currently ongoing to develop a common European assessment method (King et al., 2011). For the current case study, the UK Calculation of Road Traffic Noise (CRTN) method was used to calculate noise levels.[3] These were than validated using measurements to ensure the model provided an accurate representation of the urban sound environment.

## Noise mapping and population exposure estimation

In order to produce a strategic noise map, the process proceeds by calculating noise levels at receiver points on regular grids placed over the study area (Figure 7.2). In terms of representation, the grids range from five to twenty square metre resolutions. Normally, noise maps are then completed through a process of spatial interpolation within a GIS.[4] For the current study, a standard grid spacing of 10 metres was chosen. All calculations were performed at the standard receiver height of 4 metres above the ground. The results from the strategic noise mapping exercise are shown in Figure 7.2. In order to estimate exposure, the noise level at the most exposed façade must be determined (European Union, 2002). Thus, for the current study separate calculations were undertaken for the completion of strategic noise maps and for estimates of noise at building façades. For façade calculations the recommendations outlined in the Good Practice Guide for Noise Mapping (WGAEN, 2006) were followed. Receiver points were placed at 0.1 metres in front of the façade; a spacing of 3 metres between calculation points was used.

Population exposure was estimated by determining the number of residential units for each building in the study area. Once determined, each residential unit was assigned an average household size value equivalent to

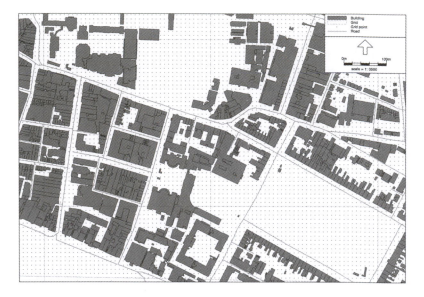

**Figure 7.2**  Constructing a uniform receiver grid for noise calculation.

the census enumerator area (EA) where the building was located. This value was obtained from the 2006 Census of population data for 162 EA's falling within the study area. Information on the number of residential units in each building was acquired from the Irish GeoDirectory database for 2007. The GeoDirectory is a complete database of every building in Ireland, among other things it contains information detailing the number of residential units in each building. It is updated on a quarterly basis by the Irish Postal Service and is the most complete building database available in Ireland. Given the number of residential units for each building in the study area and the average household size associated with each building location, it is possible to compute estimates of the residential population for each building.

Figure 7.3 shows the results of the strategic mapping procedure for the night-time period in Dublin. The key reason for mapping environmental noise lies in the ability of policy makers to easily identify 'noise hotspots' – areas where noise pollution is greatest – so that noise mitigation measures can be put in place. These may include anything from reducing travel demand, reducing speeds, implementing traffic calming measures, to noise attenuation by erecting noise barriers along roadsides.

It is notable from Figure 7.3 that very high levels of noise are evident along the main routeways for the night-time period because these are the routes with the greatest road traffic volumes. The results for population exposure are quite striking. They suggest that 27.2 per cent of residents are

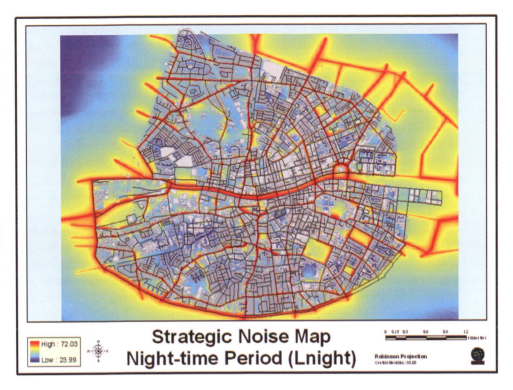

**Figure 7.3**   Strategic night-time noise map for Dublin.

exposed to noise levels exceeding 70 dB(A) for $L_{Den}$ while the corresponding figure for night-time noise exposure ($L_{night}$) greater than 40 dB(A) is 84.3 per cent. The results indicate that the rates of exposure are high in Dublin, and this is particularly the case for night-time noise where the adverse public health implications are considerable within the context of public health sustainability.

## Caveats for noise mapping research

As with the vast majority of approaches relying heavily on numerical modelling, there are some methodological limitations with the existing approach. First, in the case of strategic noise mapping it is common for commercial software packages to be used for calculating noise levels. While most of these packages offer a mapping component within the software, they fall far short of the capability of a GIS for digital mapping and spatial data manipulation. Indeed, the quality of the mapping components can vary considerably between the various software offerings, and this can cause difficulties for standardised comparisons between cities within the EU and regionally within individual nations.

There is a further issue relating to the use of spatial interpolation. The mapping component in commercial software does not provide the user with a choice of spatial interpolation method to be used. In fact, many of them do not specify the method being utilised in the mapping process at all. However, within a GIS there is a choice of a number of interpolation methods, and the EU Directive does not provide guidance on what method to use. Thus different approaches towards interpolation are being used across the EU, adding further to the difficulty of comparison across EU states.

Visualisation is also an issue. In the first phase of noise mapping, numerous colour schemes have been used between and within states to graphically represent the noise environment. However, this can be quite confusing for the general public, and the absence of guidance on a standardised colour scheme for noise mapping fails to aid public understanding of environmental noise as a health concern. Murphy and King (2010) have pointed out that an ISO standard exists and this standard, until it was revised recently, specified a colour scheme for the presentation of acoustic graphics (see ISO, 1996). The adoption of such a standardised approach towards the visual representation of noise mapping information would certainly help to increase understanding of noise mapping representation across the EU.

There are also methodological problems with regard to the estimation of population exposure. Despite the methodology outlined previously, there is no standardised methodology for the estimation of population exposure as part of the Directive. Thus, different approaches have been used in different member states and some are wholly inadequate. In fact, some states have not used façade calculations at all to estimate exposure but have simply used noise maps (see King et al., 2011). Clearly, the variation in approaches creates significant difficulties in terms of preventing any direct comparison of the scale of the exposure problem across the EU. Thus, for a variety of reasons (see Murphy and King, 2010), it is likely that significant over-estimation of exposure has occurred in most EU states and as a result there is the potential for policymakers to over-estimate the health risks associated with noise exposure resulting from the noise mapping process. Given that the estimation of exposure is directly related to dose–effect relationships associated with environmental noise exposure, this concern should be addressed as a matter of priority.

As mentioned already, the Directive requires that noise mitigation measures should be implemented in areas considered to be of poor sound quality. These mitigation measures tend to be traffic and land-use planning measures, technical measures to reduce noise sources, reduction of sound transmission or regulatory measures/economic incentives. Overall, the most important issue for policy makers is to ensure that they take account of the severity of the noise situation under consideration and the potential implications for implementing any measure in a local context. Moreover, policy makers must take care to preserve areas of good sound quality. There is a temptation in noise mapping studies to ignore areas that are of good sound quality and concentrate on 'noise hotspots'. However, areas of good sound quality should be monitored on an ongoing basis to ensure satisfactory standards are being maintained.

A key goal of the END is to raise awareness of the issue of environmental noise in the EU. To this end, the efficient dissemination of noise mapping information to the general public is crucial if this awareness-raising agenda is to be achieved. To date, it seems that this element of the noise mapping process, which should occur in conjunction with the emergence of population exposure results and the development of action planning (see Figure 7.3), has been given little serious consideration in relative terms in the noise mapping process (see King et al., 2011; Murphy and King, 2010). This is something of a concern, and it is important that serious engagement of the public in relation to the results of noise mapping needs to occur, using various different dissemination avenues and technologies.

## Conclusion

One of the key points to take from this chapter is that the issue of environmental sustainability is wide-ranging. The scope of human–environment interactions to negatively impact upon the environment is considerable. Thus, sustainability issues need to be at the forefront of all considerations where human activities have the potential to affect the environment. While this approach is important in all areas, it is particularly pertinent for public health. The foregoing discussion has focused on noise pollution as an issue for environmental and public health sustainability. The sustainability of public health implies that environmental quality should not only be maintained at standards that ensure the preservation of good quality public health but that policies should be put in place to improve environmental quality and its impact on the well-being of individuals. Within this context, new and existing approaches applied in different settings that aid the uncovering of potential threats to environmental sustainability are highly important.

The methods outlined in the current study rely heavily on cartographic approaches to understanding environmental problems. More specifically, they highlight the potential of digital cartography, and in particular, Geographic Information Systems for acting as a storage, data manipulation and data representation system for environmental research in the social sciences. In the specific case of noise mapping, the methodology conveys the role of mapping techniques in exploring the extent of the problem of noise pollution from transportation in cities, an issue which had previously not been very well understood by the general public or policy makers. While there are still concerns in this regard, it is clear that the use of mapping techniques to graphically represent the scale and extent of the level of population exposure to noise in cities has served to raise public awareness about noise pollution as an environmental and public health sustainability issue. Thus, by improving our understanding about the nature and scale of the exposure problem in cities, policies can and have been formulated and implemented to support the mitigation of noise in vulnerable areas while protecting those areas of good sound quality.

An important point for the reader to bear in mind is that the techniques used here are not specific to noise research, but can be more or less universally applied in any research which involves the utilisation of spatial data, mapping and technology to improve our understanding of environmental and related phenomena. Perhaps most importantly, it is the employment of mapping, and digital maps in particular, which allows researchers, policy makers, local communities and the public more generally to visually inspect and identify interesting trends in data that can aid our present and future understanding of environmental issues and potential solutions.

## Notes

1   This includes the four administrative authorities of Dublin and the surrounding counties of Meath, Kildare and Wicklow.
2   The first phase of noise mapping was completed in 2007. The second phase is due to be completed in 2012.
3   This method has been used as the default noise calculation method in Ireland for many years. See O'Malley et al. (2009) for more information.
4   The main interpolation methods available within a GIS framework are nearest neighbour, kriging and inverse distance weighting.

## References

Alijani, B., Ghohroudi, M. and Arabi, N. (2008) 'Developing a climate model for Iran using GIS', *Theoretical and Applied Climatology*, 92: 103–12.

Babisch, W. (2006) 'Transportation noise and cardiovascular risk: updated review and synthesis of epidemiological studies indicate that the evidence has increased', *Noise Health*, 8: 1–29.

Babisch, W., Beule, B., Schust, M., Kersten, N. and, Ising, H. (2005) 'Traffic noise and risk of myocardial infarction',. *Epidemiology*, 16: 33–40.

Babisch, W., Ising, H. and, Gallacher, J.E.J. (2003) 'Health status as a potential effect modifier of the relation between noise annoyance and incidence of ischaemic heart disease', *Occupational and Environmental Medicine*, 60: 739–745.

Ball, J. (2002) 'Towards a methodology for mapping "regions for sustainability" using PPGIS', *Progress in Planning*, 58: 81–140.

Belojevic, G., Jakovljevic, B., Stojanov, V., Paunovic, K. and Ilic, J. (2008) 'Urban road-traffic noise and blood pressure and heart rate in preschool children', *Environment International*, 34: 226–31.

Berglund, B., Lindvall, T. and Schwela, D.H. (1999) *Guidelines for Community Noise*. Geneva: World Health Organization.

Bernhardsen, T. (1999) *Geographic Information Systems: An Introduction*. New York: Wiley.

Burrough, P.A. and McDonnell, R.A. (1998) *Principles of Geographic Information Systems*. New York: Oxford University Press.

CALM (2007) Research for a quieter Europe in 2020. Strategy paper of the 519 CALM II network; Brussels: European Commission.

Carter, N.L. (1996) 'Transportation noise, sleep, and possible after-effects', *Environment International*, 22: 105–16.

Central Statistics Office (2011) *Census of Population*. Dublin: Stationery Office.

Chertov, O., Komarov, A., Mikhailov, A., Andrienko, G., Andrienko, N. and Gatalsky, P. (2005) 'Geovisualization of forest simulation modelling results: a case study of carbon sequestration and biodiversity', *Computers and Electronics in Agriculture*, 49 (1): 175–91.

Chrisman, N.R. (1999) 'What does "GIS" mean?', *Transactions in GIS*, 3 (2): 175–86.

Daly, H. E. (1993). Sustainable Growth: An Impossibility Theorem. In H. E. Daly and K. N. Townsend, *Valuing the Earth: Economics, Ecology, Ethics* (pp. 267–274). Cambridge, MA: The MIT Press.

Drettakis, G., Roussou, M., Reche, A. and Tsingos. N. (2007) 'Design and evaluation of a real-world virtual environment for architecture and urban planning', *Presence: Teleoperators and Virtual Environments*, 16 (3): 318–32.

Dublin City Council Traffic & Transportation Strategic Policy Committee (2009) 'College Green Bus Priority Scheme (Public Transport Gate)'. Dublin: Quality Bus Network Project Office.

European Commission (1996) Green Paper of the European Commission: Future noise policy, COM (96)540.

European Commission (2002) 'Directive 2002/49/EC relating to the Assessment and Management of Environmental Noise', *Official Journal of the European Communities*, No. L 189.

European Community (1993) The Firth Environmental Action Programme of the EU. *Official Journal of the European Communities*, No C 138.

Evans, G.W., Hygge, S. and Bullinger, M. (1995) 'Chronic noise and psychological stress', *Psychological Science*, 6: 333–8.

Evans, G.W., Lercher, P., Meis, M., Ising, H. and Kolfer, W.W. (2001) 'Community noise exposure and stress in children', *Journal of Acoustical Society of America*, 109 (3): 1023–7.

Evans, G.W. and Lepore, S.J. (1993) 'Nonauditory effects of noise on children', *Children's Environment*, 10: 31–51.

Evans, G.W. and Maxwell, L. (1997) 'Chronic noise exposure and reading deficits: the meditating effects of language acquisition', *Environment and Behaviour*, 29: 1514–23.

Fahy, F. and O'Cinneide, M. (2009) 'Re-constructing the urban landscape through community mapping: an attractive prospect for sustainability', *Area*, 41 (2): 167–75.

Fidell, S., Barber, D.S. and Schultz, T.J. (1991) 'Updating dosage–effect relationship for the prevalence of annoyance due to general transportation noise', *Journal of Acoustical Society of America*, 89: 221–33.

Fields, J.M. (1998) 'Reactions to environmental noise in an ambient noise context in residential areas', *Journal of Acoustical Society of America*, 104: 2245–60.

Goodland, R. (1995) 'The concept of environmental sustainability', *Annual Review of Ecology and Systematics*, 26: 1–24.

Goodland, R. and Daly, H. (1996) 'Environmental sustainability: universal and non-negotiable', *Ecological Applications*, 6: 1002–17.

Ingle, S.T., Pachpande, B.G., Wagh, N.D. and Attarde, S.B. (2005) 'Noise exposure and hearing loss among the traffic policemen working at busy streets of Jalgaon urban centre', *Transportation Research D*, 10: 69–75.

International Organisation for Standardisation (1996) International Standard ISO 1996–2. Acoustics – Description and measurement of environmental noise – Part 2: Acquisition of data pertinent to land use; 1987. Geneva: ISO.

Jarnevich, C.S., Holcombe, T.R., Barnett, D.T., Stohlgren, T.J. and Kartesz, J.T. (2010) 'Forecasting weed distributions using climate data: a GIS early warning tool', *Invasive Plant Science and Management*, 3: 365–75.

King, E.A., Murphy, E. and Rice, H.J. (2011) 'Implementation of the EU Environmental Noise Directive: lessons from the first phase of strategic noise mapping and action planning in Ireland', *Journal of Environmental Management*, 96 (3): 756–64.

King, E.A., Murphy, E. and MacNabola, A. (2009) 'Reducing pedestrian exposure to environmental pollutants: a combined noise exposure and air quality analysis approach', *Transportation Research Part D: Transport and Environment*, 14 (5): 309–16.

Michaud, D.S., Keith, S.E. and McMurchy, D. (2005) 'Noise annoyance in Canada', *Noise Health*, 7: 39–47.

Lewis, D.M. (1995) 'Importance of GIS to community-based management of wildlife: lessons from Zambia', *Ecological Applications*, 5 (4): 861–71.

Linsbauer, A., Paul, F., Hoelzle, M., Frey, H. and Haeberli, W. (2009) 'The Swiss Alps without glaciers – a GIS-based modelling approach for reconstruction of glacier beds', In R.S. Purves et al. *Proceedings of Geomorphometry*. Zurich, pp.243–47.

Lydon, M. (2003) 'Community mapping: the recovery (and discovery) of our common ground', *Geomatica*, 57 (2): 131–44.

Mazaris, D.A., Kallimanis, S.A., Chatzigianidis, G., Papadimitrious, K. and Pantis, J.D. (2009) 'Spatiotemporal analysis of an acoustic environment: interactions between landscape features and sounds', *Landscape Ecology*, 24: 817–31.

Meadows D., Meadows D. and Randes J. (1992) *Beyond the Limits: Global Collapse or a Sustainable Future*. Post Mills, VT: Chelsea Green.

Meadows D., Meadows D., Randes J. and Behrens, W. (1972) *The Limits to Growth*. New York: Universe.

Michaud, D.S., Keith, S.E. and McMurchy, D. (2005) 'Noise annoyance in Canada', *Noise Health*, 7: 39–47.

Miedema, M.E. (2003) Relationship Between Exposure to Single or Multiple Transportation Noise Sources and Noise Annoyance. World Health Organisation and European Centre for Environment and Health Report on the Technical meeting of Exposure–response Relationships of Noise on Health. Bonn, Germany: WHO.

Mo, X, Liu, S., Lin, Z. and Guo, R. (2009) 'Regional crop yield, water consumption and water use efficiency and their responses to climate change in the North China Plain', *Agriculture, Ecosystems and Environment*, 134: 67–78.

Murphy, E. and Killen, J.E. (2010) 'Reflections on the science and art of using a GIS to locate a new national children's hospital in Ireland: comments on Houghton', *Irish Geography*, 43 (2): 201–04.

Murphy, E. and King, E.A. (2010) 'Strategic environmental noise mapping: methodological issues concerning the implementation of the EU Environmental Noise Directive and their policy implications', *Environment International*, 36 (3): 290–8.

Murphy, E. and King, E.A. (2011) 'Scenario analysis and noise action planning: modelling the impact of mitigation measures on population exposure', *Applied Acoustics*, 72 (8): 487–94.

Murphy, E., King, E.A. and Rice, H.J. (2009) 'Estimating human exposure to transport noise in central Dublin, Ireland', *Environment International*, 35 (2): 298–302.

Naitoh, P., Muzet, A. and Lienhard, J.P. (1975) 'Effects of noise and elevated temperature on sleep cycle'. Second International Congress of Sleep Research. *Sleep Research*, 4: 174.

O'Malley, V., King, E., Kenny, L. and Dilworth, C. (2009) 'Assessing methodologies for calculating road traffic noise levels in Ireland – converting CRTN indicators to the EU indicators (Lden, Lnight)', *Applied Acoustics*, 70: 284–96.

Ohrstrom, E. and Skanberg, A. (2004) 'Sleep disturbances from road traffic and ventilation noise – laboratory and field experiments', *Journal of Sound and Vibration*, 271: 279–96.

Ohrstrom, E., Skanberg, A., Svensson, H. and Gidlof-Gunnarsson, A. (2006) 'Effects of road traffic noise and the benefit of access to quietness', *Journal of Sound and Vibration*, 295: 40–59.

Papadimitriou, K.D., Mazaris, A.D., Kallimanis, A.S. and Pantis, J.D. (2009) 'Cartographic representation of the sonic environment', *The Cartographic Journal*, 46 (2): 126–35.

Prasher, D. (2003) Estimation of Hearing Damage from Noise Exposure. World Health Organisation and European Centre for Environment and Heath Report on the Technical Meeting of Exposure–response Relationships of Noise on Health, Bonn, Germany, 17–19 September 2002. Bonn, Germany: WHO.

Schafer, R.M. (1994) *The Soundscape: Our Sonic Environments and the Tuning of the World*. Rochester, NY: Destiny Books.

Schafer, R.M. (1977) *The Tuning of the World*. New York: Knopf.

Shaban, M., Urban, B., El Saadi, A. and Faisal, M. (2010) 'Detection and mapping of water pollution variation in the Nile Delta using multivariate clustering and GIS techniques', *Journal of Environmental Management*, 91: 1785–93.

Sheppard, S.R.J. (2006) 'Bridging the sustainability gap with landscape visualisation in community visioning hubs', *The Integrated Assessment Journal*, 6: 79–108.

Thiessen, G.J. (1988) 'Effect of traffic noise on the cyclical nature of sleep', *Journal of the Acoustical Society of America*, 84: 1741–3.

Tran, P., Shaw, R., Chantry, G. and Norton, J. (2009) 'GIS and local knowledge in disaster management: a case study of flood risk mapping in Viet Nam', *Disasters*, 33: 152–69.

Visvalingam, M. (1989) 'Cartography, GIS and maps in perspective', *The Cartographic Journal*, 26: 26–32.

Working Group on Assessment of Exposure to Noise (WGAEN) (2006) *Presenting Noise Mapping Information to the Public*. European Commission Working Group.

World Health Organisation (2011) *Burden of Disease from Environmental Noise*. Bonn: WHO and JRC.

Yuan, F. (2008) 'Land-cover change and environmental impact analysis in the Greater Mankato area of Minnesota using remote sensing and GIS modelling', *International Journal of Remote Sensing*, 29 (4): 1169–84.

# PART IV

## Time in Focus

# 8

# Everyday Life in Transition: Biographical research and sustainability

*Melanie Jaeger-Erben*

## Introduction

Everyday consumption patterns are widely seen as a key issue in social-scientific sustainability research (e.g. WBCSD, 2008). What we eat and buy, how we heat our homes and what mobility options we choose contribute to the level of (un) sustainability of everyday living. Moreover, the everyday behaviour of individuals and households determine the success or otherwise of measures designed to reduce the environmental impact of human consumption.

But consumption patterns are rarely consistent over a person's lifetime: contexts, wishes, needs, social influences and financial resources change as people move through different life phases. Consumption patterns thus need to be conceptualised and studied empirically as a continuous process rather than a stable trait.

This chapter focuses on changes in everyday consumption that follow important life events, such as the arrival of the first baby or relocation, that are relevant to sustainability for a number of reasons. First, normative life events and rites of passage such as moving out of the parents' home as part of the transition to adulthood are socially negotiated and tend to affect the majority of people. They thus produce significant overall effects for society and setting. Studying changes in consumption that coincide with these life events reveals how people develop consumption patterns during different life stages. For example, after leaving school and home, adolescents are often confronted with decisions concerning hitherto taken-for-granted aspects of their everyday lives. This in turn may shift their consumption patterns towards more unsustainable patterns, at least initially. Home-made meals are replaced with fast food, car ownership turns public transport into a much less attractive option and accommodation changes from quality full board to low budget self-supply.

Second, consumption studies very often concentrate on different lifestyles and neglect the transformation of consumption patterns over the life course. Biographical approaches to social-scientific sustainability research that take life-course transitions seriously offer a viable alternative to more 'static' models of human behaviour that underpin much of the lifestyle research today.

Third, studying life courses also helps to better grasp the influence of sociocultural and structural contexts and how they both reinforce or impede sustainable behaviour. We cannot understand stability and change in consumption patterns if we focus only on individual needs and choices. Social, cultural and infrastructural conditions exert considerable influence over people's life course as well as their everyday lives. For example, how young people manage their move away from home is contingent upon the availability and cost of infrastructure, the views and practices of their peers and societal rules and standards concerning gadgets, clothes, or food choices. Finally, life events may offer 'windows of opportunity' for changing unsustainable routines and may open up possibilities for targeted sustainability communication or interventions.

The remainder of this chapter is divided into two parts. The first part offers a critical examination of key approaches to life course research in the social sciences and their relevance to sustainability studies. Subsequently, the chapter focuses on one specific approach to life-course research – problem-centred interviewing (PCI) – and its application in a sustainable consumption study carried out in Germany from 2008 to 2011 which investigated changes in everyday consumption after the birth of the first child or relocation.

## Biographical research as methodological approach

Biographical research is not one coherent method (see Roberts, 2002 for a detailed overview) but describes a plethora of approaches which are used individually or together depending on the research questions and which frequently cut across academic disciplines. Although being quite heterogeneous, biographical approaches share some key characteristics:

1 Many biographical studies adopt a qualitative approach to social research and draw on diverse research methods such as interviewing, participant observation and ethnographic fieldwork.
2 The collection and interpretation of 'personal documents' such as transcripts of narratives, interviews, autobiographies, diaries, chronicles, letters, photographs, historical documents or ethnographic field notes.
3 The in-depth interpretation and comparison of a small sample of cases that yields rich and detailed data.
4 Individuals are seen as the 'creators of meaning which forms the basis of their everyday lives' (Roberts, 2002: 6). Therefore, biographical research frequently (not always) adopts a constructivist approach that focuses on how individuals and social groups ascribe meaning to particular social

phenomena; forms of social (inter)action and biographic experiences. For example, biographical studies ask how certain social experiences and structural conditions shape people's ways of thinking, acting and decision making.

Doing biographic research means to 'enter' an individual's life, to take over their position and to follow them through their life, at least to some extent. How deep and far-reaching this process of entering someone else's life-world must be and, consequently, what methods to choose for data collection and analysis, depends on the research questions. While there are no general rules in qualitative research that connect a particular kind of research question to a specific 'research plan', both the scope of the research question and ideas about the desired outcome nevertheless provide a general orientation. Concerning both aspects, we can very broadly differentiate between three *levels of scope*, each with specific methodological implications.

## Focus on life phases

Here, the researcher is interested in a specific topic that shapes different people's lives and the creation of meaning around it. Exemplary questions are: how does a specific institution shape the working conditions of people? What are relevant influences on people's educational choices and options? The researcher focuses on a specific phase in people's lives rather than their entire biography, to reduce the amount of analytical work required in a single case. This makes it possible to compare specific life phases of a larger number of people. Semi-structured interviews can be used to gather data, combining open and narrative questions with more focused ones. As will be described in more detail below, a problem-centred interview (PCI) can be a suitable option, followed by a grounded theory approach to theory formation and data analysis. Observations and surveys may complement the interview data. Pregernig (2002), for example, used a problem-centred approach to explore the decision-making processes of forestry professionals concerning the restoration on degraded forest ecosystems. He revealed among others that besides the 'objective' urgency of the degradation, the subjective perceptions as well as social interactions of professionals play an important role for environmentally relevant decisions. The study presented below is a further example of this type of approach.

## Life story

If the researcher is interested in how people view their life and tell their life story, they can use a narrative interview and narration analysis (cf. Schütze, 2006). The aim is not to collect 'objective' information about one's life but to investigate subjective perceptions of social reality and a person's construction of meaning and identity. In the interview situation the researcher only provides 'narration stimulus' in the beginning and tries to remain in the background. Interviewees are invited to talk as much and as long as they want. A core idea behind this approach is that people do not tell their story randomly, but that they select and connect events to develop a more or less coherent storyline. This reveals much about their conscious and unconscious interpretations, attitudes and ways of handling experiences. To give coherence to their story, people are sometimes forced to either divulge more personal information than they had anticipated or to condense some parts of their life story. Here, the 'logic' behind the selection of details is of great interest to the researcher. This approach especially can reveal how learning processes evolve over a lifetime and how peoples' attitudes, meanings and practices were formed in their biography. Vandenabeele and Wildemeersch (2010), for example, used a biographical approach to study how farmers learn about environmental issues and how these become part of their professional life (or not). They found that environmentally conscious farmers develop richer narratives than less conscious farmers concerning their learning about environmental issues, and are, for example, more willing to incorporate and accept different perspectives on agriculture and environment.

## Life history

Life history approaches broaden the scope of the research to include the individual's social group and position within society. Here, the researcher aims to 'objectify' the stories told and to reconstruct how life has been lived. This means to go beyond interviewees' own accounts to try to discover how the person 'really' felt or acted in the past, which has at least two major implications. First, complementary data is needed to contextualise the life story told, including historical archives, testimonies of other people, or personal documents from the interviewee. Second, it is assumed that people construct their own account of how things 'really happened', which may or may not be accurate, and that their subjective point of view needs to be made explicit vis-à-vis more factual accounts of the same event. Rosenthal's (2004) biographical case reconstruction approach exemplifies life history research that attempts to compare subjective perceptions to 'objective' historical facts. Her research (e.g. Rosenthal, 2010) focuses among others on how the history of survivors and perpetrators of the Nazi regime was passed on to and negotiated within the next generations of their families. This approach gives a deep insight on the social construction of meaning of the Shoah as well as the negotiation of responsibility, guilt and atonement.

## Summary

Overall, the choice of scope very much depends on the researcher's interest and research questions. As the empirical examples show, a life-phase approach can answer questions concerning (everyday) decision making and the individual construction of meaning, whereas a focus on life story can reveal (lifelong) processes of learning and socialisation. Life-history approaches lend themselves to the investigation of specific phases in history or historical processes and their impact upon people. The broader the level of scope, the more complex and time-consuming data collection and analysis become. For example, life-history studies are often carried out by teams of experts from different disciplines (e.g. history, sociology, political science) who have research experience with different types of data (e.g. documents, group discussion).

The next section will focus on an empirical study of everyday consumption and its transformation after major life events, namely the arrival of the first baby and moving house. The project concentrated on life phases (see above) and adopted a problem-centred approach that yielded valuable results to guide the design of sustainable consumption interventions in the future. It formed the qualitative, sociological part of an interdisciplinary multi-method project, *Life events as windows of opportunity for change towards sustainable consumption patterns* (LifeEvents), which was carried out in Berlin, Germany between 2008 and 2011.[1]

## Case study: Everyday consumption and life events

The LifeEvents project addressed two main research questions:

1  How do everyday consumption patterns change as result of critical life events, such as relocation? And
2  Following these life events, are people more susceptible to campaigns that aim to change consumption habits towards sustainability?

The second question was addressed using a quantitative approach that evaluated the effectiveness of a three-pronged intervention based on targeted telephone conversations, an information package and a control group. This part of the study involved over 1,000 participants and covered three domains of everyday consumption – mobility, food and energy – where more sustainable alternatives (e.g. public transport, less meat, energy saving) were promoted.

The qualitative part of the study investigated how people's everyday consumption patterns change as a result of major life events. Here, participants and non-participants of the quantitative campaign were interviewed about their experiences and their conduct of everyday life before and after the life event, the evolution of their consumption habits as well as the role of the intervention during that time. Sustainability was used as a 'normative foil' to assess the activities mentioned as a part of everyday life before and after the life event. This strand of research is now described in more detail.

### Sample and choice of methods

Forty persons who either had their first child or moved house during the previous 6 to 13 months took part in the interviews that lasted up to

2 hours. Twenty-three of them participated in the sustainability campaign (see above) while 17 did not. Among them were 23 new parents and 17 people who recently moved whose age ranged from 17 to 89 (Mean 34.2). Women (72 per cent) and respondents with an academic background (65 per cent) were in the majority. Most of the parents (16) were on maternal leave at the time of the interview: 12 were full-time employed, 2 without a job, 3 had already retired and 3 participants were still students. Overall, the sample was very heterogeneous with regard to participants' attitudes, knowledge and activities concerning sustainability, their life situation and their residential neighbourhoods, without being representative in the quantitative sense of the term.

## Interview technique and complementary methods

The project adopted a problem-centred approach to interviewing (PCI), a technique that was originally developed by Andreas Witzel and that is now widely used in many areas of social research, especially in German-speaking countries (Scheibelhofer, 2005). PCI constitutes a specific method in life-course research that combines open-ended questions with more concrete, targeted questions concerning a specific topic such as consumption (Witzel, 2000). A key characteristic of PCI is its focus on understanding interviewees' perception of and experiences with *a specific topic or problem*. Another related characteristic is its *object orientation*, which means that the researcher's choice of methodology is guided by the object under study. To facilitate a more thorough investigation, PCI is thus often complemented by other methods such as participant observation. A third main characteristic of PCI is its *process orientation*. This stipulates that the interviewer needs to provide interviewees with ample opportunities to make their views known and to be sensitive to and accept 'the flow' of the interview. Even if the interviewer has some concrete question prepared, they should not ask them line by line but in ways that fit the situation.

According to Scheibelhofer (2005: 27), the PCI allows the interviewer to move gradually from a more passive to a more active, intervening role, which clearly distinguishes PCI from narrative and semi-structured approaches to qualitative interviewing. One main role of the interviewer in the LifeEvents project was to encourage interviewees to go beyond general comments or standard explanations such as 'one needs to eat healthily but I have no time' and to ask for more concrete examples and explanations to uncover the structure of a specific everyday problem.

Overall, PCI was chosen for the LifeEvents project for two main reasons. First, changes in mobility, food consumption and energy use in during specific life-course transitions were important; therefore a more structured, topic-oriented approach was necessary. Second, PCI represents a more interactive method that enables participants, at least to a certain extent, to participate in the formulation of results; this makes it highly relevant for sustainability research as a transdisciplinary science (Elzinga, 2008). Since everyday routines are not necessarily open to conscious reflection or immediate verbalisation, the interview as a mainly language-based approach was complemented by observation as well as a creative method (see description below).

Following Witzel's approach (2000), each individual interview in the LifeEvents project incorporated four distinct phases (see Table 8.1). To explore the influence of a life event on everyday life to the fullest extent possible, the interview started off with an invitation to participants to tell 'their story'. This story-generating part is intended to capture how interviewees perceive the life event themselves. In LifeEvents, the interview was opened up as follows:

> I am interested in how everyday life changes when people have their first child/move house. Could you please tell me your story, starting from when having a child/moving house first emerged as a topic of conversation, and then tell me everything that happened until now.

After this initial phase, during which the interviewer adopts a more passive role, the PCI continues with a 'general exploration' where the interviewer asks questions about the interviewee's story and tries to discover patterns in their arguments and stories. In this phase the interviewer develops some initial interpretations of the topic and tests them in the subsequent 'specific exploration' phase. This phase is most dialogical because both interviewee and interviewer bring their expertise to bear on the topic. In the LifeEvents project this phase was used to shed light on people's mobility, food consumption and energy use. For example, interviewees were asked to describe a typical weekday in detail, from getting up in the morning to going to bed at night, and to specify how they move around, what they eat or drink and how they use energy to do these things. They were also asked to detail their use of financial, material and time resources and to describe what activities they do on their own and when they cooperate with others.

The concluding part of the PCI – phase four – is used for questions that have not been addressed before but that are of interest to the interviewer. If they have not been mentioned before, participants were encouraged to comment on what role the environment and global concerns as well as health issues play in their everyday lives. The interview should be closed in unison when both partners have nothing else to ask or add.

Witzel (2000) recommends that PCI be complemented with other methods. In the LifeEvents project a short questionnaire was used to collect sociodemographic data (age, professional background, household composition). In addition, the researcher carried out participant observations in the households and the neighbourhood in order to be able to connect respondents' everyday activities to (the design of) places where they happen and to observe aspects that people would or could not talk about, such

**Table 8.1**  The four phases of PCI, as applied in the LifeEvents project

| Phase | Characteristics | Focus in LifeEvents |
|---|---|---|
| One: narrative start | Open, story-generating questions, structuring by interviewee; passive role for interviewer | Individual story after decision for having a baby/relocating; influences and contexts of decision making; preparation before and adaptation after event |
| Two: general exploration | Questions about the story aiming to understand the perspective of the interviewee and discover patterns; interviewer–interviewee dialogue | Asking details about specific situations (focus on consumption-relevant decisions); exploration of the role of social networks and infrastructures |
| Three: specific exploration | Testing/negotiation of interviewer's interpretations, 'dialogue between experts' | Focusing everyday mobility, food consumption and energy use as well as relevant influences (e.g. different kinds of resources) on related practices |
| Four: conclusion | Asking of remaining questions; finding a conclusion in unison | If not mentioned before: exploring the role of environmental issues/sustainability |

as characteristics of their homes in comparison to other households. Interviewees were also encouraged to draw their personal city map and to describe how they move through the city, what places they visit, why they visit them and what places they like or do not like. Finally, the researcher collected additional information on places and sources of information mentioned by interviewees (e.g. workshops, web forums, specific infra-structures or meaningful places).

## Data analysis using Grounded Theory

According to Witzel (2000: 3) 'the concept of a PCI borrows largely from the theory-generating procedure of grounded theory', one of the most widely used techniques for data collection, analysis and interpretation in qualitative social research. Grounded Theory (GT) was chosen as the method of data analysis because it allows a thorough analysis of the contexts of and influences on behaviour. It was initially formulated by Glaser and Strauss (1967) and subsequently developed into two competing schools of thought. Despite this diversification, most GT approaches display two key features:

1  A general 'logic of research' whereby theoretical models are developed from empirical data through inductive and deductive reasoning.

2   A concrete analytical process: a three-stage coding system based on constant comparison of observations which moves from 'open codes' to categories and dimensions to a theoretical model.

The LifeEvents project utilised Strauss and Corbin's (1990a, b) approach to GT and adopted its general logic as well as its coding system. The remainder of this section will detail the use of the three-stage coding system in the LifeEvents project.

## Coding in Grounded Theory

Coding in GT represents a way of translating empirical data, for example interview texts, into more abstract terms. This in turn facilitates the comparison of individual cases. The GT coding system encourages the development of increasingly abstract and aggregated terms that make it possible to understand, describe and differentiate an increasing number of social phenomena. GT coding starts off with *open coding* where the researcher interprets and codes the text very broadly and remains relatively close to the phenomenon under study. This is followed by *axial coding*, where codes generated during the open coding phase are systematised. Axial coding paves the way for *selective coding* in which theoretical models are developed and refined. These three steps cannot always be clearly separated from one another. For example, it is possible that the researcher develops some theoretical concepts at the start of the coding process, which are then used to refine these theoretical concepts rather than develop them from scratch. Ideally, the coding process ends with a general model or a 'theory grounded in data' which answers the research questions.

## Open coding

Open coding encompasses a first sorting of the data to reveal significant, interesting and remarkable aspects. Despite this general openness, it is important to always keep the research question in mind and to try to focus on phenomena that are related to it. This focus should not be seen as limiting but rather as a way of framing empirical research without eclipsing potentially important aspects. In the LifeEvents project, interview sequences that covered consumption activities and their contextual conditions were coded particularly thoroughly. Here, the researcher's theoretical and practical knowledge, including insights generated through the use of complementary methods (see above), proved particularly useful. Overall, open coding produced a large number of codes. The following excerpt from an interview with a 34-year-old mother exemplifies how open coding may be done (see Box 8.1). The vertical lines indicate the coded sections, the numbers highlight where they start and end and refer to the code names listed below.

---

**Box 8.1   Example of open coding in the LifeEvents project**

'|$_1$ We $_1$| have|$_2$ particularly searched for fridge-freezer $_2$| to |$_3$ be able to freeze her |$_4$ baby food $_4$| $_3$|. Before we had a |$_5$ normal fridge $_5$| – and we thought: "Should we buy |$_6$ a normal fridge-freezer that is |$_7$ cheaper $_7$| and |$_8$ needs more energy $_8$| or should we buy an A++, which is |$_7$ more expensive $_7$| but |$_8$ uses less energy $_8$| $_6$|." And then we really – you always find |$_9$ these numbers on the devices $_9$| – |$_{10}$ |$_1$ we $_1$| really calculated how many years it takes until such a fridge-freezer pays itself back $_{10}$|. [...] and then somehow calculated |$_3$ it takes five or six years or so, than it's amortised $_3$| and |$_{11}$ then we bought an A++ fridge-freezer $_{11}$|.'

   1  joint preparation
   2  clear focus
   3  long-term preparation
   4  special food for babies
   5  normal device, definition of normality
   6  comparison of advantages and disadvantages
   7  characteristic of electrical device: price
   8  characteristic of electrical device: energy consumption
   9  energy labels
  10  price consciousness
  11  special devices, definition of speciality

---

This example illustrates how codes developed during open coding may either overlap or recur, which is important for the analysis. Even if the quantity of codes (or better: how often the researcher applies a particular code) does not necessarily signify its conceptual importance, it gives the impression of relevance. Moreover, codes that are only used a few times in a sample of ten interviews are not useful for carrying out comparisons between these interviews. Overlapping codes can reveal relationships between codes, which in turn is important for theoretical reflections and subsequent analytical steps.

The above sequence reveals how the respondent and her partner assessed different arguments for and against purchasing an energy-efficient fridge-freezer for preserving home-made baby food. The respondent's decision seems to be relatively rational, comparing advantages and disadvantages and deciding on the basis of technical information and numbers. A possible title for this sequence could be: 'Making a clever long-term decision' bearing in mind that 'clever' refers to how *she* evaluates and presents her decision. 'Clever' could mean making a decision that takes into account the long-term costs of a purchase. Even though the respondent's account suggests that she and her partner are interested in saving energy (and maybe also in protecting the environment), it is the actual cost of the purchase that counts the most. Perhaps her decision would have been different if the energy-efficient fridge-freezer had not paid for itself after a reasonable time period. In other words, prices and costs appear to be the most relevant factors in her assessment. Interestingly, she also distinguishes between a 'normal' fridge-freezer (i.e. cheaper and less energy-efficient) and a 'special one' with an A++ energy label. This suggests that for her, saving energy is something out of the ordinary rather than a normal part of everyday life. Naturally, this initial interpretation by the researcher needs to be substantiated with further examples. In addition, this interview sequence raises further questions. Why does she have to freeze the baby food? And why is she already so far ahead, namely for a time at least half a year after the birth when the baby starts to eat baby food? The researcher notes these questions to answer them during subsequent stages of the GT process. For example, other interview and documentary data material revealed that many people view home-made baby food as 'natural' and 'healthy'. The freezing of pre-cooked portions offers an efficient way to provide home-made baby food every day. The above excerpt shows how a 'norm' concerning the preparation of baby food influences the participant's preparation for the birth of her child. The importance of this particular finding will be discussed in more detail below.

After developing a considerable number of codes on the basis of three interviews, these codes were grouped together to get an overview of their quality and content and to organise them into 'code families'. Figure 8.1 shows how codes identified in the fridge-freezer example above could be grouped. Grouping codes is not a mandatory step in GT, but appears to be particularly useful whenever the number of codes is high. Coding as well as grouping should always be guided by the research question.

The grouping of codes shown in Figure 8.1 provides a first impression of the kinds of *strategies*, *criteria* and *structures* that participants draw on when preparing for the arrival of their first baby. These code families were further refined later on in the project through a comparative analysis of the interview data collected.

## Axial coding

In the *axial coding* phase, codes were grouped together into categories. Categories are 'higher-order' codes or 'conceptual umbrellas' that subsume various individual codes and that are more nuanced than code families. Categories are used later on in the research to define conceptual models that explain the phenomena under study. Again, it is important to identify categories that capture significant patterns. It is not the aim of GT to develop as many codes and categories as possible, but to construct codes that facilitate comparison between cases and that describe different types of empirical phenomena. Here, the researcher tries to discover connections between codes, such as possible links between codes for attitudes and coded behaviours, or significant patterns of codes. In the LifeEvents project, axial coding resulted in the reclassification of codes and categories into three

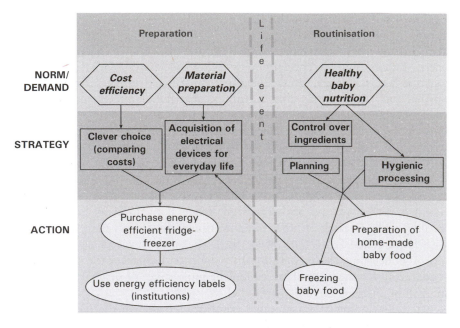

**Figure 8.1** Connections between codes and categories following axial coding (based on the fridge-freezer purchasing decision discussed in the text).

chronological phases before and after the life event: (1) preparation, (2) adaptation and (3) re-routinisation. Life events such as the birth of the first child or moving house are preceded by a preparation phase during which people 'get ready' both mentally and physically. Re-routinisation involves the establishment of new everyday routines, and occurs after an initial adaption phase that follows immediately after the life event. Evidence from the LifeEvents project shows that this preparation phase is quite important because many changes that occur *after* the life event are 'prefigured' by activities *prior* to the event. Codes and categories were organised into these three chronological phases. This was followed by an in-depth analysis of the connections between codes *within* these three phases.

Figure 8.2 shows the connections between codes and categories that are relevant to the fridge-freezer example discussed above, and reveals the connections between preparation and re-routinisation. More precisely, it illustrates the link between preparation (the purchase of an energy-efficient fridge-freezer) and a new routine established a considerable time after the event (the preparation and freezing of home-made baby food). Importantly, this visualisation exercise allowed the researcher to clarify the link between an energy-related activity before the life event and a newly established daily nutritional routine after the event. Since the adaptation is not relevant for this connection, it has been left out in the figure.

As regards the grouping of codes, the code family 'evaluation criteria/norms' from the open coding phase was subsequently refined into 'norm/demand', subsuming all codes related to different tasks and requirements that the respondents were confronted with before, during and after the life event (the first layer in Figure 8.2). The strategy level shows what strategies the respondent deployed to fulfil those tasks (the second layer in Figure 8.2). Finally, the bottom layer covers concrete actions undertaken. The actions 'purchase of energy-efficient freezer' and 'preparation of home-made baby food' are related to each other through a number of interconnected strategies and demands. The important demands are 'cost efficiency', 'material preparation' and 'healthy baby nutrition'. They form three distinct categories that subsume several codes each. Connected to 'cost efficiency' is the strategy-code 'clever choice', which in this specific case implied comparing costs. Material preparation emerged as a category in the axial coding phase and subsumes all activities in the preparation phase that serve the acquisition of material things (e.g. appliances, utensils, furniture) deemed relevant to life after the event. In this case the strategy code 'acquisition of electrical appliances for everyday life' is connected to material preparation. These two strategies taken together explain why the purchase of an energy-efficient fridge-freezer was important. However, they do not explain why such an appliance was deemed necessary in the first place. This can be explained by considering practices that are relevant in the re-routinisation phase. The preparation of home-made baby food emerged as a relevant issue in a considerable number of interviews with parents (especially mothers) and was frequently connected to the norm/demand 'healthy baby nutrition' through the strategies 'ingredient control' and 'hygienic processing of food'. All interviewed parents wanted to provide a healthy diet for their baby, and some parents decided to prepare baby food themselves to be able to choose the best ingredients, to avoid additives and to adopt the healthiest way to prepare the meals. They also learned that it is less time-consuming

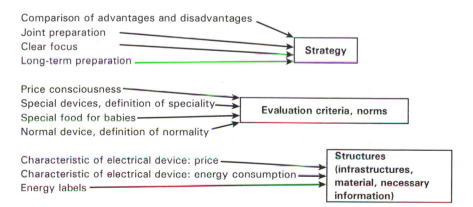

**Figure 8.2** Example of grouping of codes into 'code families'.

and even more hygienic to prepare a bigger amount of food at one time and freeze it. Freezing baby food therefore is an important practice for different purposes, and created the demand to buy a freezer or fridge-freezer in households without such an appliance.

To summarise, Figure 8.2 illustrates how demands associated with caring for a baby (in this case the need to provide the 'right' diet) influence plans for everyday life in the future. This in turn influences investments in electrical appliances and other material objects prior to the life event. The example also illustrates the creation of a 'material reality' during the preparation phase that prefigures everyday activities as well as energy consumption in the future. Once the freezer is bought, the person is more inclined to implement her plans to prepare and freeze baby meals, even if she realises that this is not as easy as she had hoped.

The above example illustrates the emergence from the data of a key dimension, namely *social norms, expectations* and *roles*. Even before their first child was born, parents in the sample encountered a plethora of information about their child care responsibilities as well as hitherto unfamiliar sociocultural norms that stipulate what a 'caring parent' does and does not do. Information related to parenting and child rearing is partly communicated 'officially', for example through books, web pages, flyers or professionals like midwifes or medicals. However, social norms regarding parenthood and 'doing family' are often communicated in more subtle ways, for example through informal peer pressure exerted by friends, neighbours and family members. These subtly expressed expectations may be both shaped by and reinforced through stories in newspapers, Internet forums and movies.

*Structural influences and conditions* make up a second dimension that is only marginally reflected in the above example but that emerged from other interviews in the LifeEvents project. In the above example, the interviewee needed access to relevant information, in her case energy labels and prices, to be able to compare different offers. This information is generally provided by institutions and the market. This dimension also encapsulates spatial and infrastructural aspects such as mobility options and places for recreation, shopping or work that characterise a person's living environment. How parents view and use their surroundings changes significantly depending on whether their living environment does or does not meet their own and their child's needs. For example, the interviewed parents started to avoid 'dirty' or 'insecure' places and discovered others (alongside shops and public traffic options in that area). Unavailable and/or inaccessible public transport also influenced some new parents' decision to use their car more often following the arrival of their child.

Overall, observable changes in consumption patterns following an important life event can be largely attributed to both sociocultural norms and (infra) structures These are influenced by people's socio-economic status, cultural background and living environment. For example, highly educated mothers are more likely to cook baby food themselves because they see it as 'more natural' and 'healthy'. For less educated parents, this specific practice was less relevant. These kinds of observations are important for the last step in the GT process, namely selective coding and the formulation of general models.

## Selective coding

During this phase of the research process all interview data was analysed again to test the idea that both sociocultural norms and (infra)structures fundamentally influence people's responses to major life events. This reflects the final aim of GT, which is the formulation of a general model that answers the research question, as far as possible, on the basis of the given data.

*Social practices* emerged as the *key construct* which links both sociocultural norms and (infra)structural influences and conditions to concrete behaviour. Social practices can be described as a set of interwoven activities (or 'doings') which have a certain spatial and temporal order and which utilise certain tools or equipment (cf. Schatzki, 1996; Shove and Pantzar, 2005). Practices are also intrinsically social because they are endowed with shared meanings and are connected to roles, positions, or specific fields. For example, the preparation of home-made baby food serves as a 'marker' for new parents with a specific educational background and knowledge. To cook baby food at home thus serves two main functions: it satisfies a 'real' need (feeding the baby) and it gives some parents the feeling of 'being a good/caring mother or father'. By adopting an established social practice people can show their ability and willingness to embrace certain cultural and social norms. This in turn has consequences for their practical everyday life, including their material consumption patterns. The mother discussing her decision to purchase an energy-efficient fridge-freezer needs to organise her everyday life around the meals. She has to source the ingredients (which need to be organic if she follows the recommendations), ensure that appliances and utensils needed for food preparation (fridge-freezer, hand blender) are available and in working condition, and spend a certain amount of time each day in and around the kitchen.

The last aspect – the allocation of temporal resources – is particularly relevant to an improved understanding of changes in everyday life and their relevance for sustainability, even though this has not yet been adequately recognised in the consumption literature (see also Rau and Edmondson, Chapter 9 in this volume). In the case of new parents, who participated in the LifeEvents project, a shift in practices led to more structured and healthy eating by all family members and the purchasing of organic products. At the same time, these families consumed more energy than before. Not only because they spent more time at home, but also because they had bought new appliances. Some also used their car more often (or bought a car) because they felt that this would enable them to better meet the demands of rearing a child.

Overall, selective coding culminated in the classification of various social practices whose transformation as a result of major life events coincided with observable behavioural changes. Table 8.2 covers three of these practices – the preparation of porridge, breastfeeding and participation in baby courses – to illustrate their social meanings, their connections to social roles and their consequences for people and setting.

## Key results

The qualitative part of the LifeEvents project revealed that people who experience significant life events have to process and respond to large amounts of socially relevant information. They become more aware of social demands, expectations and norms, all of which both shape and reflect prevailing social practices. On the one hand, these social influences can offer guidance and help to meet the challenges of the new life phase. On the other hand, they can also have significant material, temporal–spatial and organisational impacts on everyday life and on the (un)sustainability of people's consumption patterns.

Social-scientific inquiries into the (un)sustainability of people's consumption patterns that aim to be both theoretically rigorous and policy relevant will benefit from a social practices framework. The LifeEvents project indicated that campaigns to encourage new parents to adopt more sustainable consumption patterns would benefit from a social practice approach that highlights both opportunities for, and barriers to, successful policy intervention. It is argued that many conventional consumption studies that focus exclusively on what people (say they) do or think can be misleading because attitudes and behaviour frequently combine, sometimes in seemingly incongruent or unpredictable ways, to shape people's responses to life events. It would be difficult to persuade a mother to choose an alternative to the car to bring her baby to swimming classes if the car is the most comfortable option and if taking part in the baby swim is deemed to be very important. A social practice approach, on the other hand, can help identify aspects of the practice that *can* be changed, such as the availability of public transport options or the scheduling or location of the course. It can also point to cases where the social meaning of a practice ought to be changed. For example, some parents who participated in the project adopted child care practices that are potentially harmful and that are based on false information, such as the 'myth' that babies need a bath every day or require a constant indoor temperature of 23 degrees centigrade. These kinds of practices do not only increase household energy consumption but can also negatively affect the baby's health.

# Capturing changes in social practices: Benefits and drawbacks of a problem-centred biographical approach to sustainability research

A major outcome of the qualitative part of the LifeEvents project was the identification of significant changes in social practices that accompanied key life events. By adopting a biographical approach, the study revealed

**Table 8.2**   Characteristics of some identified social practices

| Everyday relevant practice | Meaning | Social role | Spatial–temporal/ material/physical/ cognitive components |
|---|---|---|---|
| Self-made porridge | Healthy baby nutrition ('better' baby nutrition) | Caring parent; possibly belongingness to milieu with orientation towards 'naturalness/purity' | Fresh ingredients (organic); preparation time; time in kitchen; devices (e.g. hand blender); 'nutrition competence' |
| Breastfeeding | Healthy baby nutrition | Caring, 'natural' mother/woman | Female body, physical 'skills'; planning and timing |
| Go to baby swim (or other baby courses) | Early learning, early childhood intervention | Caring, supportive parent | Availability of time, accessible infrastructure, modes of transport (mostly car) |

important processes of learning during life-course transitions and also highlighted the significance of learning contexts and information sources. At the same time, it was possible to ascertain when, where and how the participants appropriated and performed (un)sustainable practices and how (changing) infrastructural contexts, social discourses and norms influenced them. Studying life phases and significant life-course transitions such as the arrival of the first child through the lens of social practices thus helps to make visible dialectic interactions between historical conditions and societal structures on the one hand, and individual biographies on the other hand. This makes it possible to ascertain, at least to some degree, whether structural measures or social interventions or a combination of both are effective in promoting more sustainable consumption patterns.

The complexity of consumption practices also throws up significant challenges for sustainability research. Interview data from the LifeEvents project shed light on people's self-reported daily consumption decisions and habits. Given that some features of personal consumption may not lend themselves to immediate verbalisation during an interview, the collection of complementary observational data could further enhance the quality of sustainable consumption research in the future. New and innovative time-geographical approaches that focus on both the social and the physical environment within which individual consumption occurs could be useful in this context. Additional quantitative data such as electricity meter readings, mileage figures or supermarket receipts could add depth and rigour to future sustainability studies by capturing important aspects of people's consumption-related 'ecological footprint' that would otherwise remain invisible.

## Note

1   This three year project was funded by the German Federal Ministry of Education and
Research under the socio-ecological research programme (www.lifevents.de).

# References

Elzinga, A. (2008) 'Participation', in G. Hirsch Hadorn, H. Hoffmann-Riem, S.
Biber-Klemm, W. Grossenbacher-Mansuy, D. Joyce, C. Pohl, U. Wiesmann and
E. Zemp (eds), *Handbook of Transdisciplinary Research*. Berlin: Springer. pp. 343–60.

Glaser, B.G. and Strauss, A.L. (1967) *The Discovery of Grounded Theory. Strategies
for Qualitative Research*. Chicago, IL: Aldine Publishing Company.

Pregernig, M. (2002) 'Perceptions, not facts: how forestry professionals decide on
the restoration of degraded forest ecosystems', *Journal of Environmental
Planning and Management*, 45 (1): 25–38.

Roberts, B. (2002) *Biograpical Research*. Buckingham: Open University Press.

Rosenthal, G. (ed.) (2010) *The Holocaust in Three-Generations. Families of Victims
and Perpetrators of the Nazi-Regime*. Opladen: Barbare Budrich.

Rosenthal, G. (2004) 'Biographical research', in C. Seale, G. Gobo, J.F. Gubrium
and D. Silverman (eds) *Qualitative Research Practice*. London: Sage. pp. 48–64.

Schatzki, T. (1996) *Social Practices – A Wittgensteinian Approach to Human
Activity and the Social*. Cambridge: Cambridge University Press.

Scheibelhofer, E. (2005) 'A reflection upon interpretive research techniques: the
problem-centred interview as a method for biographic research', in N. Kelly,
C. Horrocks, K. Milnes, B. Roberts and D. Robinson (eds), *Narrative, Memory
and Everyday Life*. Huddersfield: University of Huddersfield. pp. 19–32.

Schütze, F. (2006) 'Biography analysis on the empirical base of autobiographical narratives – how to analyse autobiographical narratives interviews. Parts, in *INVITE –
Biographical Counselling in Rehabilitative Vocational Training – further education
curriculum, Module 1 - B2-1*. Available at: http://www.uni-magdeburg.de/zsm/projekt/
biographical/1/B2.1.pdf.

Shove, E. A. and Pantzar, M. (2005) 'Consumers, producers and practices understanding the invention and reinvention of Nordic walking', *Journal of Consumer
Culture*, 5 (1), 43–64.

Strauss, A.L. and Corbin, J. (1990a) *Basics of Qualitative Research. Grounded
Theory Procedures and Techniques*. London: Sage.

Strauss, A.L. and Corbin, J. (1990b) 'Grounded theory research: procedures, canons
and evaluative criteria', *Qualitative Sociology*, 13 (1): 3–21.

Vandenabeele, J. and Wildemeersch, D. (2010) 'How farmers learn about environmental issues: reflections on a sociobiographical approach', *Adult Education Quarterly*,
December 2010. Published online before print: doi: 10.1177/0741713610392770.
Also available at: https://lirias.kuleuven.be/bitstream/123456789/291423/1/artikelfarmer
completeapril2010end.pdf.

World Business Council for Sustainable Development. (2008). *Sustainable Consumption:
Facts and Trends from a Business Perspective*. Geneva: WBCSD.

Witzel, A. (2000) 'The problem-centered interview', *Forum: Qualitative Social
Research*, 1 (1): 22. Available at: http://nbn-resolving.de/urn:nbn:de:0114-fqs0001228.

# 9

# Time and Sustainability

## Henrike Rau and Ricca Edmondson

## Introduction

While the term 'sustainability' remains highly contested with regard to its definition and meanings, commentators would probably agree that *time* forms one of its central dimensions. Most definitions of sustainability prescribe the adoption of a long-term view of social and political life that focuses on the fair, just and viable distribution of economic, social and environmental resources both within *and* across generations (e.g. World Commission on Environment and Development, 1987; Ott, 2009). Similarly, many mainstream indicators of (sustainable) human development focus more or less explicitly on aspects of time, including people's life expectancy (see Khoo, Chapter 5 in this volume). Some efforts to further advance the sociological investigation of time-related views and habits have touched on environmental issues and are thus relevant to the sustainability debate. Recent socio-ecological work to do with time focuses on the effects on society and the environment of a growing discrepancy between natural cycles and social pacers that is apparent in many modern capitalist societies (Adam, 1996, 1998; see also Elias, 1984). Others seek to highlight the relationship between time politics and resource consumption, for example in relation to the centrality of acceleration in transport planning and policy (Adam, 2009; Peters, 2005). The ways in which different (sub-)cultural relationships to time can affect attitudes and behaviour relating to the environment is also highly relevant in this context. For example, how is people's interest in the social and ecological behaviour of the past – shown, not least, in enthusiasm for national or local heritage – connected with support for future-oriented policies aimed at enhancing sustainability (Edmondson and Rau, 2008)?

Efforts to address widespread problems of ecological (un)sustainabil-
ity associated with the rise of consumerism and the emergence of the
'throwaway society' have challenged the spread of instantaneous time
that accompanies these consumption-centred forms of sociocultural
organisation. What people buy and what kinds of social meanings they
attribute to their purchases are inextricably linked to time-related structures in society, including the allocation of time to work and leisure
activities respectively. Recent attempts in some European countries to
reduce working hours and increase leisure time as a way of increasing
domestic consumption of goods and services reflect this link. This said,
the connection between work, leisure and consumption is often much
more complex than these time-political efforts suggest, which partly
explains its resistance to simplistic forms of social engineering. How
people live, work and shop may be affected, among other things, by their
location within the human life course. For example, life satisfaction
among people over the age of 50 has been shown to involve different
forms of 'attachment to place' (Gilleard and Higgs, 2002) and to the
environment. The effects of 'the baby boom generation' are frequently
discussed: both in terms of the deleterious ecological impacts of lifestyles attributed to this generation in particular, and in terms of the
possibility of using the power of politically active older people to
defend the environment.

Key contributors to sustainable consumption debates have argued for
fundamental changes in how individuals, households and societies view
and use time (e.g. Jackson, 2008, 2009; Shove et al., 2009; Schor, 2010).
They have also offered time-related solutions to the 'wicked problem' of
economically and socially significant, yet ecologically disruptive patterns of (over-)consumption, albeit often as part of a broader range of
prescribed measures for restructuring how people view and interact with
their physical and social environment. Juliet Schor (2010) identifies a
fundamental shift in how we use time as one of the four main principles
of *plenitude*, which involves living in such a way as to treat time as an
'abundant resource' rather than a source of pressure. According to Tim
Jackson (2008), the 'paradox of well-being' frequently revolves around
issues of production and consumption and the allocation of time. He
asks why people continue to work and consume too much instead of
spending time on less resource-intensive activities such as exchanges
with family and friends (see also Jackson, 2009). Similarly, a recent proposal by the New Economics Foundation for a 21-hour working week
was intended to demonstrate a possible way of breaking the self-
perpetuating cycle of over-production and over-consumption that is
now a major cause of both social inequality and ecological degradation,
both in the UK and other societies (Coote et al., 2010). It should however be noted that many social developments associated with late

modernity, from women's heightened participation in the workforce to increased longevity on the part of both sexes, have been accompanied by suggestions that they could furnish the wherewithal for a shorter statutory working week. Strong resistance to such proposals, not least on the parts of employers, underlines the complexity of socio-economic relationships in relation to work-time, production and consumption (Ausubel and Grübler, 1995; Beder, 2004). Coote et al. (2010) outline some of the problems to be anticipated:

> Of course, moving from the present to this future scenario will not be simple. The proposed shift towards 21 hours must be seen in terms of a broad, incremental transition to social, economic and environmental sustainability. Problems likely to arise in the course of transition include the risk of increasing poverty by reducing the earning power of those on low rates of pay; too few new jobs because people already in work take on more overtime; resistance from employers because of rising costs and skills shortages; resistance from employees and trade unions because of the impact on earnings in all income brackets; and more general political resistance that might arise, for example, from moves to enforce shorter hours. (2010: 3)

This is clearly a scenario with ramifications that need exploration on multiple levels.

Initially, this chapter will focus on some recent developments with regard to the theoretical treatment of time in the context of social-scientific sustainability debates and its implications for future social research practice. Here it will be argued that growing engagement with the topic of time among those interested in sustainability questions has yet to be matched by more time-sensitive research designs and research methods. In section three, some alternative ways of using qualitative and quantitative time-use data will be explored. It will be shown that linking questions of time use and issues of sustainability in novel and creative ways can open up exciting opportunities for a sustainability-centred analysis of existing time-use data. The benefits and weaknesses of time-sensitive ethnographic approaches to the study of social groups and their social and physical environment will be demonstrated in section four. The concluding part of this chapter attends to possible future trends towards more time-sensitive sustainability research.

## Time and sustainability: Linking theory and research

Given the centrality of time for sustainability, it seems odd that much social-scientific work on the topic remains atemporal in terms of both its theoretical focus and methodological orientation. Sociological debates on how to transform people's time-related views and practices remain scarce, which actually reflects a broader tendency within the social sciences to treat time rather unsystematically, if at all (Edmondson, 2000; Rau, 2004). The absence of an explicit engagement with the issue of time seems all the more surprising given that future scenarios and long-term trends are central to many current sustainability debates, most notably in relation to climate change and technology adoption. For example, social research has shown that judgements regarding the consequences of a new technology for society and setting can often only be made after a substantial amount of time has passed (Wajcman, 2008). A more in-depth engagement with how people view and use their time and how these time-use patterns become influenced by a plethora of social and ecological pacers is urgently required.

This engagement would lock into the growing interest in sustainability that has sparked debates about the creation of alternative futures for people and planet in order to reconcile economic development with social justice and ecological integrity and to promote the adoption of new practices that work *with* nature rather than against it (e.g. Jackson, 2009; Schor, 2010). Most importantly, the establishment of a sustainable society is widely expected to require the adoption of distinct time perspectives and temporal practices, including a propensity towards long-term thinking, a strong orientation towards the future and the application of the precautionary principle, among others. Interestingly, many of these are in direct opposition to the preoccupation with novelty, short-termism, instant gratification and the present that characterises many modern capitalist societies and their focus on economic growth as a driver of development. For example, Jackson observes how 'two interrelated features of modern economic life ... drive the growth dynamic: the production and consumption of novelty' (2009: 9). In other words, the transition to sustainability is expected to require *a fundamental shift in time culture* which may or may not be compatible with existing social systems of time-space regulation.

Questions immediately arise with regard to whether such a fundamental shift in how people view and use time is achievable, or indeed desirable. To what extent is it possible to achieve a fundamental restructuring of people's time horizons and practices, in particular in the context of current economic systems that favour instantaneity, acceleration and immediate gratification of material wants? Can people be expected to adopt time-use patterns that almost immediately consign them to the margins of most developed societies? Calls for the adoption of alternative time-related practices such as an embrace of slowness, 'downshifting' or the celebration of idleness assume that people are willing and able to voluntarily opt out of the current temporal order, which may or may not be the case. These and other related sociological questions are hardly ever adequately problematised in the sustainability literature, which represents a major gap in the debate.

The basic problem this exposes is that calls for socio-economic and political change which are central to debates on sustainability too often assume either a voluntarism on the parts of individuals with regard to time use – an assumption that they can simply decide to change time-related habits and practices, even though they might scarcely be aware of where these habits have arisen and what they imply – or the possibility of effective forms of social engineering which there is little historical evidence to support. Recent research by Goodin et al. (2008) reveals that levels of temporal autonomy and the distribution of control over the resource of 'time' vary significantly both within and between countries. They maintain that differences in the availability of 'discretionary time', that is, the amount of time per day that people are able to allocate more or less freely, are a central measure of freedom and (in)equality in society. Their analysis of time-use data from six countries representing three distinct welfare and gender regimes clearly shows that people's time-use patterns are shaped in fundamental ways by public and social policy.

Studies such as this, which adopt a time-sensitive approach to key sociological debates around welfare and equality and which use conventional time-use data in new and innovative ways, demonstrate the potential of 'temporalising' traditional socio-political subject areas. It should be possible to augment their methodological armoury by adapting approaches to human lifetime such as Baars' 'triple temporality', which intertwines chronology, personal experience and 'narrative articulation' (Baars, 2007). We would argue, however, that the consequences of people's time-use patterns for society *and* the environment requires equally urgent attention, and that the 'temporalisation' of sustainability theory and research needs to be advanced without delay.

Similarly, it needs to be recognised that all forms of human resource consumption, including the use of time as resource, are primarily *social processes* that produce very real material consequences. How people use their time both shapes and reflects prevailing social conditions, world-views, meanings, cultural norms and conventions, and (re-)produces tangible material realities at the same time. Interdisciplinary studies that combine mainstream temporal–social indicators with indices of human impact on the environment to investigate the relationship between time use and resource consumption are urgently required if future sustainability efforts are to succeed. These in turn must be complemented with qualitative social–ecological research that connects insights into people's

time perspectives and temporal practices with data on everyday conceptu-
alisations of sustainability across different social and cultural groups and
settings. The remaining sections of this chapter will expand on these
methodological issues.

## Measuring the sustainability of time perspectives and temporal practices

The question of how to measure sustainability in ways that take time
seriously has yet to be taken up by social scientists with the necessary
rigour and attention. For example, while time-use diary data have been
shown to be extremely useful for answering pressing sociological questions such as those concerning gender and the division of labour or
changes in the nature of (un)paid work and care, their potential for the
investigation of sustainability issues has yet to be fully exploited. We still
know very little about the implications for sustainability of people's self-
reported time use. How does the energy consumption of households
relate to the actual time-use patterns of their members? Which activities
are more or less resource-intensive and what social and cultural functions
do they fulfil? The relative dominance of quantitative tools for measuring
people's time use has the consequence that many social and cultural
aspects of human time use remain invisible. While existing qualitative
social research on time perspectives and temporal practices reveals their
relevance to questions of sustainability (Edmondson and Rau, 2008;
Rau, 2008), there has been little empirical work that systematically connects time and sustainability.

Advocates of post-normal science and transdisciplinary research see the
development of alternatives to conventional ontological–epistemological
and methodological approaches as an important step towards an enhanced
social-scientific understanding of sustainability issues (e.g. Hirsch Hadorn
et al., 2006, 2008). It is argued here that the problem of people's time
perspectives and temporal practices represents one key area of research
that urgently requires a transdisciplinary turn. For example, existing time-
use data such as the UK-based Multinational Time Use Study (http://www.
timeuse.org/mtus) clearly lends itself to more resource-focused secondary
analysis that links time-use patterns to environmental sustainability indices, such as the level of carbon dioxide emissions or overall resource
consumption attributable to a particular set of activities. The resulting socio-
ecological information would facilitate a more enhanced 'sustainability-
proofing' of current and future policies that impact directly on people's
time use, most notably in the area of working time but also in relation to

school and university schedules or public transport timetables, to name but a few.

Indicators of (un)sustainable human development used by large global organisations such as the UN or the OECD have also undergone significant revisions of late, which partly reflects successful efforts by advocates of alternative development models to re-define *what it means to lead a good life and live sustainably* and *how to measure it* (cf. New Economics Foundation, 2009; see also Khoo, Chapter 5 and Gaube et al., Chapter 6 in this volume). Proposals for alternative measurements of human development that recognise the multifaceted nature of human flourishing and sustainability more generally, and that move beyond the mere quantitative assessment of a country's economic performance using GDP, GNP or other indicators, have emerged (New Economics Foundation, 2009; Pillarisetti and van den Bergh, 2010). For example, the Human Development Index (HDI) – perhaps the most widely used index of human well-being today – combines measurements of life expectancy at birth, education and income to express both inter- and intranational differences in development. Its application in research and policy making has been significant and suggests it may be useful as an alternative to GDP-only measures. Similarly, the Happy Planet Index (HPI) developed by the New Economics Foundation (NEF) in 2006 includes sustainability considerations in its measurement of well-being (New Economics Foundation, 2009).

What remains peculiarly absent from the HDI and other alternative sustainability indicators is a measure of the quality and distribution of people's temporal resources, which limits their explanatory power considerably. More wide-ranging indices such as the Canadian Index of Wellbeing (CIW),[1] which covers a range of social and environmental factors including Canadian people's time use, remain the exception. This lack of recognition for the key role of time in sustainability seems all the more surprising given that many of those involved in researching and regulating people's time use consider a high-quality temporal environment to be a fundamental aspect of human well-being. There is a plethora of studies that reveal the negative impacts of stress and harriedness on people's mental and physical well-being and that argue for high levels of temporal autonomy, time diversity, the 'reclamation' of 'quality time' and the introduction of measures to reduce the risk of time poverty (e.g. Geißler et al., 2006; Goodin et al., 2008; Mückenberger, 2011).

A commitment to 'temporalising' sustainability research throws up a number of methodological questions and challenges. What might a future indicator of sustainable time use look like? And what can more conventional social research methodologies such as (time use) surveys and qualitative interviews bring to the debate, given their focus on individuals' self-reported attitudes and behaviour? After all, how people say they use their time does not necessarily correspond to their everyday time practices and their interpretation of them, a fact that has been well documented in the time-use literature (Pentland et al., 1999; Brenner, 2011). It is possible that the growing emphasis in public debate and policy on pro-environmental attitudes and behaviour will increase the social desirability of sustainable lifestyles and thus the reporting of activities associated with such lifestyles (e.g. recycling, buying organic food). This in itself raises important questions about the measurement of attitudes and (self-reported) behaviour and their transformation over time.

Based on these considerations, we would argue that primary social research that connects time and sustainability needs to meet at least three criteria. First and foremost, it needs to be set within a theoretically informed framework that connects social theories of time with contributions from social scientists to current sustainability debates. Recent social-scientific work in the area of sustainable consumption offers interesting starting points because of its inherent interest in material consequences of human actions and their social and political underpinnings (cf. Pape et al., 2011). For example, how people buy, prepare, consume and discard food is inextricably linked to prevailing time-use patterns in society (as well as global systems of food production and marketing). Some of the material consequences of this relationship include the amount of food waste produced per household as well as the availability of certain utensils and appliances for food preparation and their spatial arrangement within the kitchen. The growing popularity of 'wasteful' ready meals and the increasing use of resource-intensive time- and labour-saving devices for food preparation such as microwave ovens exemplify this (see also Jaeger-Erben, Chapter 8 in this volume).

Second, an engagement with questions of time and sustainability also requires concepts of human time use that include both behaviour *and* meanings. The operationalisation and empirical investigation of such complex concepts in turn requires the application of *multi-method approaches* to social research that combine verbalisation and observation and that facilitate creative forms of relational data analysis (cf. Mason, 2002). Both similarities and contradictions between qualitative and quantitative time-use data can offer important insights into how people use their temporal (and material) resources and how they make sense of their own and other people's time-use patterns, which may or may not be culture-specific (Rau, 2004).

Third, we argue that measuring sustainable outcomes requires time-sensitive social research, whose epistemological underpinnings rest on a *long-term approach to the study of human social life* and whose research practice incorporates *longitudinal elements*, either in terms of actual data collection or in their methodological focus, to capture change (see also Jaeger-Erben, Chapter 8 in this volume). For example, much existing time-use research continues to provide quantitative 'snapshots' of human behaviour at certain points in time. Bytheway (2011: 28) argues forcefully that, without a longitudinal dimension, such research fundamentally misconceives what human experience involves. But cross-sectional data such as the 2005 Irish Time Use Survey (McGinnity et al., 2005) remain commonplace and inform time-political debates in many developed (and some developing) countries. Similarly, longitudinal qualitative research on time remains relatively rare. This said, there are plenty of examples of recent research work that have adopted a longer-term perspective, for example by deploying historical analyses, modelling or forecasting. For example, Steinberger and Roberts's (2010) longitudinal analysis of changes in resource consumption measures, HDI scores and other indicators of human development between 1975 and 2005 demonstrates patterns of association between resource use and human flourishing that challenge commonly-held ideas. Their work reveals that increasing resource consumption does not necessarily increase people's living standards, and that a more equitable global distribution of currently available resources would be sufficient to meet human development needs. Although the success (or otherwise) of these longitudinal studies in informing wider sustainability debates remains to be determined, they offer a welcome alternative to more conventional 'snapshot' research work.

However, what has been recognised in many policy circles is that efforts to promote more sustainable patterns of resource consumption can take considerable time to implement, if they are practised at all, and that they therefore require long-term monitoring. This in turn has significant implications with regard to the evaluation of initiatives such as local sustainable transport interventions. Conventional forms of sustainability assessment may need to be either replaced or complemented with innovative longitudinal approaches to interviewing and participant observation, backcasting based on local expertise and secondary analysis of historical data (see Box 9.1). Of course, such a novel approach to sustainability assessment is likely to have considerable financial implications and to provide challenges for decision makers whose position as public representatives is contingent upon re-election every few years (cf. Sprinz 2012). This illustrates the often highly political nature of sustainability assessments, in particular when they involve a rethinking of taken-for-granted approaches to time (Rau, 2008). The next section will focus on ethnography as a form of social research that is closely associated with the investigation of (un)familiar time perspectives and temporal practices and that potentially provides important impulses for the development of time-sensitive approaches to sustainability research and assessment in the future.

---

**Box 9.1   Smart Moves – temporary shift or lasting change in how people travel to work?**

As part of a research project on sustainable consumption, employees of a large firm in the west of Ireland were asked to participate in the *Smart Moves Challenge* (http://smartermovement.org/) and to make their trip to and from work more sustainable by leaving the car at home at least once a week. Nine teams consisting of three members of staff each (n = 27) took part in the competition in spring 2011. Team members were required to self-report their daily travel patterns online, and a winning team was selected based on how many car trips they collectively saved over a period of thirty days. The *Smart Moves Challenge* was accompanied by two waves of data collection, one prior to commencement (T1) and one immediately after the programme had ended (T2). This was intended to capture any changes in how people viewed and carried out their travel to work. A third wave of data collection (T3) took place three to four months after completion to establish whether participants had kept up their new travel practices. Data collection included both qualitative and quantitative interviews and observation. This innovative longitudinal research design recognised the time-related aspects of attitudinal and behavioural change as well as the need to assess the effectiveness of sustainability initiatives over longer periods of time. The *Smart Moves Challenge* was part of a large-scale social research project on household consumption on the island of Ireland (www.consensus.ie).

---

# Benefits and challenges of ethnographic methods: Longitudinality and time

A major advantage of using ethnographic methods in sustainability studies – at least in principle – is that these techniques are intended to trace attitudes and habits which may be too profoundly taken for granted to be easily verbalised by the people who hold them. Much behaviour connected with time, work, consumption and the environment falls into just this category. It can be difficult to access simply by *asking* people: respondents may feel uneasy about adjusting the tempos of their lives to a slower (or a faster) pace, for example, but find it hard to say precisely why. What they do say – 'I wouldn't feel comfortable like that', perhaps – does not necessarily tell us much, and there may be few available conventions for clothing such feelings in more detailed descriptions. Moreover, human behaviour is characteristically social: at least some of the reasons for it derive from interaction with others, or from socially shared and evolved worldviews, rather than solely from individual decisions. This is evidenced, for example, by the dominance of the car over other modes of transport, which has produced social and cultural conventions (as well as economic and infrastructural conditions) that promote car-based mobility across generations and that are proving to be very resistant to sustainability interventions. Hence, the reasons why people engage in particular consumption patterns, for instance, even those which are extremely important to them, such as car-driving, may not be easy for them to divulge. Habits of consumption may arise less from conscious choice and more from membership of interwoven networks of activity, which themselves generate further wants and desires. Being a biker, or a banker, is likely to put someone in a position where given ranges of consumption appear natural. 'It is the fact of engagement in the practice, rather than any personal decision about a course of conduct, that explains the nature and process of consumption' (Warde 2005: 138). In tracking and explicating such complexes of feeling and behaviour, ethnographic methods themselves depend heavily on time. They entail protracted periods of 'participant observation', face-to-face with the people whose attitudes and behaviour are being studied, living their lives as far as possible (Atkinson et al., 2001: 4; Lofland and Lofland, 1984), in order to translate this behaviour into terms that readers can also understand (Asad, 1986/2010).

Practices relating to work, family or everyday living, then, belong to complex fabrics of meaning – which themselves have developed over time, whether among different generations, for example, or within work groups, or in whole subcultures. They make sense to those involved, partly because they expect them to make sense to each other. The ethnographer's task is to spend enough time immersed in the social setting under study not only to discover what its inhabitants do in their everyday lives but to excavate down to the underlying reasons which make it seem reasonable, rewarding or apparently inevitable to them to do it. It is central to such work that it cannot easily be hurried, or even carried out according to a strict time-plan. It is hoped that allowing research-time to be dictated by the subject rather than the researcher in this way will generate insights which may be hard to acquire using speedier methods.

By locating these insights in terms of overall complexes of behaviour, ethnographic methods have the power to explicate aspects of how people adapt to different settings as they go from one to another. It may 'make sense' for someone to conform to speedy, efficient work practices in the office, but the same conduct would appear meaningless or absurd on a kindergarten picnic, making it much less likely to be engaged in. In this way, at least some inconsistencies in behaviour can be explained by restoring to them their social dimensions – a key approach to understanding incongruences between people's expressed desires for more sustainable approaches to living and their actual conduct. The assumptions underlying ethnographic methods do not entail that individuals *cannot* 'downshift' or 'embrace idleness' (see above), but ethnographic analysis offers a powerful and sometimes indispensable approach to identifying some of the problems in the way of their doing so.

Ethnographers tend to be relatively strongly attuned to the ways in which past attitudes impact on current ones in the settings they are studying – where particular positions are 'coming from'. However, closer examination of ethnographic material can show that people's habits and behaviour can be strongly oriented to the *future* as well as the present and past. An example can show that ethnographic study is needed to expose time-trajectories in relation to the environment which operate in a different way from what their 'surface' expressions would seem to imply. Edmondson (2000) studied attitudes to time among farmers in the west of Ireland, showing that reluctance to embark on precipitate change is not necessarily the same as conservatism. Farmers here were in fact relatively quick to change their policies or techniques if they considered it reasonable. Their verbal expressions might, in effect as a form of shorthand, refer to the past – 'That's not how things were always done.' But responses like this can be intended to refer to the fruits of experience, rather than offering a literally historical reason for action. Subsistence farmers could not afford to take unnecessary risks, for they seldom possessed financial bulwarks in case of disaster; but their concerns were not to show respect for past traditions, rather to preserve their crops in the *future*.

Ethnographic approaches involving participant observation are not hermetically sealed from other methods. Crate (2006), for instance, uses perspectives from political and cultural ecology, geography and environmental studies among others to connect discourses about global sustainability with her ethnography of a Siberian people attempting to adapt to sudden change thrust onto their lifestyle by outside forces. Or, in the example from Ireland mentioned above, documentary methods could usefully supply details of changing forms of land use. Interviews – when the interviewer is sufficiently au fait with local usage to conduct them effectively – supply detailed histories which could be interpreted in the light of local knowledge. What is less often emphasised, even by ethnographers, is the need to explore all relevant time-dimensions of the attitudes and behaviour in particular settings. Ethnographers, first, may fail to explore rigorously all that their observations could tell us about time-related views and behaviour; like other social scientists, they may simply omit to take an interest in time, or focus only on selected aspects (such as seasonality or responses to imposed change). Second, partly as a consequence, they may fail to notice the ways in which respondents' views themselves develop. Exceptions include studies of environmental *movements* and community changes such as Finn's (1998) account of the effects of a strike in the 1960s on later events in a copper-mining community (see also Garavan, Chapter 4 in this volume). This dimension is crucial in relation to sustainability, where views may develop and change relatively fast. An example is taken from the words of an environmental scientist who had, at the time of the interview, worked for three years on a permaculture farm in the Middle East.

> I used to think more like a top-down person. When I started working in the water sector I really believed you needed a centralised system, because if you let people use any water they like they'll over-draw the aquifers. I still think you need someone to manage the system. But the more you get into it, the more you can see that the people who really have power here are the people who use the resources all the time. Everyone can preserve water, or stop using bleach. If you add up all this power it's far more effective than walking in with 20 million and putting in a massive system. The power of individuals is more important. (Interview by R. Edmondson, 27 March 2011)

First, note that time, and constant interaction with farmers, has changed the speaker's view of what sustainability is and how it can be achieved. Second, her current meaning actually binds time and sustainability together. She no longer defines sustainability as a set of abstract principles, but thinks in terms of the people who might carry it out over time. Third, the type of time-related human agency she associates with sustainability has changed: we are not dealing with action involving schematic, technical approaches to time, but with an 'inhabited' form of time. Moreover, the agents whose timescales she has in mind here include natural as well as human ones. In the rest of the interview, the speaker says a great deal about the people she is working with, their daily struggles to make a living, and how they see the world. She says, 'They work to a different timescale here. Everyone plants trees, it's like an investment in the future, everyone values trees. They're still living off trees planted by their great-grandparents, and understand the value of leaving trees for their great-grandchildren.' 'Trees are one of the most powerful symbols here,' living proof that farmers own their land and are tending it. 'Trees are fabulous. They outlive us and stay on in the environment and provide so many possibilities for so many people.' These may be views about sustainability which the speaker would not have voiced during the phase in her life-course when she worked as a scientist. This is not to imply that her views of sustainability have necessarily changed *solely* in response to her personal experiences as they have evolved in the course of interacting with new people and predicaments. Broader social assumptions about sustainability are also constantly changing, providing fluid networks of opinion which inform behaviour in different ways. But nor are this speaker's conceptual changes *simply* conceptual: they mean that she behaves in many different ways whose ramifications need to be explored empirically. A range of other viewpoints and ways of acting will now make sense to her although they did not before, while positions she formerly saw as reasonable will no longer seem so.

These observations underline the need for ethnographers to be highly conscious of time in their work, in a variety of senses. They need to be attuned to its implications both about the ways in which time-related features are bound into people's behaviour, and to the ways in which the passing of time produces changes in the attitudes and behaviour of those they are studying. Even though ethnographic methods are intrinsically longitudinal in the sense that they take longer to practise than do most others, they do not always set out to study change longitudinally (Simonton, 2010). Repeat studies in ethnography are relatively rare, partly because of this method's own time-consuming nature; but this can have the unintended effect that ethnographic accounts may 'preserve in aspic' the versions of social settings they produce (Clifford and Marcus, 2010; cf. Fabian, 1983; Adkins, 2011). It would be particularly important to avoid this in relation to sustainability studies, which make constant mention of changes in environmental and related opinions over recent decades. Ethnographic methods could in the future be highly significant in understanding these changes further.

## Discussion and Conclusion

While it would be hard to deny the centrality of time in sustainability research and debate, nonetheless it is often overlooked. As this chapter has revealed, time-sensitive approaches to inter- and transdisciplinary sustainability research still demand further development. We have also indicated some of the issues that need to be recast in such a way as to emphasise their relationships to time and to outline some of the methods than can be adopted in exploring them. Examples of time-use survey research and time-sensitive ethnography used in this chapter demonstrate the relevance of these two major social research methods to sustainability research. Their application in various settings and disciplinary fields reveals diverse and at times conflicting time perspectives among both researchers and researched. As we were able to show, effective engagement with time-related issues requires awareness of these differences (as well as similarities), in particular in the context of interdisciplinary projects where diametrically opposed views about human society, sustainability and the nature of society–environment relations may come to the fore and even clash during the research process. Interestingly, such clashes and incompatibilities may not always be recognised by those involved, which suggests that interdisciplinarity itself is more often acclaimed as an aspiration than observed in a thoroughgoing and theoretically aware manner. On the other hand, there have been some significant theoretical and methodological developments in trans- and postdisciplinary research whose advocates promote greater reflexivity and engagement with the philosophical and ethical underpinnings of research into human and non-human worlds. This is beginning to shape the sustainability research landscape in fundamental ways, albeit rather slowly, and may aid the integration of time-related topics in the future.

Other remaining problems with regard to the 'temporalisation' of sustainability research include the question how time-related methods are to be integrated both with each other and with other approaches in this radically interdisciplinary field. As far as methods are concerned, it is rare to find examples of empirical research (whether or not connected with sustainability) which show an equal understanding of both qualitative and quantitative methods and their implications. As far as integrating methods derived from different disciplines is concerned, there are genuine conflicts of interest to be overcome. The models of human behaviour which different disciplines embrace and the types of explanation they think appropriate for it are sometimes in genuine conflict and cannot simply be amalgamated without further ado.

Sustainability transitions can take a long time to materialise and become observable, which makes them difficult to capture using 'snapshot' approaches to research. This has significant implications for future sustainability research, especially with regard to medium- to long-term funding. It also means that hasty political decisions made today, perhaps even with sustainability goals in mind, can produce unintended outcomes at a much later stage. Human–environment interactions that were deemed 'safe' 20 or 30 years ago have been shown to be seriously disruptive for people and planet. Lessons need to be learned about how to furnish sustainability research to ensure that long-term consequences are discovered and that timely action is taken to mitigate their impact, especially on vulnerable social groups and natural habitats.

One of the main contributions that more time-sensitive approaches can make is to highlight the intrinsically time-bound nature of sustainability research itself and to challenge more traditional, linear notions of 'progress' in human knowledge, understanding and expertise that often (not always) dominate the field. We do not claim that it will always be easy to add time-dimensions to the mixture of approaches needed to explore and promote issues relating to sustainability. But we hope that, besides being – we believe – necessary, examining the operation of time, and views, habits, structures and practices associated with time will prove illuminating to this field.

## Note

1  http://www.ciw.ca/en/TheCanadianIndexOfWellbeing.aspx (accessed 15 August 2011).

# References

Adam, B. (1996) 'Re-vision: the centrality of time for an ecological social science perspective', in S. Lash, B. Szerszynski and B. Wynne (eds), *Risk, Environment and Modernity: Towards a New Ecology*. London: Sage. pp. 84–103.

Adam, B. (1998) *Timescapes of Modernity*. London: Routledge.

Adam, B. (2009) 'Zeit ist Geld: Geschwindigkeit aus zeitökonomischer und zeitökologischer Sicht'. Paper presented at the conference Jenseits der Beschleunigung. Zeitpolitische Perspektiven postfossiler Mobilität, 30 April–2 May 2009, Evangelische Akademie Tutzing, Germany.

Adkins, L. (2011) 'Practice as temporalisation: Bourdieu and economic crisis', in B. Turner and S. Susen (eds), *The Legacy of Pierre Bourdieu*. London: Anthem Press. pp. 347–365.

Atkinson, P., Coffey, A., Delamont, S., Lofland, J. and Lofland, L. (eds) (2001) 'Editorial introduction', in *Handbook of Ethnography*. London: Sage. pp. 1–7.

Asad, T. (1986/2010) 'The concept of cultural translation in British social anthropology', in J. Clifford and G. Marcus (eds), *Writing Culture: The Poetics and Politics of Ethnography*, 2nd edn. Berkeley, CA: University of California Press. pp. 141–65.

Ausubel, J. and Grübler, A. (1995) 'Working less and living longer: long-term trends in working time and time budgets', *Technological Forecasting and Social Change*, 50 (3): 195–213.

Baars, J. (2007) 'Introduction: chronological time and chronological age: problems of temporal diversity', in J. Baars and H. Visser (eds), *Aging and Time*. Amityville, NY: Baywood. pp.15–42.

Beder, S. (2004) 'Consumerism: an historical perspective', *Pacific Ecologist*, 9 (1): 42–8.

Brenner, P.S. (2011) 'Exceptional behavior or exceptional identity? Overreporting of church attendance in the US', *Public Opinion Quarterly*, 75 (1): 19–41.

Bytheway, B. (2011) *Unmasking Age: The Significance of Age for Social Research*. Bristol: Policy Press.

Clifford, J. and Marcus, G. (eds) (2010) *Writing Culture: The Poetics and Politics of Ethnography*, 2nd edn. Berkeley, CA: University of California Press.

Coote, A., Franklin, J. and Simms, A. (2010) *21 hours: Why a Shorter Working Week can Help us All to Flourish in the 21st Century*. London: New Economics Foundation.

Crate, S. (2006) *Cows, Kin and Globalization: An Ethnography of Sustainability*. Lanham, MD: AltaMira Press.

Edmondson, R. (2000) 'Rural temporal practices: future time in Connemara', *Time and Society*, 9 (2/3): 269–88.

Edmondson, R. and Rau, H. (2008) 'Introduction: environmental arguing and interculturality', in R. Edmondson and H. Rau (eds), *Environmental Argument and Cultural Difference: Locations, Fractures and Deliberations*. Oxford: Peter Lang. pp. 11–34.

Elias, N. (1984) *Über die Zeit*. Frankfurt am Main : Suhrkamp.

Fabian, J. (1983) *Time and the Other: How Anthropology Makes its Object*. New York: Columbia University Press.

Finn, J. (1998) *Tracing the Veins: Of Copper, Culture and Community from Butte to Chuquicamata*. Berkeley, CA: University of California Press.

Geißler, K., Kümmerer, K. and Sabelis, I. (eds) (2006) *Zeitvielfalt: Wider das Diktat der Uhr*. Stuttgart: Hirzel.

Gilleard, C. and Higgs, P. (2002) 'The third age: class, cohort or generation?' *Ageing and Society*, 22 (3): 369–82.

Goodin, R.E., Mahmud Rice, J., Parpo, A. and Eriksson, L. (eds) (2008) *Discretionary Time: A New Measure of Freedom*. Cambridge: Cambridge University Press.

Hirsch Hadorn, G., Hoffmann-Riem, H., Biber-Klemm, S., Grossenbacher-Mansuy, W., Joye, D., Pohl, C., Wiesmann, U. and Zemp, E. (eds) (2008) *Handbook of Transdisciplinary Research*. Dordrecht: Springer.

Hirsch Hadorn, G., Bradley, D., Pohl, C., Rist, S. and Wiesmann, U. (2006) 'Implications of transdisciplinarity for sustainability research', *Ecological Economics*, 60 (1): 119–28.

Jackson, T. (2008) 'The challenge of sustainable lifestyles', in The Worldwatch Institute (ed.) *State of the World: Innovations for a Sustainable Economy*. London: The Worldwatch Institute. pp. 45–60. Available from http://courses.umass.edu/plnt397s/SustainableLiving.pdf (accessed 12 August 2011).

Jackson, T. (2009) *Prosperity without growth?* London: Sustainable Development Commission.

Lofland, J. and Lofland, L. (1984) *Analyzing Social Settings*, 2nd edn. Belmont, CA: Wadsworth.

Mason, J. (2002) *Qualitative Researching*, 2nd edn. London: Sage.

McGinnity, F., Russell, H., Williams, J. and Blackwell, S. (2005) *Time Use in Ireland 2005: Survey Report*. Dublin: ESRI.

Mückenberger, U. (2011) 'Local time policies in Europe', *Time and Society*, 20 (2): 241–73.

New Economics Foundation (2009) *The Happy Planet Index 2.0: Why Good Lives Don't Have to Cost the Earth*. London: NEF.

Ott, K. (2009) 'On substantiating the conception of strong sustainability', in R. Döring (ed.) *Sustainability, Natural Capital and Nature Conservation*. Marburg: Metropolis Verlag. pp. 49–72.

Pape, J., Rau, H., Fahy, F. and Davies, A. (2011) 'Developing policies and instruments for sustainable household consumption: Irish experiences and futures', *Journal of Consumer Policy*, 34 (1): 25–42.

Pentland, W., Harvey, A.S., Powell Lawton, C. and Mc Call, M.A. (1999) *The Application of Time-use Methodology in the Social Sciences*. New York: Plenum.

Peters, P.F. (2005) 'Exchanging travel speed: time politics in mobility practices', *Configurations*, 13 (3): 395–419.

Pillarisetti, J.R. and van den Bergh, J.C.J.M. (2010) 'Sustainable nations: what do aggregate indexes tell us?', *Environment, Development and Sustainability*, 12 (1): 49–62.

Rau, H. (2004) Time perspectives and temporal practices: a cross-cultural, comparative study of time cultures in Ireland and Germany. Ph.D. thesis, National University of Ireland, Galway.

Rau, H. (2008) 'Environmental arguing at a crossroads? Cultural diversity in Irish transport planning', in R. Edmondson and H. Rau (eds), *Environmental Argument and Cultural Difference: Locations, Fractures and Deliberations*. Oxford: Peter Lang. pp. 95–124.

Schor, J. (2010) *Plenitude: The New Economics of True Wealth*. New York: The Penguin Press.

Shove, E., Trentmann, F. and Wilk, R. (eds) (2009) *Time, Consumption and Everyday Life: Practice, Materiality and Culture*. Oxford: Berg.

Simonton, M. (2010) Ageing as navigating the life course: a longitudinal social–anthropological exploration in the west of Ireland. Ph.D. Thesis, National University of Ireland, Galway.

Sprinz, D.F. (2012) 'Long-term environmental policy: challenges for research', *The Journal of Environment and Development*, 21 (1): 67–70.

Steinberger, J.K. and Roberts, J.T. (2010) 'From constraint to sufficiency: the decoupling of energy and carbon from human needs, 1975–2005', *Ecological Economics*, 70: 425–33.

Wajcman, J. (2008) 'Life in the fast lane? Towards a sociology of technology and time', *The British Journal of Sociology*, 59 (1): 59–77.

Warde, A. (2005) 'Consumption and theories of practice', *Journal of Consumer Culture*, 5 (2): 131–53.

World Commission on Environment and Development (1987) *Our Common Future: A Global Agenda for Change*. Oxford: Oxford University Press.

# PART V

## Current Developments and Future Trends

# 10

## Researching Complex Sustainability Issues: Reflections on current challenges and future developments

### *Frances Fahy and Henrike Rau*

Undoubtedly, sustainability research has gained considerable momentum in recent times in both the natural and social sciences, partly because academics, policy makers and the public have grown increasingly aware of pressing social and environmental problems. This rapid transformation of the research landscape has coincided with significant changes in institutional structures, funding opportunities and research training. As detailed in our introductory chapter, whether or not one agrees with the dominant sustainable development agenda, it is evident that its adoption has promoted the social-scientific investigation of human development and its environmental causes and consequences.

Arguments for and against empirically researching human social life and related methodological questions concerning the 'what' and 'how' are central to the development of the social sciences more generally, and social-scientific sustainability research in particular. This suggests that questions of methodology not only relate to practical matters, i.e. how to best carry out a specific project, but also reflect broader questions about the logic of research per se. As outlined by the various authors throughout this volume, one encounters *specific* challenges that go beyond discussions about the nature of social research. These emerge whenever attempts are made to investigate people, societies *and* their biophysical and material environments through tailored social-scientific or interdisciplinary approaches. Efforts to integrate indicators of human development and measures of resource use discussed in Part III of this collection, emphasise the difficulties of capturing economic, social and environmental trends in an integrated manner.

But what makes sustainability research different from other types of social research? And what might the future of the field look like, given current developments outlined both in the introduction and in various contributions to this book? This concluding chapter critically examines the distinctive position of sustainability research at the interface between academic inquiry and policy. Drawing on all contributions to the collection, the remainder of this chapter will focus on three key aspects of the research process which are directly shaped by this position: (1) the development of a theoretical framework and its translation into research questions, (2) methodological choices, and (3) the production and dissemination of research findings.

Initially, we will critically discuss conceptual opportunities and challenges that arise from a commitment to policy-relevant research that aims to provide concrete solutions to real-world sustainability problems. Social scientists working on sustainability issues are frequently required to engage in debates on the role, purpose and nature of (social) science and its ontological and epistemological foundations and to defend their own position against those in more established fields of research. Similarly, limitations exist with regard to the introduction and adoption of new terminology and concepts, partly because diverse audiences have very different communication cultures, needs and expectations that may or may not be open to change. We consider to what extent the desire to be policy-relevant requires researchers to compromise in terms of both their theoretical outlook and their conceptual orientations.

Subsequently, we will consider how some new and innovative methodological approaches to sustainability research can challenge common perceptions of what constitutes 'proper science' that exist among fellow academics, policy makers, sustainability practitioners and members of the public. Here we will draw on our own experiences conducting research on sustainable consumption as well as those detailed in this collection.

Balancing the need to produce scientific knowledge with the increasing demands for evidence-based policy presents major opportunities and challenges for those engaged in sustainability research, particularly in relation to how results are generated and distributed. The need to appeal to diverse audiences requires sustainability researchers to develop innovative and sophisticated dissemination strategies that may or may not fit within established work practices in a university context. In this section we question the nature of knowledge and its transmission in society.

The concluding section summarises possible directions for the conceptual and methodological development of social-scientific sustainability research in the future.

# Reflections on the opportunities and challenges of policy-relevant sustainability research

Over the past two decades there has been increasing pressure on academics to demonstrate the value and impact of what they do. Importantly, there has been a marked shift towards policy-relevant research that meets the expectations of various policy actors and communities. It is increasingly expected that academic research must produce concrete and directly implementable answers to 'real-world problems' such as over- and underdevelopment and environmental degradation. National governments across Europe, for example, have set ambitious targets for public research funding bodies to demonstrate the impact or application of their research (see Gibbons et al., 1994; EEA, 2005). While this emphasis on policy relevance has proven beneficial in many respects, including increased awareness of and funding for sustainability research that engages with relevant policy communities, significant drawbacks have emerged at the same time. As academics actively involved in the field of sustainability research, all authors in this volume are acutely aware of the demands for, as well as of, policy-relevant work. In this section we will critically reflect on some of the opportunities and challenges that they face in their research.

Contributions to this book more or less explicitly point towards three key aspects of the research process that are impacted by the desire to produce findings that are relevant to policy makers and other non-academic audiences: (1) the formulation of research questions and their theoretical underpinnings, (2) the methodological design of a study, and (3) research outputs and their dissemination. Drawing on our experience of working for the Irish Environmental Protection Agency on a project investigating sustainable consumption in households across the island of Ireland (see Box 10.1) as well as on the various chapters in this edited collection, the following subsections aim to present some critical reflections on the implications of embarking on policy-relevant research for these three aspects. Where appropriate, we will connect our own observations to points made elsewhere in this collection.

## Box 10.1   Undertaking policy-relevant sustainability research for Ireland's EPA: Introducing the ConsEnSus project

The ConsEnSus (Consumption, Environment and Sustainability) project is a four-year large-scale project (2009–2013) and it is the first of its kind to explore at sustainable consumption on the island of Ireland; in both Northern Ireland and the Republic of Ireland. The project involves eight researchers with expertise in the fields of geography, information technology, political science, psychology and sociology. Research is divided between two leading universities in the Republic of Ireland, Trinity College Dublin and National University of Ireland, Galway. The project was awarded as part of the Science, Technology, Research and Innovation for the Environment (STRIVE) Programme 2007–2013, which is financed by the Irish Government under the National Development Plan. It is administered on behalf of the Department of the Environment, Heritage and Local Government by the Environmental Protection Agency (EPA) which has the statutory function of coordinating and promoting environmental research.

The research proposal for ConsEnSus project was submitted in 2008 in response to a socio-environmental call from the EPA to investigate household sustainable consumption in Ireland. There was no prescriptive research design outlined by the funding agency. However, given the urgent need for research in this topical field, one of the key outputs of this research was to make recommendations for local and national sustainable consumption policies. Other key aims of the ConsEnSus Project include:

- gathering of baseline data for Ireland in the areas of transport, energy, water and food
- reviewing of key issues for sustainable consumption of measurement, evaluation, behavioural analysis, quality of life and governance
- facilitating cooperation between stakeholders involved in consumption practices (e.g., regulators, businesses, consumers, civil society organisations); and
- establishing an international Sustainable Consumption Research Network.

The interdisciplinary approach adopted for the ConsEnSus Project draws on a mixture of conventional and innovative research methodologies, including surveys, interviews, participatory action research and visioning techniques.*

The advisory board for the project is composed of international researchers in the field of sustainable consumption as well as representatives of state and semi-state agencies responsible for policy development in the fields of energy, food, water and transport (www.consensus.ie)

*For a detailed description of these methods see Davies et al. (2011) and for an overview of the overall project see www.consensus.ie

## Theoretical and conceptual challenges: Developing research questions for policy-relevant research

The merits of conducting policy-relevant research have been well catalogued over the past decade (for good reviews see Ward, 2005 or Pain, 2006). Similarly, there is an extensive body of literature extolling researchers' hostility towards policy research (see Allen and Imrie, 2010 for a review). While it is clearly beyond the remit of this chapter to reiterate these debates, it is nevertheless useful to critically assess some of the conceptual implications of a commitment to policy relevance. To what extent is there a reduction in conceptual complexity that affects what kind of questions can be explored in the context of research? What are the effects of policy-relevant expectations on academic freedom and integrity? These and related considerations clearly point towards the *need for compromise* when undertaking such research, a topic which has hitherto been noticeably absent from discussions in the field. Contributions to this collection point, more or less explicitly, to the tensions between what kinds of questions sustainability researchers can meaningfully ask and their attempts to contribute to policy development.

Existing debates about the merits and demerits of policy-relevant research frequently remain rather narrow and one-sided. According to Woods and Gardner (2011), many discussions to date regarding policy relevance have tended to either imply, more or less explicitly, that being policy-relevant and maintaining critical integrity is relatively unproblematic (see Murphy, 2006), or else have emphasised the value of alternative forms of policy making, for example, participatory research and activism outside of academia (see Pain and Francis, 2003). More nuanced debates are needed that address the role of power and participation in social-scientific sustainability research and decision making.

To what extent does an (over)emphasis on policy relevance bring about a *reduction in complexity* with regard to choice of research topics and their conceptual and theoretical underpinnings? As Sharp et al. note, there has been a trend towards claims to know the world and to provide 'reliable rules of thumb through which policy makers can see what is important' (2011: 505). When designing the research questions for ConsEnSus (see Box 10.1), the researchers had to debate and discuss the framing of the concept of sustainable consumption. This occurred in the context of a funding organisation that traditionally supported natural science research and had limited experience in supporting and managing large-scale social-science projects. Faced with the issue of responding to what is widely perceived to be a pressing policy problem caused by individuals' unsustainable material practices, one of the primary aims of the project is to explore how a shift towards more sustainable consumption might be encouraged, measured and governed. In this respect, the remit of this project reflects the traditional patterns in policy-relevant research that prioritise the issue of measurement over theory building and conceptual explorations. The ConsEnSus project addresses issues in household consumption that emerged from recent national and international policy documents (European Commission, 2004; EPA, 2006) as well as international research (see Seyfang, 2006 for a review).

In this context it was essential to balance commonly-held notions of consumption as an economically necessary, but environmentally problematic, activity carried out by individual householders, with concepts that emphasised its wider social and cultural significance, its multiscalar effects and its structural root causes. The resulting challenges of integrating conflicting conceptual and theoretical frameworks within a single research project are also dealt within a number of chapters in this book. Khoo's account in Chapter 5 of the evolution of development indicators, away from narrow economistic measures towards more inclusive indices that integrate economic, social and environmental dimensions, exemplifies this. Her chapter demonstrates how hegemonic conceptual and methodological frameworks can be highly resistant to change, partly because they are firmly embedded in policy and decision-making arenas. The danger of perpetuating, rather than challenging, established ways of thinking about and measuring sustainability remains a critical issue for sustainability researchers and their audiences (cf. Cohen 2006).[1]

## Between convention and innovation: Combining methodological approaches

Regarding the key methodological implications of undertaking policy-relevant sustainability research, we reflected in the opening chapter on the persistent dominance of quantitative approaches to data collection and analysis in this field. In fact, numerous authors have highlighted that policy actors tend to prefer large-scale quantitative studies based on representative samples, that is, work that is easy to replicate, over qualitative approaches which are often perceived as 'soft' and 'not rigorous'. This emphasis on quantification is also mirrored in public debates and policy discourses that prioritise *directly measurable aspects of resource efficiency, material consumption and environmental degradation* such as noise pollution (cf. Murphy and King, Chapter 7 in this volume), water and air quality, energy use in the home, or fuel consumption in the transport sector. In Chapter 2 of this volume Barr and Prillwitz clearly show the merits and drawbacks of quantitatively measuring individual pro-environmental behaviour, the promotion of which forms a central pillar of many sustainability efforts today. They are particularly concerned about the potential decontextualisation of these measurements whereby social and environmental drivers of human behaviour are largely ignored and individuals are studied in isolation from the wider sociocultural, political and material context they find themselves in.

While critiquing the bias towards quantification in sustainability research, it is nevertheless important to recognise the significance of large data sets for a critically inspired, progressively orientated research agenda. For example, the ConsEnSus project introduced earlier in this chapter rests on a large-scale survey of 1500 households on the island of Ireland that explores lifestyles and everyday consumption practices. This was done with a view to recording baseline behavioural data in key areas of consumption that impact directly on the environment (see Pape et al. 2011). This survey was complemented with a review of international good practice for governing sustainable consumption as well as a critical assessment of Ireland's performance in this area. Both the large-scale ConsEnSus survey and the cataloguing of good practice examples serve to accommodate policy actors' requirements for – 'solid' data. However, combining these rather conventional approaches to data collection and analysis with four exploratory studies that deployed novel participatory methods ensured a balance between methodological innovation and funders' requirements.

Many complex socio-ecological phenomena such as linkages between place, landscape and identity or cultural meanings of consumption practices frequently occupy a much less prominent position in public debate, policy making and on research programmes such as the European Union's Framework Programme, partly because they tend to resist immediate testing and quantification. Moreover, it is often the case that social relations are crucial to the formation, perpetuation and decay of such linkages between society and the physical environment. These and related issues have significant consequences for the choice of methodology as well as decisions regarding research design. It is argued here that many sustainability-related research questions could best be answered by looking at groups and networks rather than individuals. This, however, requires particular types of methodologies that are able to capture social linkages and synergy effects. Anna Davies' contribution (Chapter 3) on focus group research clearly demonstrates the importance of social interaction and types of engagement for the formation and development of sustainability thinking, discourse and practices.

Breaking down complex problems into smaller, more manageable sub-problems also remains a strong trend in many areas of sustainability research. Even though one of the goals of sustainability research is to promote integrated thinking and a holistic perspective, the realities of designing projects adheres to the convention of breaking them down into discrete 'work packages' that may or may not be (re-)integrated during the research. The creation of sectoral 'silos' within sustainability projects, whereby different dimensions of human resource use such as energy and water consumption are dealt with separately, exemplifies a dominant trend. In the context of ConsEnSus this is certainly discernable; mechanisms to link and integrate different work packages have been incorporated into its design. For example, the collection of baseline consumption data for four key sectors (water, food, energy and transport) that are subsequently fed into the different work packages has been one of the cornerstones of the project.

Innovative relational analyses of qualitative findings from different work packages feature strongly in ConsEnSus project plan.

Another key issue to consider in the initial stages of project planning is the time frame of the study, with cross-sectional designs favoured over longitudinal designs because the former are perceived to pose fewer practical and financial problems. In addition, given the limited time frame adopted for many of these projects and, indeed, the topical nature of the subject under investigation, policy makers often indicate a clear preference for research designs that deliver results quickly. Researchers can have a difficult time attempting to balance the demands of a rapid turnaround of results with the growing workloads of academics in university environments. Academics are often accused of offering 'too-complex views, too-time-consuming methods, too-contingent conclusions' (Bell 2011: 217).

Given the *centrality of time* in sustainability thinking, policy and research that has been detailed in Chapter 9 in this collection, this emphasis on short-term fact delivery of research results appears to undermine efforts to mitigate short-termism in research policy and practice. Rau and Edmondson argue that growing engagement with the topic of time among those interested in sustainability questions has yet to be matched by more time-sensitive designs and research methods. This is particularly relevant in relation to impact assessment studies which have to deal with the fact that the economic, social and environmental consequences of today's policy decisions may only become visible many years from now. Similarly, it seems difficult to adequately evaluate the effectiveness (or otherwise) of sustainability programmes such as information campaigns to promote sustainable consumption without adopting a long-term view. In Chapter 8 of this collection Melanie Jaeger-Erben clearly demonstrates some of these time-related issues which affect the investigation of daily practices around food preparation and mobility and their potential transformation towards sustainability. Nevertheless, much policy-relevant research in the area of sustainable consumption remains firmly wedded to cross-sectional designs that yield large amounts of data in a short space of time.

More generally, a key dilemma inherent in the arguments made for policy-relevant research is that there is an assumption that the relevance (or otherwise) of the work is known from the very inception of the project – and this is often not the case. The trajectory of a research project is contingent upon historical conditions and contemporary events, including learning processes among all relevant parties. As noted by Ward (2005: 315), while 'a commissioned piece of work might not end up being relevant in the sense that it was envisaged', another piece of research that initially appeared unlikely to generate relevant findings might end up being used in the most unlikely of circumstances.

Another methodological issue that deserves attention in this context is the question of scale. Barr and Prillwitz's plea for survey-based sustainability assessment to move beyond the household level and to explore 'alternative sites of practice' reveal the importance of different socio-geographical scales (Chapter 2). Here, conventional distinctions in the social science literature between micro-, meso- and macro-level social phenomena (and associated concepts and theories) offer a point for discussion. Traditionally, work on meso-level phenomena has been overshadowed by research focusing on both the micro and macro level. Organisation and community studies remain on the margins of sustainability research in the social sciences, with work on individual attitudes, motives and behaviour and studies of national and international sustainability performance dominating the field. A strong focus on institutions and organisations such as large employers (meso-scale) formed a central element of the transport and mobilities sub-project within ConsEnSus (see Chapter 9 for details).

Detailed case studies are an increasingly popular choice of research design because they can shed light on social structures, processes and inter-relations between different social groups that would otherwise remain invisible (cf. Flyvbjerg, 2004). This is particularly evident in the context of social and environmental protests where individual cases can reveal specific conditions that influence their outcomes, at least to some degree. In Chapter 4 Mark Garavan offers some reflections on how best to investigate a specific case of local resistance to a socially and ecologically disruptive gas project. His contribution to this collection clearly shows the merits and demerits of case study research for both participants and researcher.

On the other hand, as detailed throughout this book, opportunities for multi-method research and methodological innovation have been a key feature of sustainability research. In fact, many of the contributions to this volume have highlighted the benefits of developing and deploying innovative methodological approaches, partly because they may challenge expectations among many policy makers about *how* research should be conducted. Similarly, serious gaps remain between verbal commitments to inter- or transdisciplinarity as part of funding applications and actual evidence of successful disciplinary integration, for example through relational data analysis and innovative presentation of findings (cf. Hirsch Hadorn et al., 2008; also Chapters 1 and 6 in this collection). This reflects an ongoing commitment among policy makers and researchers to established ways of conducting research and implementing findings through policy. Backcasting workshops conducted in the ConsEnSus project to develop verbal and visual scenarios for heating, washing and eating in 2050 and to find ways to achieve them illustrate the potential benefits, as well as drawbacks, of adopting such innovative methods. It remains to be seen whether policy makers in Ireland and internationally will be prepared to accept both qualitative and quantitative data that are collected using novel cross-disciplinary methodologies such as backcasting and visioning.

Many researchers have expounded the challenges of persuading policy makers of the value of particular techniques (for a good review see Burgess,

2005). As Burgess (2005: 277) reflects on 30 years of policy-relevant research, 'persuading them [policy makers] to contemplate the idea of qualitative research and then, even more riskily from their perspectives, to use the evidence from qualitative research studies in decision making has been a real challenge'. Overall, the need to bridge the gap in expectations with regard to suitable methodologies between those who research sustainability issues and those who are tasked with developing sustainable development policies remains a considerable challenge (cf. Cohen 2006).

## Making an impact? Sustainability-research outputs and dissemination of results

The expectation to produce research outputs that are relevant to those who draft and implement policy responses is another inherent feature of much sustainability research in the social sciences. Indeed the European Commission's (2006a) White Paper on Communication states that the scientific community has a duty to share its newfound knowledge with a broader public. However, this raises pressing questions about academic freedom and professional integrity, the distribution of power in the realms of science and policy making as well as about the nature of knowledge itself. Who decides what counts as acceptable evidence? Are actors in the policy-making arena really willing to either radically reform existing policy if evidence is produced that these measures are either ineffective or counterproductive? After all, social scientists may only be willing to compromise on aspects of their academic freedom and voluntarily limit their conceptual and methodological choices if they are able to see a real, tangible impact of their work on relevant policy fields.

Interestingly, demands with regard to research outcomes often emerge *during* a project rather than being set out explicitly at the beginning (Ward, 2005). It may be very difficult to gauge or anticipate an audience's interest in the research findings and subsequently incorporate enough time into the project design for appropriate dissemination. In the same vein, anticipatory budgeting for extensive dissemination of research results at the project's inception may prove problematic.

Occasionally, emerging tensions between those who produce the findings and those who are expected to implement them force all involved to clearly spell out their expectations and reservations, which may or may not occur in a constructive and amicable atmosphere. As Rau and Edmondson illustrate in Chapter 9 in this volume, there are often divergent views among interested parties involved in sustainability projects regarding how much time it takes to bring about change that is beneficial for local people and the environment.

The need to reach a wide and varied audience and related demands to meet a number of divergent goals, can present a daunting task. For example, the European Commission's recent publication *Communicating research for evidence-based policymaking* (2010) outlines five key priorities that socio-economic sciences policy makers expect to have met. These range from the provision of valid and timely evidence and the identification of major trends and potential challenges to improved measurement capabilities and evaluation of policy effectiveness (European Commission, 2010: 20). Researchers frequently encounter challenges when attempting to coordinate the dissemination of research findings among audiences with different skill sets and degrees of engagement. The need to appeal to policy makers, practitioners, publics and academic audiences can create tensions over terminology used, visual representation of results, or the choice of media used to publicise data.

The most traditional method of research dissemination is via peer-reviewed publishing, and academics in the field of sustainability acknowledge that this is a critical outlet and an essential demand on active researchers. These publications enable sustainability researchers to share experiences, success and approaches to sustainability research and problem solving (Wiek et al., 2011). However, increasing pressure on researchers to demonstrate the value of what they do in terms of contributions to public policy is juxtaposed with the growing recognition of the relative inaccessibility of this traditional research outlet (scientific journals) to wider audiences. The ongoing dominance of relatively conventional forms of presentation in the sustainability literature, including the rather uncritical incentivisation of single-authored, peer-reviewed articles in discipline-specific, high-ranking journals fuelled by academic performance metrics illustrates this disjuncture between vision and practice.

This said, the availability of more innovative and accessible communication tools such as online fora and social media has opened new and fruitful avenues for effective dissemination of research findings to audiences outside the realm of academia. In addition to international peer-reviewed journal articles, ConsEnSus team members presented at academic and practitioner workshops and conferences, delivered oral and poster presentations and produced policy reports and factsheets. Public dissemination of research findings to date include the production of press releases, monthly online newsletters, interviews with local and national radio stations, public seminars, on-street research stands, as well as an interactive exhibition in a national science gallery. Such dissemination, while time-consuming and challenging, can clearly provide opportunities by opening up spaces for communication.

Increasingly, state bodies and other research funders require detailed dissemination plans and actors like the European Commission have published a plethora of guidelines for disseminating research, including *Communicating science – a scientist's survival kit* (2006b) and *Communicating research for evidence-based policymaking – a practical guide for researchers in socio-economic sciences and humanities* (2010). National funding agencies, such as the Irish EPA (2011) are encouraging the production of short synthesis reports and practitioners' guides or policy briefs, in addition to the traditional extended end-of-project reports. The rationale behind the call for accessible summary statements rather than lengthy reports implies consideration of policy makers' limited time. The suggestion regarding brevity outlined in the European Commission guidance document illustrates this: 'Bear in mind the possibility that some members of your policymaking audience may skim the brief or read only the first page before delegating the task of detailed examination' (European Commission, 2010: 16).

Some academic literature in the field of sustainability research examines the virtues of undertaking wide dissemination of research results, and a large number of studies focus on attempts to measure the impact of research (for a good review see Bell et al., 2011). Yet others warn of the limitations of linear dissemination (see Scott, 2000) and stress the need to engender interest and trust (see for example Tydén and Nordfors, 2000). Comparatively few researchers appear to reflect critically on the practical constraints when disseminating sustainability research results, such as the large amount of the researcher's time which can be consumed by these innovative dissemination activities. This is further exacerbated by the contingent nature of sustainability research and the unpredictability of research outcomes. Reiterating Ward's (2005) sentiment, when one embarks on a policy-relevant research study; one may end up generating findings that are quite unexpected. In the context of the ConsEnSus project, it was interesting to observe the broadening of the research dissemination remit as the project progressed. From the initial research design stage, the key research objectives included production of recommendations for local authorities and national decision makers concerning sustainable consumption policies. However, funder requests for wider dissemination increased dramatically in the third year of the project, perhaps reflecting the importance of increasing accountability for public funds in a changing economic climate. This further highlights how the timing and context of a project can be vital in sculpting the research process.

Undoubtedly, debates around sustainability have opened up spaces for diverse academic and non-academic contributors to exchange ideas and to communicate their visions of sustainability. It is important to exercise caution, however, when judging the apparent success or failure of any extensive and innovative dissemination strategy. While intensive and indeed extensive dissemination of results to targeted communities (e.g., policy makers, practitioners) may or may not affect change (see Lyall et al., 2004 for an in-depth discussion), there are often unintended benefits of policy-relevant research which may never enter academic assessment models. For example, the use of the research by local networks of NGOs or campaign groups and community projects (see Walter et al., 2007 for a comprehensive review of direct impacts, e.g. new knowledge, and other relevant impacts, for example capacity building). Students and scholars of sustainability research will be aware that current and traditional academic reward systems are based on peer review publication records and, indeed, specific objectives of individual disciplines. This echoes our opening arguments in Chapter 1 on the unique challenges of working in the distinctly interdisciplinary field that is sustainability research. The under appreciation of user-valued research is evident in, for example, the Research Assessment Exercise (RAE) in the UK (Woods and Gardner, 2011). As funding agencies appear to follow a similar system, sustainability researchers have begun to call for a research agenda that looks beyond the acquisition of research funding and publishing to value all activities related to developing and implementing solution strategies for solving and mitigating sustainability problems.

## Concluding reflections and key considerations for future sustainability research

Commonly-held ideas among policy makers and members of the public about *what social scientists actually do* frequently remain wedded to traditional images of social research that incorporate taken-for-granted assumptions about the nature of science. As a result, conventional methodologies continue to dominate the field of sustainability research. Recent trends towards more integrated, innovative approaches, such as those examined in this collection, including participatory and action research, technology-aided forms of inquiry such as the use of GIS in the production and dissemination of socio-environmental maps, or inter- and transdisciplinary designs have not yet entered the public's imagination to the same extent. These disparities between images of social research and actual research practice impact on social-scientific sustainability research in a multitude of ways, including decisions about what types of research projects do and do not receive funding.

Illustrating the variety of insights and approaches to sustainability research, this book has demonstrated the enormous contribution made by social scientists to the investigation of sustainability problems. Importantly for students and scholars of social-scientific sustainability research, each chapter has focused on the application of these methodological approaches and tools in actual empirical projects, providing practical advice as well as theoretical guidance for those embarking on research in this field.

The challenges of sustainability research continue to be significant, and require concerted efforts and creative and innovative solutions by the social science community. Reflecting on all the contributions to this collection, a number of key considerations for future sustainability research emerge. First and foremost, it seems important to move sustainability questions to the centre of social-scientific theorising, research and debate. Second, there needs to be a much more nuanced debate around issues of inter- and transdisciplinarity that focuses on conceptual, methodological as well as practical issues. Tensions clearly remain, and perhaps will become further exacerbated, between traditional orientations towards discipline-specific specialisation and emerging discourses of interdisciplinarity. These tensions cannot be resolved easily and require a much more thorough engagement with ontological and epistemological dimensions of social research as well as examining their practical implications. Finally, as highlighted in this concluding chapter, there is a clear need to reconsider the channels and mechanisms for supporting sustainability research and to strive for more inclusive ways of measuring the impacts of social-scientific research efforts in this field.

Overall, the collection we have assembled here offers a diversity of methods from a variety of perspectives and provides a practical and informative guide for students and scholars in the field of sustainability research. We hope that this collection will consolidate some of the research done to date and, furthermore, we anticipate that it will inform and inspire future researchers to investigate and explore this critical area of social scientific research.

## Note

1 For example, Cohen (2006: 68) observes that 'The last decade has seen considerable progress in the development of an expansive technical repertoire with which to [*diagnose*] currently unsustainable consumption patterns. [...] These developments, however, have not been matched by commensurate progress devising actual policy initiatives to foster more socially and ecologically benign provisioning practices.'

# References

Allen, C. and Imrie, R. (2010) *The Knowledge Business*. Aldershot: Ashgate.

Bell, D. (2011) 'Grey area', *Dialogues in Human Geography*, 1 (2): 215–18.

Bell, S., Shaw, B. and Boaz, A. (2011) 'Real-world approaches to assessing the impact of environmental research on policy', *Research Evaluation*, 20 (3): 227–37.

Burgess, J. (2005) 'Following the argument where it leads: some personal reflections on "policy-relevant" research', *Transactions of the Institute of British Geographers*, 30: 273–81.

Cohen, M.J. (2006) 'Sustainable consumption research as democratic expertise', *Journal of Consumer Policy*, 29 (1): 67–77.

Davies, A. R., Doyle, R. and Pape, J. (2011) 'Future visioning for sustainable household practices: spaces for sustainability learning?', *Area*, 44(1): 54–60. doi: 10.1111/j.1475-4762.2011.01054.x

EEA (European Environmental Agency) (2005) *Household Consumption and the Environment*. EEA Report No. 11/2005. Copenhagen: European Environmental Agency.

EPA (Environmental Protection Agency) (2006) *Environment in Focus: Environmental Indicators for Ireland*. Dublin: Environmental Protection Agency.

EPA (Environmental Protection Agency) (2011) *Guidelines for Submissions of Final Reports*. Available from www.epa.ie

European Commission (2004) *Sustainable Production and Consumption in the EU*. Brussels: European Commission.

European Commission (2006a) White Paper on a European Communication Policy, COM(2006)35. Luxembourg: Office for Official Publications of the European Communities.

European Commission (2006b) *Communicating Science – A Scientist's Survival Kit*. Luxembourg: Office for Official Publications of the European Communities.

European Commission (2010) *Communicating Research for Evidence-based Policymaking – a Practical Guide for Researchers in Socio-economic Sciences and Humanities*. Luxembourg: Office for Official Publications of the European Communities.

Flyvbjerg, B. (2004) 'Five misunderstandings about case-study research', in C. Seale, G. Gobo, J.F. Gubrium and D. Silverman (eds), *Qualitative Research Practice*. London: Sage. pp. 420–34.

Gibbons, M., Limoges, C., Nowotny, H., Schwartzman, S., Scott, P. and Trow, M. (1994) *The New Production of Knowledge*. London: Sage.

Hirsch Hadorn, G., Hoffmann-Riem, H., Biber-Klemm, S., Grossenbacher-Mansuy, W., Joye, D., Pohl, C., Wiesmann, U. and Zemp, E. (eds) (2008) *Handbook of Transdisciplinary Research*. Dordrecht: Springer.

Lyall, C., Bruce, A. Firn, J., Firn, M. and Tait, J. (2004) 'Assessing end-use relevance of public sector research organisations', *Research Policy*, 33 (1): 73–87.

Murphy, A.B. (2006) 'Enhancing geography's role in public debate', *Annals of the Association of American Geographers*, 96: 1–13.

Pain, R. (2006) 'Social geography: seven deadly myths in policy research', *Progress in Human Geography*, 30: 250–59.

Pain, R. and Francis, P. (2003) 'Reflections on participatory research', *Area*, 35: 46–54.

Pape, J., Fahy, F., Davies, A. and Rau, H. (2011) 'Developing policies and instruments for sustainable consumption: Irish experiences and futures', *Journal of Consumer Policy*, 34 (1): 25–42.

Scott, A. (2000) *The Dissemination of the Results of Environmental Research*. EEA Environment Issues Series, 15. Brighton: SPRU.

Seyfang, G. (2006) 'Sustainable consumption, the new economics and community currencies: developing new institutions for environmental governance', *Regional Studies*, 40 (7): 781–91.

Sharp, L. McDonald, A., Sim, P. Knamiller, C., Sefton, C. and Wong, S. (2011) 'Positivism, post-positivism and domestic water demand: interrelating science across the paradigmatic divide', *Transactions of the Institute of British Geographers*, 36 (4): 501–15.

Tydén, T. and Nordfors, D. (2000) 'INFOPAC – researchers learn research dissemination by doing', *Science Communication*, 21 (23): 296–308.

Walter, A., Helgenberger, S. Wiek, A. and Scholz, R.W. (2007) 'Measuring societal effects of transdisciplinary research projects: design and application of an evaluation method', *Evaluation and Program Planning*, 30 (4): 325–38.

Ward, K. (2005) 'Geography and public policy: a recent history of policy relevance', *Progress in Human Geography*, 29 (3): 310–19.

Wiek A., Withycombe, L., Redman, C. and Mills, S.B. (2011) 'Moving forward on competence in sustainability research and problem solving', *Environment: Science and Policy for Sustainable Development*, March–April, available from www.environmental magazine.org

Woods, M. and Gardner, G. (2011) 'Applied policy research and critical human geography: some reflections on swimming in murky waters', *Dialogues in Human Geography*, 1 (2): 198–214.

# Index

*Agenda 21* 53
agriculture 58
    farmers 158
    food production 114
anthropocene 122
axial coding 163, 165–7

backcasting 10, 181, 201
basic needs concept 96
Bedfordshire study 60–6
behaviour *see* human behaviour
biodiversity 115, 122
biographical research 155–6, 172
    focus on life phases 157
    life history 158
    life story 157–8
    research study *see* LifeEvents
biomass 119–20
birth control 97
Brazilian Miracle, The 95
British Empire 93
Brundtland report 5, 6

Canadian Index of Wellbeing 179
carbon capture 59
Carbon Flow Accounting 120
citizen–consumer approach 30–2
Cleveland, C. 9
climate change 114
    and migration 7
    reports 8
Club of Rome 97
coding 163
    axial 166–9
    open 163–5
    selective 169
collaborative research 4, 7
    *see also* interdisciplinarity
colonialism 92–3, 108–9
community studies 201

comparative studies 6, 16, 17
ConsEnSus project 196, 197, 199
    Smart Moves project 182
consumption 12
    consumer–citizen approach 30–2
    households as mobile units 49–50
    and life events 155–6
    and use of time 174–5, 180, 182–3
Copenhagen Summit 101–2
Corrib gas dispute 72, 74–6
    research study *see* dialogic research
culture 7, 9–10
    and consumption 12, 169, 171, 199
    cultural invasion 75
    and perspectives of time 16, 176
    society–nature interactions 115–16

data collection 5–6, 7
deforestation 121
developing countries 93
development 6, 91–2
    colonial and post-colonial legacy
        92–3, 108–9
    the human development paradigm
        92, 100–2, 108
    measures of 103–7, 108
    sustainability concept contested 96–9
    welfare capitalism and human rights
        94–6
dialogic research 19, 72–4
    language sets and oppositional
        discourse 74–6
    listening and giving voice 78–80
        citations from *Our Story* 81–5
        temporal transformation of views
            78–80, 85
    methodology and assessment
        key questions examined 81–5
        limitations and dangers 85–6
digital mapping 135

dissemination, research output 202–5
Dublin noise study
  noise mapping methodology 141
    data acquisition and study area 142
    noise modelling 142–3
  population exposure and mapping
    145–6
  summary and conclusions 145–8

ecology
  Ecological Debt Day 99
  ecological footprint 99, 103, 105, 106
    as biophysical indicator 115,
      123–7
    strengths and weaknesses 125
  ecological overshoot 99
  Ecological Space 20
  ecological sustainability 96–7, 98,
    133–4
economics 6–7, 20, 92–3, 106
  dominance of 9, 14
  New Economics 92, 103–4
  socio-economic metabolism 115–20
Energy Flow Analysis 20, 115,
  116–18, 128
environment
  Environmental Noise Directive (END)
    139–40, 143, 146, 147
  environmental space 92, 99, 103
  EU policy 139–40
  poor blamed for degradation of 97
  pro-environmental behaviour 32–3
    measuring 36–7
  public environmental values 60–6
  sustainability 28, 96–7, 98, 133–4
  Sustainability Index 105, 106
Environmental Protection Agency (EPA)
  Ireland 195, 196
environmentalism, in Ireland 76–8, 86–7
ethnography, time-sensitive 182–6

famine 97
farmers 158
focus groups 18–19, 53–5
  characteristics and nature of 55–7
  merits and limitations 66–8
  use in studies
    brief review of 57–9
    environmental values 60–6
fossil fuels 118

gas pipeline project 19
Genuine Progress Indicator 105, 106
Genuine Savings measure 105
Geographic Information Systems (GIS)
  21, 135–6, 143, 145–6
global hectares 124
global warming 114
Great Xhosa Cattle Killing 76
greenhouse gases 114
Gross National Happiness
  104, 107
gross primary production 119
grounded theory 163

Happy Planet Index 9, 20, 104–5,
  106–8, 179
household research 17–18, 27–30
  background
    disciplinary/interdisciplinary
      perspectives 29–30
    green lifestyles 28–9
    households defined 27
  changing consumption and life-events
    155–6
  citizen–consumer constructs 30–1
  ConsEnSus project 196, 197, 199
  households as mobile units of
    consumption 49–50
  methodological approaches
    biographical research 156–9
    broad traditions of study 32–3
    the survey approach 34–41
Human Appropriation of Net Primary
  Production 20, 21
  as biophysical indicator 120–3, 128
  ecological footprint compared 125
human behaviour 15, 19
  behavioural change 17
  pro-environmental 31–2
    measuring 36–7
  varying views of 11, 12
human development approach 20, 92,
  100–2, 105–9
Human Development Index 9,
  100, 179
*Human Development Reports* 101–2
human rights 95–6

ICCPR 96
ICECSR 96

imperialism 92–3
Index of Sustainable Economic
    Welfare 106
indicators 114–15
    ecological footprint 123–6
    human appropriation of net
        primary production (HANPP)
        120–3
    material and energy flow analysis
        (MEFA) 115–20
Institute of Social Ecology 14
interdisciplinarity 11–14, 23, 178
    challenges of combined approaches
        198–202
    distinguished from transdisciplinarity
        13, 23
    incentives for and against 29–30
International Labour Organization 96
interviews
    narrative 157–8
    problem-centred 259–62

Johannesburg World Summit 99

land-use
    developments 60, 65, 118–19
    and ecological footprint 124–5
    and net primary production
        119–25
life stories 157–8
LifeEvents project 159–60
    grounded theory data analysis 163
        coding 164–71
    problem-centred interviewing 160–3
    sampling 159
    summary and results 170–1
lifestyles 28–9
    green lifestyles 28, 30–1
    life-course research see LifeEvents
longitudinal approaches 5–6, 8,
    22, 85, 180–2
    time-sensitive ethnography 182–6
Luton study 60, 60–6

mapping 21, 133–4
    digital mapping 134–6
    noise 136–40
    research study see Dublin
        noise study
market research 56

Material Flow Analysis 20, 115,
    116–17, 128
measurement
    and methodological challenges
        8–10
    of sustainability 7, 20–1,
        103–7, 108
    see also indicators
methodology 5–6
    challenges 8–10
migration 7
Multinational Time Use Study 178

Nansen Conference 7
narrative interview 157–8
nature conservation 58
neocolonialism 93
Net Primary Production (NPP)
    119–21
New Economics Foundation 20
New International Economic
    Order 93
noise pollution 21
    EU policy 139–40
    mapping research see mapping
    and public health 136–9
    traffic 136, 137, 139, 140, 143

observation see participant
    observation
opinion polls 54
Our Common Future 5
Our Story 78–9, 81–5

participant observation 73, 156, 160,
    161, 183, 184
participation see public participation
peer group approach 6
People and Participation Portal 68
Physical Quality of Life Index 95
place, sense of 82
    place names 72, 80
planning decisions 60, 65–6
policy
    European Union 139–41
    policy-relevant research 195
pollution 114
population growth 96–7
Potsdam Institute for Climate Impact
    Research (PIK) 14

poverty 94, 97
Preston 57
problem-centred interviewing 156
    four phases of 162
public participation 53–4
    ladders of participation 54
    Participation Portal 68
    public meetings 83
publications and publishing 203

qualitative research 67–8, 198, 202
quality of life 95, 97, 99
quantitative studies
    dominance of 8, 14, 54, 178,
        198–9
    survey design 34–5, 48
    and time-use data 178, 180, 186
questionnaires 34–5
    data sampling and collection 40
    design 38–40
    travel questionnaire 43–6

reality tours 9–10
refinery project see Corrib gas
    conflict
refugees 7
research challenges 193–4, 205–6
    methodology and combined
        approaches 5–11, 198–202
    policy-relevant research 195–7
        developing research questions
        197–8
    research outputs and dissemination
        202–5
Right to Development 95–6, 109
Rio Earth Summit 53

selective coding 163, 169
sleep, disturbed 137–8
Smart Moves project 182
social constructivism 10
social movements
    arising from local campaign 84–5
    characteristics of 77
society, sustainable 96–7, 98
socio-economic/ecological metabolism
    115–20
Stockholm Environment Institute 14
STRIVE programme 196
substance flow see material flow

surveys 4, 7
    flow diagram and survey
        process 34–5
    household surveys
        construction 38–40
        design considerations 36–7
        sampling and implementation 40–1
        survey analysis 48–9
    and opinion polls 54
    see also travel behaviour study
sustainability 3–4
    agricultural sustainability 58
    challenges for research methodologies
        5–7
    definitions of 4–5, 91, 133
    ecological 96–7, 98, 133–4
    environmental 28, 96–7, 98, 133–4
    measuring 7, 20–1, 103–7, 108

The Limits to Growth 97
The Other Economic Summit 104
The Population Bomb 96–7
three pillars concept 98–9
time 16, 17, 21–2, 173–87, 200
    longitudinal approaches 5–6, 8,
        22, 85, 180–2
    temporal transformation of views
        78–80, 85
    theory and practice 200
        ethnographic methods 182–6
        measures of sustainable time
            178–82
        time-sensitive social practices
            175–7
transdisciplinarity 4, 10, 11, 14, 205
    distinguished from interdisciplinarity
        13, 23
    and problem-centred interviewing
        161
    and time 178, 186
Transition Towns 6–7
travel behaviour study 18, 41–2
    and interdisciplinarity 29–30
    objectives and survey design 35,
        36, 42–7
    sampling and implementation 47–8
    survey analysis 48–50

United Nations Development Programme
    100–2

visioning 8, 10, 54, 196, 201
visualisation methods 7

waste-management 58–9
WCED 5, 6, 99
welfare capitalism 94–6
working hours 174–5
World Commission on Environment and
  Development (WCED) 5, 6, 99

World Conservation Strategy 98
World Council of Churches 98
World Health Organization
  (WHO) 136
  noise study 138, 139
World Social Charter 102
World Summit on Social
  Development 101
Wuppertal Institute 14